Human Rights Horizons

Human Rights Horizons

The Pursuit of Justice in a Globalizing World

Richard Falk

Routledge
A member of the Taylor & Francis Group
New York   London

Published in 2000 by
Routledge
29 West 35th Street
New York, NY 10001

Published in Great Britain in 2000 by
Routledge
11 New Fetter Lane
London EC4P 4EE

A member of the Taylor & Francis Group

Printed in the United States of America on acid-free paper
Design and typography: Jack Donner

Library of Congress Cataloging-in-Publication Data

Falk, Richard A.
Human rights horizons : the pursuit of justice in a globalizing world / by Richard Falk.
p.   cm.
Includes bibliographical references.
ISBN 0–415–92512–6   ISBN 0–415–92513–4 (pbk.)
1. Human rights. I. Title.
JC585.F35 2000
323—dc21   99–088210
CIP

For Edward Said
a brave, heroic, and inspirational friend

Contents

Acknowledgments

As with any book, the debts of an author are numerous and largely unpaid. There has been a flourishing literature of human rights over the course of the last decade that has liberated this subject matter from westernizing moralists and propagandists. Coming to terms with the legal and political implications of human rights in an era of globalization and of multi-civilizationalism is the dominant world order challenge in the period following the fall of the Berlin Wall.

I would like to thank, in particular, a series of friends and scholars from non-Western backgrounds who have opened my eyes wide to the view of "the other": Rajni Kothari, Jacques Baudot, Upendra Baxi, Chandra Muzaffar, Mohammed sid Ahmed, Kader Asmal, Yasuaki Onuma, Walden Bello, Maivan Lam, Deepak Nayar, Radha Kumar, Lester Ruiz, Edward Said, and the late Eqbal Ahmad.

The various chapters that comprise this book also reflect a series of reflections arising from controversy and collaboration with friends and scholars closer to home, including Saul Mendlovitz, Robert Jay Lifton, Charles Strozier, Burns Weston, Jacques Bandot, Barbara Baudot Sundberg, Mary Kaldor, and Rob Walker.

As so often before, I want to thank Princeton University, and especially the Center of International Studies and its supportive director, Michael Doyle, for support and milieu. Michael has himself been brilliantly exploring many of the issues that underpin the inquiry of this book. June Garson has provided me over the years with the most expert and sophisticated logistical support, and I am grateful to her for facilitating the preparation of this manuscript in many ways, from start to finish.

I also want to thank a series of editorial contributions by Routledge. Amy Shipper's enthusiasm for this project pushed me hard toward its completion. Her successor, Eric Nelson made some crucial substantive suggestions. David McAnich, the copy editor, did his best to clarify my prose, and I am grateful for this. And Liana Fredley took charge of the manuscript in its final stages in an impressively efficient manner.

My wife, Hilal Elver, has been a most loving companion and partner in all that I have done in recent years, and there are many echoes of her influence in these pages.

By acknowledging so many, I am not trying to share the blame for what remains. The subject matter I have addressed lends itself to interpretative diversity. Undoubtedly, also, my perspective is expressive of the historical context created by the developments in the 1990s. I am sure that the same motifs will look quite different to me by the year 2010.

I also wish to acknowledge with gratitude permission to draw upon previously published work in *The Australian Journal of International Affairs*, *Political Quarterly*, *Third World Quarterly*, and *Journal of International Affairs*. I would also like to thank Macmillan, St. Martin's Press, Rowman & Littlefield, Cambridge University Press, and Lynne Rienner Publishers for giving permission to rely on material previously published as chapters in edited books appearing under their imprint.

Introduction

This book seeks to encourage the continuing promotion of human rights as an integral aspect of global politics and law. To be credible, such an undertaking must confront a series of problematic and controversial issues. At the center of these investigations is the judgment that the sovereign state is changing course due primarily to the widespread adoption of neoliberal approaches to governmental function. Yet it is necessary to qualify this generalization. The role of the state is changing in response to a transformed global setting, but not uniformly. States are very differently situated and endowed, and have at their disposal a wide range of adjustment strategies and capabilities. Nevertheless, there exists a broad cumulative trend toward the social disempowerment of the state. This trend encourages private-sector "solutions" to such social issues as poverty, unemployment, and alienation, including the emergence of billionaire philanthropy as practiced by such exemplary figures as Ted Turner, George Soros, and Bill Gates.

How to advance the cause of human rights in light of this tendency toward deterritorialization of political authority and identity seems currently to be the most pressing framing question for human rights activists. Whether such a possibility is plausible or wishful thinking should be of serious concern to students of international politics, who seem to be at last broadening their inquiry from realist obsessions with power and wealth to incorporate normative matters of custom, morality, and law. This normative feature should not be romanticized, especially in relation to human rights. It can easily be confounded with the cultural arrogance of a geopolitical leadership that self-confidently disseminates its particular worldview as if it were universally valid.[1] How human rights fits into this dynamic of Western dominance in both its Eurocentric and later American phases is a critical element in any convincing claim to the effect that international human rights as now understood in the West possesses a universal applicability.

A further concern involves the economistic character of policymaking in the face of a more tightly integrated and competitive world economy. Whether the normative dimension of international relations can give "a human face" to globalization remains to be seen. Such a project would require extending the effective reach of human rights well beyond its minimal undertaking, which is to offer protection to individuals against various forms of oppressive government. It would also involve taking into account cultural pluralism, group rights, duties to the community, the unheard voices of indigenous peoples, and giving due weight to the hitherto insufficiently influential non-Western civilizations. Such ambitious goals would effectively require extending substantive democracy to global arenas of authority, as well as clarifying the scope and limits of the right of self-determination, thereby enabling some form of "humane governance" to take shape, and serve all the peoples of the world. Substantive democracy means a behavioral realization of democratic ideals: a participatory citizenry, an accountable leadership, an operative rule of law, a high degree of governmental and corporate transparency, and equitable arrangements that ensure the satisfaction of basic human needs for the entire population.[2] In this fundamental sense, realizing human rights is tantamount to achieving global justice.

POINTS OF DEPARTURE

The prominence given to human rights in all parts of the world is one of the most remarkable developments to have occurred during the last half-century. And the end of this development is not yet in sight. Support for human rights has been gathering further momentum in recent decades. This pattern of growth may reflect the overall dynamic of globalization that is creating a stronger sense of shared destiny among the diverse peoples of the world, even while it is also generating a more stressful sense of ethnic, religious, and cultural difference. The current phase of globalization reflects the victory of Western constitutional liberalism in the cold war, giving the American view of proper state-society relations, including a commitment to governmental moderation, a great deal of historical salience.

This buoyancy of human rights is undoubtedly also an aspect of the related trend toward the democratization of state-society relations, which by its very nature presupposes upholding a range of human rights standards. The rise of transnational networks of dedicated activists organized at the grassroots level on a voluntary, nonprofit basis has been a constant goad to governments and private-sector actors, who are rarely oblivious to their reputation on matters pertaining to human rights. The effectiveness of these efforts varies greatly depending on the level of grassroots commitment to human rights, the extent to which the government permits and responds to oppositional behavior, and the vulnerability of corporations and banks to consumer boycotts and other forms of pressure.

This rise of human rights has encouraged various additional and closely related normative projects. Among the most important of these is the use of force to engage in "humanitarian intervention," whether by the United Nations, by a regional actor, or by a strong state. The standard justification for humanitarian intervention is the allegation that gross violations of human rights are occurring on such a massive scale as to override the foundational principle of Westphalian world order that territorial sovereignty is inviolate. Overriding sovereignty seems increasingly acceptable in the face of human rights violations that amount to crimes against humanity or appear to constitute or verge upon genocide. NATO's seventy-eight-day air war in 1999 over the fate of Kosovo raises these concerns in a vivid, controversial, and complex fashion. Despite temptations to the contrary, however, it remains premature at this point to set forth "the lessons of Kosovo." And yet it is not too soon to offer some assessment of this dramatic instance of humanitarian intervention. In this vein, it seems useful to acknowledge that a fearful dilemma, as in relation to Kosovo, often confronts those that either endorse or criticize a particular claim of humanitarian intervention. On the one side, watching the launch of an ethnic cleansing campaign against Kosovar Albanians without acting to protect such hapless victims seemed intolerable, but on the other side, the NATO insistence that the only practical alternative to passivity involved bombing Belgrade until it submitted to a diktat seemed to entail an unacceptable use of force.

On another front, yet not too far removed from humanitarian intervention, lie several thorny questions bearing on the scope of the right of self-determination, a norm affirmed as fundamental by its placement in Article 1 of both human rights Covenants, which were drafted under the auspices of the United Nations. Yet a maximalist implementation of this norm would challenge the prerogatives of some of the largest and most powerful states in the world, and depending on circumstances, could generate serious risk of major warfare. To show that such a concern is not fanciful, think of the likely repercussions of outside military efforts to support the legally and morally compelling claims of Chechnya, Tibet, and Kashmir against Russia, China, and India, respectively. The world order tensions produced by these and many other unresolved claims are severe. If only small and weak states are expected to uphold the right of self-determination, the most fundamental claim that in law equals are treated equally becomes a mockery.[3] Yet if an effort were to be made to treat all states as equally accountable for upholding the right of self-determination, it would increase greatly the risks of major warfare, and make the global setting even more chaotic, fragmented, and menacing. In the background is the challenge of balancing a regime of rights (in this instance, the collective right of self-determination) in a political setting shaped by geopolitical status and influence.

There is a similar dilemma associated with the growing movement to hold political leaders responsible for crimes of state committed while in office. Such ideas assumed historical seriousness only in this century—especially with the indictment and prosecution of German and Japanese war leaders after World War II. During the cold war decades, the Nuremberg project was abandoned intergovernmentally. It was kept alive mainly by activists in the West, particularly in the United States, objecting under international law to the policies of their leaders with respect to the Vietnam War, nuclear weapons, and Central America. Then with the end of the cold war and the frustrations associated with the Western unwillingness to prevent ethnic cleansing in Bosnia or genocide in Rwanda, the war crimes idea was revived by initiatives underwritten by the UN Security Council.

Against such a background, pressures from global civil society, as abetted by a large group of states, are pushing these ideas of accountability far beyond their origins. The finally unsucessful effort since 1998 to detain and extradite General Augusto Pinochet, the former Chilean dictator, to face criminal charges in Spain, the war-crimes indictment of Yugoslav president Slobodan Milosevic a year later by the Hague War Crimes Tribunal, the pressure to similarly indict Iraqi president Saddam Hussein, the move to create a tribunal to review the crimes of the Khmer Rouge in Cambodia during the mid-1970s, and the campaign to establish a permanent international criminal court—all these actions flow from a wider effort to institutionalize criminal liability of leaders on a global level. The guiding idea is to fashion a framework of individual accountability that is uniformly applicable to all political and military leaders, whether in countries large or small, whether in governments that won a war or lost one. Such an ambitious extension of the rule of law involves an acceptance by leaders of the main postulates of global justice.

THE EMERGENCE OF HUMAN RIGHTS

We can also appreciate the significance of human rights by reference to its major role in three epic transnational struggles that have strongly affected the political imagination since 1945: the struggles against colonialism, against Soviet Bloc oppression, and against apartheid. In each setting, the internationalization of the conflict was morally and politically premised upon the gross abuses of internationally protected human rights. The outcome of these struggles was widely regarded as a vindication of the claims associated with the denial of fundamental rights. In light of this experience, human rights could no longer be dismissed by cynics as little more than a collection of empty and unenforceable moralisms, possibly useful in propaganda campaigns against oppressive and unjust enemies, but certainly not operative as behavioral norms that were to be seriously implemented even in the face of adverse effects.

It is important to remember that human rights were not even an active part of political consciousness until after World War II. It seems horrifying in retrospect that the blatant abuses of the Nazi regime did not on their own stir the conscience of even the liberal democracies until their own territorial security and political independence were threatened by German expansionism. The participation by the West in the 1936 Berlin Olympics remains both an awkward memory and a grim reminder that even extreme denials of human rights were at the outer margins of international concern as measured by the preoccupations of a Eurocentric world. At best, upholding elemental rights was treated as a matter best addressed between state and society. Beyond this, overseas abuse of religious and ethnic minorities only occasionally became a cause of intervention, usually when the victims were essentially regarded as cultural extensions of the intervening states. Such was the case when Western countries intervened in what is now modern Greece during the early nineteenth century to protect Christians against abuses attributed to their Ottoman rulers. But few scruples were raised by the structure of colonial oppression, which often included a spectrum of cruel abuses. In reaction, the victimized peoples developed an ethos of resistance that varied from place to place, although most patterns of resistance rested on nationalist ideas. Responding to foreign rule inevitably evoked claims to a still inchoate "right of self-determination," a formulation strongly associated with the global vision of Woodrow Wilson after World War I. Contrary to Wilson's intentions, the idea of self-determination escaped from its Pandora's Box of limited applicability, and soon expanded from its initially intended relevance to European peoples, especially the remnants of the collapsed Austro-Hungarian and Ottoman empires, to encompass all colonized peoples in the world.

It is true that certain morally objectionable international practices, most notably the slave trade, had earlier become the subject of international treaties of prohibition. Such initiatives had a definite chilling impact on the contested behavior. Note that the legal effort of the international prohibition was directed at the international slave trade, and not at the institution of slavery itself, which was left untouched by the prohibitions, remaining safely within the domain of territorial sovereignty. Of course, ideas that later formed part of the content of human rights were, even earlier, at the core of Western struggles against tyranny and royal absolutism, but these, too, were primarily domestic ideas. At the same time, the leaders of the American Revolution, and even more so the main voices of the French Revolution, believed that their proclamation of rights had a potential and deserved universal relevance, effectively defining "a legitimate state."

Despite these major preparatory political developments, the undertaking to establish the code of international human rights that eventuated in the Universal Declaration of Human Rights did not seem particularly promising when it was adopted by unanimous vote, with a Soviet abstention, of 48–0 on December 10, 1948. The document was put forward as no more than "a common standard of achievement," taking the shape of a "declaration" rather than a legally binding "agreement." It was set forth as a comprehensive image of human dignity toward which states would individually move, but at their own pace and in a manner respectful of their own *sovereignty*; the Universal Declaration was definitely not understood, despite its language of rights, as obligatory in a legal sense, or as expressing morally and politically the spirit of the time. Such modesty was appropriate given the character of international society in the 1940s. The majority of states comprising the original membership of the United Nations were not political democracies; many of them disallowed oppositional activity, punishing harshly even mild criticism and putting in jail individuals Amnesty International later came to call "prisoners of conscience." Beyond this, in a world of sovereign states, the structure of actual authority was still overwhelmingly territorial, with assurances written into the United Nations Charter that the organization was prohibited from intervening in "matters that are essentially within the domestic jurisdiction of states" (Article 2(7)). The Soviet Union and its supporters were insistent, as well, that the whole concept of human rights be developed with the clear understanding that its implementation would be left to the dynamics of self-enforcement, which in view of prevailing circumstances generally meant no enforcement at all.

The mystery that remains with us to some extent is why an assemblage of sovereign states, most of whom were at the time oppressive to some degree, would validate any call whatsoever for the realization of human rights as a matter of *international* concern. The most clarifying response is that the realities of sovereignty then seemed so entrenched in outlook and behavior that political leaders were not threatened by the utterance of a series of pieties, even if their message seemed subversive of sovereignty. What was set forth and endorsed as constituting the first comprehensive formulation of international human rights was treated by world leaders at the time as belonging on the most remote back burner of world politics, and hardly worthy of notice.

These humble origins and low expectations were reinforced by the degree to which political leaders and their advisors after 1945 increasingly looked at the world through the prism of "realism." Idealists had been deeply discredited by the failure of appeasement and disarmament to address the challenges of German and Japanese expansionism in the period between the two world wars. It was accepted by most experts after World War II that only a structure of countervailing power could keep international peace, a belief that was single-mindedly—and by most accounts successfully—applied during the cold war years.[4] This realist consensus continues to dominate the outlook of those who represent states and shape global policy, and by this logic considerations of human rights should be relevant only as an instrument of foreign policy or as a means to mobilize opposition against an international rival.

It is thus notable that despite the persistence of the state and the dominance of realist thinking, human rights have come in from the cold in the last several decades. As earlier suggested, the issue of human rights has on occasion proved useful to political actors on the global stage at various points to increase the pressures being otherwise exerted on their adversaries. Beyond this, the rise of transnational grassroots activism changed the political game of human rights. Human rights NGOs have treated parts of the normative menu contained in the Universal Declaration as expressive of obligatory standards, and pushed hard for implementation, at least with respect to such specific prohibitions as those directed against torture and racial discrimination.

Despite these positive developments, which would have exceeded all reasonable expectations fifty years ago, this is no time for celebration. Many oppressive regimes persist, and participate normally in international life. China was only momentarily and half-heartedly discredited by the bloody happenings in Tiananman Square a little more than ten years ago. The United States, once viewed as the most ardent champion of the human rights movement, has lost much of its reputation in recent years. For a variety of reasons the United States has been the slowest of major states to ratify several crucial international agreements, and to accept a series of humanitarian treaties dealing with such matters as landmines, international criminal courts, and internal conflicts. The United States is also widely perceived as using its diplomatic clout to insulate its friends from well-deserved allegations of abuse, and has itself refused to acknowledge any degree of external accountability even in relation to such internationally contested practices as capital punishment. Various unilateral uses of force by the United States in the 1990s have increasingly given this superpower the image of being an irresponsible bully in the global neighborhood, a fact that undermines its advocacy of human rights for other countries, and encourages accusations of hypocrisy. Beyond this, since its retreat from Somalia in 1994 the United States has generally weakened UN efforts to help victims of gross human rights abuse; it did so most flagrantly when it opposed a strong UN effort to curtail an unfolding genocide in Rwanda in 1994.

THE GLOBAL SETTING AFTER THE COLD WAR

During the cold war, the East-West rivalry often conditioned debate about the nature of human rights. It was widely accepted that Western liberal societies would focus on the civil and political rights of individuals, including the protection of private property. It was equally understood that the

Communist states and the Non-Aligned Movement would emphasize collective rights of social classes, highlighting rights relating to economic well-being and basic human needs. Most Third World governments have continued to put their stress on economic and social rights and, more recently, "the right to development," although a growing number have come to affirm civil and political rights as well.

There was a shared understanding that human rights had become a zone of serious ideological disagreement despite the mainly successful establishment of a common normative framework as a result of the adoption of the Universal Declaration of Human Rights, and its elaboration and refinement in the two 1966 Covenants.[5] The United Nations provided the auspices for norm-creation in relation to human rights, which managed to transcend or compromise the politics of the East-West rivalry, thereby creating a foundation in law and morality for claims that the human rights instruments resulting from intergovernmental negotiations possessed a universal validity. Eventually, this foundation also enabled a selective yet influential *politics of human rights* to flourish, and to create an evolutionary optimism about the eventual attainment of a world order embodying widely accepted notions of global justice. Such a "politics" should not, however, be confused with *a regime of effective implementation* of human rights.

With the end of the cold war, the collapse of the Soviet Union, the ideological passivity of China, and the spread of neoliberalism to the far corners of the world, the stage was set for a new phase in human rights advocacy. Francis Fukuyama caught the spirit of this new phase with his philosophically grounded contention, echoing Hegel, that "the end of history" had been achieved in the realm of ideas (without a shot being fired) as a result of the triumph of the West over the challenge mounted by Marxism/Leninism.[6]

But after 1991 the grounds of contention shifted quickly from ideology to culture, and the human rights tradition began in the early 1990s to be seriously interrogated by non-Westerners who complained about its Western bias and origins and who favored new civilizational outlooks that were proclaimed under such banners as "Asian values" or "Islamic perspectives."

The terms of debate were complex, and often convoluted. There were counterclaims made in the West (and by some activists in non-Western settings) that many of the charges of civilizational bias were being used by authoritarian governments to divert attention from their unwillingness to comply with international standards or to accept any process of internal or external accountability. It became evident in a historical sense that the human rights tradition evolved out of Western initiatives and priorities, with only nominal non-Western participation. Without such participation, the norms generated lack any real moral force, thereby eroding the voluntary bases of compliance upon which so much of the effectiveness of international law (and any law) depends. Normative bonding—that is, the dynamic of spontaneous adherence—is at least as important as formalized substantive assent and procedures of implementation. In this sense the extension of human rights from the West to the rest of the world, while superficially successful, must still be considered as largely "unfinished business."

THE NEXT FIFTY YEARS

The human rights agenda remains very full when viewed in light of the existing expectations established by international law, morality, and to some extent, politics. Among the prime challenges are improving the process of implementation, separating geopolitical practice from the domain of human rights, and enhancing the impression that leading states are subject to comparable criteria of evaluation as are weak and vulnerable states.

Beyond this, the contextualization of human rights effectiveness is critically dependent on the establishment of a functioning global democracy.[7] Such an objective is being facilitated by the further spread of constitutionalism and multiparty elections to countries that continue to be governed in an authoritarian manner, but the spread and deepening of democracy *within* states should not be confused with global democracy, although it helps sets the stage. The movement for global democracy is above all preoccupied with the democratization of global arenas of decision such as the United Nations and various regional frameworks, among them the highly evolved European Union.

The twenty-first century will also be characterized by the challenge of institutionalizing responsibility for serious abuses of human rights by leaders and others in positions of authority, including those in the private sector. Such an evolution further erodes the Westphalian image of a world of territorial sovereign states by insisting that even adherence to the "superior orders" of the state does not override the most solemn humanitarian obligations of international law.[8] One test of this dimension of the human rights movement will be whether it becomes possible to establish a permanent international criminal court that is allowed to operate free from loopholes and with a sufficient independence from geopolitical oversight to make the venture jurisprudentially credible.

Closely related to the continuing quest for an effective procedure of accountability for crimes of state is a reliable process of humanitarian intervention that is at once effective and legitimate. As Kosovo highlighted, and Rwanda and Bosnia prefigured, overlooking extreme denials of human rights can no longer be excused by deference to sovereignty, ignorance of facts, geographical remoteness, and geopolitical disinterest. But to subordinate "humanitarian intervention" to the vagaries of geopolitics is also intolerable, especially when side-issues such as "zero-casualty" tactics are relied upon to shift the risk of harm almost totally to the side of the people supposedly being rescued and to vindicate military attacks against civilian targets. Equally intolerable is allowing the economic or political "value" of the scene of the crimes to determine whether there should be an effort made to safeguard the people undergoing acute suffering. Some degree of uniformity is needed to legitimate any doctrine of humanitarian intervention, even if practice is limited to missions mandated by the United Nations.

It would seem necessary to raise the enforcement imperative in relation to such abusive circumstances above the currently prevailing level of intergovernmental ad hoc coalitions. Such an imperative exists especially in relation to the prevention of genocide and "ethnic cleansing," as well as other purification practices based on ethnic and religious ideas of exclusivity. The shocking failure to respond to the massive threat to Tutsi survival in Rwanda, compared to the overwhelming response to ethnic cleansing in Kosovo, illuminates the complementary sides of the now deficient structure of global governance in relation to the avoidance of genocidal politics. It would appear that only the creation of a volunteer standby force under the authority of the United Nations, independently financed, and with a mandate to engage without being subject to veto in the Security Council, would begin to have the means to address this critical challenge. Such a step directly confronts the present insistence by leading states, and particularly the United States, on geopolitical control. In practice, such retention of control means waiting until the catastrophe is unfolding, and then determining whether there exists sufficient political support, strategic justification, and mobilizable resources to generate a meaningful response, which if forthcoming at all, is reactive and belated. The ordeal of the people of East Timor subsequent to their opting for independence via referendum is illustrative of such a reactive response pattern. Often such a pattern is better than nothing, but it still exposes vulnerable populations to terrifying onslaughts.

It is the aim of this book to focus on these sorts of foundational human rights issues with the hope that the next fifty years will yield even more impressive results than those achieved over the course of the last fifty years. If the achievements of the twentieth century provided most of the needed normative architecture, those of the twenty-first century must provide effective and legitimate implementation via local, national, regional, and global action. It is also imperative to engender a more genuine acceptance of human rights in non-Western countries. This book proceeds on the central assumption that achieving a human rights culture and realizing global justice are intertwined and mutually reinforcing goals. The overarching aim of normative commitment is to incorporate rights and justice into a framework of humane governance.[9]

PART 1

Framing the Inquiry

Pursuing Global Justice 1

Obstacles of an ideological and structural character complicate the pursuit of global justice during this early phase of globalization. At the same time, several developments associated with globalization are encouraging to those committed to the promotion of global justice. The most salient obstacles arise from the persisting fragmentation of the world in terms of sovereign territorial states, and the widespread acceptance of efficiency and competitiveness criteria as the basis for assessing economic performance. The most promising developments arise from the plausibility of conceiving the world as a unity and from the beginnings of a global civil society due to the efforts of transnational social forces.

This chapter is intended to clarify the character of both the obstacles and the opportunities currently facing proponents of global justice. Five dilemmas are identified in this discussion; these dilemmas arise from efforts to promote global justice within the nonideal conditions of the world as we find it. This chapter concludes with a consideration of ways in which the transformation of the character of world order could greatly enhance the realization of global justice with far fewer of the disappointments and debilitating compromises that characterize the present global setting.

Part of the undertaking of this book is to consider the contribution being made by international institutions, including the United Nations, with respect to global justice. The role of institutions is central to all aspects of this inquiry, but it is also ambiguous. International institutions definitely promote and consolidate the ends of global justice in various respects, but they are also vulnerable to manipulation and control by political forces that are responsible for some of the worst forms of injustice, including patterns of domination, exploitation, and victimization. International institutions, while they merit appreciation for their achievements, must also be criticized for their deficiencies.

At present, the most promising avenues for the immediate actualization of global justice involve sensitive adjustments to variations of state and society makeup, as in the numerous peace, reconciliation, and accountability procedures established in a number of countries. Also encouraging are various collaborations between transnational social forces and those governments that are more value-oriented and sensitive to the claims of global justice, as opposed to those that define their role according to the maximization of power, wealth, and influence. Such projects include a push for treaties that prohibit antipersonnel landmines, outlaw reliance on nuclear weaponry, and establish an international criminal court. Each of these initiatives has its own distinct character, but all of them disclose a new form of global politics in which states are more motivated by values and human solidarity than by narrowly conceived national interests. Such encouraging developments treat global security as based on a demilitarizing respect for law in relation to effective international institutions that are constitutionally oriented.

It is also important to acknowledge the contributions being made within regional frameworks, particularly the European Union. European regionalism in relation to economic cooperation and the protection of human rights is undoubtedly the boldest world order experiment currently under way. If the European Union is perceived as successful in other parts of the world, it could rapidly lead to the extension of a regional approach to neglected instances of injustice. Especially in view of the current mood of disillusionment with the United Nations, it seems likely that, institutionally and substantively, regional arenas will provide the most promising opportunities in the near future to pursue global justice in contexts beyond the boundaries of territorial states.

FRAMING GLOBAL JUSTICE

The background of analysis and reflection about the nature of global justice mainly derives from earlier efforts to conceive of justice in relation to a specific community. This tradition in the West can be traced back to ancient Athens and the conceptions of justice set forth by Plato and Aristotle, and carried forward to our contemporary circumstances perhaps most prominently by John Rawls.[1]

The evolution of thought about justice as it applies to political communities has been the central preoccupation of political philosophy through the centuries. Such thought relies on a dualism, most clearly evident in the *Leviathan* of Thomas Hobbes; specifically, justice and ethics are inapplicable in the absence of a viable international community. Without community sentiments and institutions, separate sovereign states will continue to pursue their own ends unconditionally.[2] The idea of a just society of sovereign states was initially embedded in the medieval universalism of the Roman Catholic Church. It was also embodied in the shared Christendom of European states, which established the modern system of world order in the mid-seventeenth century. The concept of justice coexisted with the idea of sovereignty, which in effect relegated most dimensions of justice to the internal relations between state and society. With the separation of church and state that accompanied the rise of the modern state, the notion of justice assumed a specifically and predominantly secular character that could no longer be interpreted merely as an extension of religious thought.[3]

Two developments are crucial to the framing of global justice: the idea and practice of sovereignty at the level of the territorial state, and the increasing secularization of the most influential forms of speculation about the nature of justice. At the same time, various schools of natural law associated with Catholicism and other formulations of rights and laws rested on divine revelation, the timeless intuitions of rationality, and the objective order of the universe. These approaches persisted as minority countertraditions that challenged the view of justice as socially constructed by human will in the specific settings of historical societies.[4] It is arguable that the positing of the Universal Declaration of Human Rights as a moral and legal foundation for political, social, economic, and cultural behavior amounts to the reassertion of natural law as a legitimate underlying arrangement of governance.

A series of prominent jurists tried to make the transition to modernity, taking account of the rise of secularism and territorial sovereignty. Pre-Westphalian thinking about the nature of international political life was particularly well developed by the Spanish school of international law, especially by Francisco de Vittoria and Francisco Suárez. Their outlook was essentially an extension and application of Catholic jurisprudence to the special circumstances of international life.[5] The birth of modern international law is generally associated with the treatise *The Law of War and Peace*, written by the Dutch jurist Hugo Grotius in reaction to the destructive and barbarous Thirty Years War.[6] Grotius has remained a pivotal figure in international studies because his historical and intellectual location—with its appropriate particular emphasis on war—spanned the transition from medieval to modern times.[7] His insistence that the just-war doctrine formed an essential part of international law was an attempt to find an acceptable means of combining the realities of sovereign, secular statehood with the normative—in both the moral and legal sense—aspirations of the European system of world order.

This order presumed to impose limits on behavior even under conditions of warfare. Grotius also wrote at a time in which the common adherence to Christendom gave credence to the view that statehood could be combined with a sense of an international community that could, over time, establish a true international society. As the state gained in strength and capability, the notion of some sort of solidarity based on a shared cultural or religious background faded, and more absolute notions of sovereignty prevailed. These views were expressed most influentially by the seventeenth-century political philosopher Jean Bodin, and by the Swiss jurist Emmerich de Vattel in the mid-eighteenth century.[8]

Whether the Grotian evolutionary outlook was "utopian" has been subsequently debated in many settings, but most significantly in terms of whether the statist idea set definite limits on the degree of solidarity that could be effectively established in the relations among states.[9] The minimalist view that persists to this day is that a world of states can operate successfully only if it accepts such restraining ideas as nonintervention, the failure of efforts to outlaw war, and the nonaccountability of leaders.[10] The contending view, which can be identified as the evolutionary or progressivist view, envisages steady progress toward a well-ordered international community premised on the supranational implementation of human rights (inherently interventionist), the prohibition of war, and the accountability of leaders. A revival of interest in Grotius is partly occasioned by the ambiguity of the present historical circumstance, namely, whether we are situated in a great transition from a statist world to some type of emergent global village.[11]

Aside from the relevance of justice to the international law tradition, there is the further preoccupation about how to escape from the core predicaments of an anarchical international society—especially from the Hobbesian idea of the war of all against all—without ignoring the structural reality that interacting sovereign states are grossly unequal in their capabilities.[12] Even before emergence of the modern state, visionary thinkers conceived of a world more structured around some central institutional authority. Justice was mainly conflated with order, and order was so highly valued because it was conceived to be the indispensable foundation for a durable peace.[13]

This tradition has been expressed in this century mainly in postwar settings that advanced plans for world government.[14] In effect, global justice was associated almost exclusively with the problem of war, and the solution was sought by institutionalizing the rule of law with respect to the use of force in international relations. The basic conception of world government evolved from state-society relations that conformed to a federalist model. The main anxiety among advocates and critics of world government, aside from the difficulty of its attainability, was the danger that such a centralization of authority would likely, or even inevitably, degenerate into a demonic superstate that would establish a totalitarian reign of global scope.[15] Thus the challenge for advocates of world government, or enhanced central guidance, was to design a constitutional structure of checks and balances that was effective enough to prevent war, yet decentralized enough to resist morphing into the ultimate Frankenstein's monster of global authoritarianism.[16]

In an important sense, the establishment of the League of Nations after the First World War, and the United Nations after the Second World War, represented diluted moves in this direction of institutionalized authority. Beset both by problems associated with the unwillingness of states to renounce their own sovereignty (the problem of attainability), and by a concern about the menace of premature centralization of authority (the problem of global authoritarianism), these steps toward creating the structures of global justice disappointed visionaries and disillusioned even those neo-Grotians who took refuge in optimistic expectations associated with an evolutionary view of global political development. At the same time, these moves toward the establishment of an organized international community disappointed world federalists who regarded such steps as far too modest to achieve the goal of war prevention. They also frightened ultranationalists who saw these steps as moving inexorably toward a diabolical world state. But such moves generally satisfied liberal internationalists who, placing particular hope in the eventual prospect of ever greater cooperation of a functional character, believed that progress at the global level could be achieved only by small, incremental steps.[17]

INSTITUTIONALIZING THE QUEST FOR GLOBAL JUSTICE

As a result, there have been three adaptations of a system designed to pursue global justice. First, there have been those who viewed the UN system as containing an evolutionary promise that could be fulfilled by bold action to convert the organization from its relatively impotent present character into an entity of sufficient capabilities and authority to bring peace—and thereby justice—to the world. Grenville Clark and Louis B. Sohn, in *World Peace through World Law*,[18] proposed the most widely articulated version of this reformist strain, although this line of thought has not persisted essentially because it has failed to attract adherents. This may well reflect the perception that its solution to the problem of attainability did not seem at all commensurate with the severity of the resistance arising from an attachment to sovereign rights and the creeds of nationalism. Additionally, the United Nations, although the site of many notable innovations at the margins of world politics, has not provided a receptive arena for any further structural modifications that moved away from a sovereignty-centered world.[19] Such institutional rigidity has been especially manifest with respect to the inability of the United Nations to "fix" the composition of the permanent membership of the Security Council in a manner that better reflects the changes in the character of international society since 1945, particularly the impact of decolonization on the participation of the non-Western world.

A second and more promising line of adaptations involves a different way of envisioning evolution and progress in state relations—an approach that goes back to Immanuel Kant's immensely suggestive essay *Perpetual Peace*, first published in 1795.[20] Although the interpretation of Kant's worldview remains contested, one idea has been derived and recontextualized in the conditions of the late twentieth century—the idea of "democratic peace," which has been invoked in many guises and has generated an enormous body of recent literature, particularly in the United States.[21] The essential claim of this theory is that democratically organized states do not wage war against one another, and that democracy is spreading throughout the world as the basis of legitimate government.[22] The attractiveness of the idea is that it seems empirically grounded and follows the course of history. Also relevant is the liberal idea that support for international human rights creates a just world society that extends its reach beyond the external relations of states to encompass the relations between governments and their citizens. Present in this idea is the expectation that a democratized world community would be able to agree upon far more ambitious institutional arrangements. This possibility is given added plausibility by the institutionalization of relations in the European regional context, even on sensitive issues of rights and money.[23]

Whether these views on democracy can be extended to non-Western countries and regions remains in doubt. It may turn out that a democratic peace holds only among Western democracies. Furthermore, the rise of global market forces is challenging the centrality of the state in the construction of world order, specifically by emphasizing the priorities of global capital as opposed to individuals within a given territorial community, and by generating policies in arenas that are beyond state control.[24] As such, the degree of institutionalization represented by the UN system seems to be slipping into the abyss of globalization despite the notable progress of recent decades toward democratization at the state level.[25] The United Nations may be too statist in conception to serve a world order in which both global market forces and transnational social actors are playing increasingly significant roles.[26] The seductive premise in the presumption of the democratic peace approach is that institutionalization at regional and global levels is not indispensable for a just world order. Rather, the inner orientation of states (especially, states' commitment to democracy and human rights) is what forms their pattern of behavior in world society. This adaptation also tests the limits of plausibility, given the rising levels of interconnectedness that characterize so many aspects of international life and that produce intractable problems ranging from the control of transnational crime and international migration to the rise of international terrorism, the spread of weapons of mass destruction, and the protection of the global commons.

The third line of adaptation takes the form of normative adjustment—deliberate transformative changes made in different arenas of authority to lessen human suffering. The World Order Models Project (WOMP) was initiated in 1967 to encourage systematic thinking by leading academics in different cultural and ideological settings about how to achieve a just world order. In the course of more than thirty years of activity, WOMP has generated a series of distinct perspectives on how to proceed toward the realization of global justice, but it has significantly failed to agree upon a single approach.[27] Although WOMP has avoided much of the Eurocentrism that appears to have afflicted earlier efforts to shape a just world order, it is vulnerable to allegations of utopianism for not having addressed the attainability problem in a convincing fashion. It does, however, move the global justice concern off an exclusively war/peace axis to embrace global concerns about poverty, inequality, environmental protection, and social, economic, and cultural rights.

WOMP's attitude toward international institutions is diverse and ambivalent. Aside from its main organizational leader, Saul Mendlovitz, the other main participants in WOMP have been skeptical about an enhanced United Nations, both for reasons of attainability and appropriateness (i.e., the perception that the United Nations in its current form is too statist and too susceptible to geopolitical domination to serve consistently the interests of the peoples of the world in a just world order).

The notion of global justice has also been articulated in terms of achieving what could be called "humane governance." This point of view examines positive and negative trends along several main axes of normative concern: security in relation to international and intranational violence; economic well-being in relation to basic human needs and degrees of inequality within and among societies; and the depth and breadth of democratization, including economic and social aspects of human rights and the extent of environmental protection as it relates to present and future conditions.[28] Humane governance is also conceived in relation to "inhumane governance," a reference to degrees of insecurity, deprivation, exploitation, inequality, marginalization, and environmental decay. An important line of inquiry examines the tensions between "globalization-from-above" (capital-driven market forces seeking a maximally efficient world) and "globalization-from-below" (people-oriented transnational and grassroots social forces seeking a maximally humane and sustainable world).

Where the state fits into this drama of globalization will depend on how this essential encounter between contending forces of globalization resolves itself over the next decade. The outcome is likely to determine the extent to which international institutions play an enhanced role in the future, and if so, whether they will play a positive role from the perspective of humane governance. The critiques of the policies of the Bretton Woods institutions, especially the International Monetary Fund's stress on structural adjustment programs and the World Bank's promotion of megaprojects, were based on their alleged inhumane impacts.[29] The transnational project to establish an international criminal court is premised on its expected contribution to the realization of a more humane world order.[30] Each institutional aspect of the world system needs to be interpreted from the perspective of global justice to assess whether its promise and performance is to be viewed positively.[31]

The choice of the term *governance* rather than *government* is important for several reasons. First, *governance* calls attention to various forms of institutional and collective efforts to organize human affairs on a global scale, encompassing the global institutions of the UN system, various regional actors, and transnational and local grassroots initiatives. Second, the specific initiative of The Commission on Global Governance responded to a perceived window of opportunity to improve the world's peace and security infrastructure in the aftermath of the cold war. Third, the idea of governance was intended to be flexible and analytical, avoiding the anti-sovereignty connotations of "global" or "world" government. And fourth, the focus on global governance addresses a concern that a statist world order framework would no longer capture the reality being created by the rise of market forces and the transnational activities of voluntary civic associations.[32] It represents the conviction that self-organizing systems (such as the market or the Internet) and other nonbureaucratized modes of authority (such as those of environmental or human rights activists and organizations) may achieve beneficial results without institutionalization. Furthermore, the beginnings of an existent global civil society are more easily encompassed within a governance structure for world society than they are within a traditional statist framework.[33] There is also the related idea that fears and objections associated with world government may be dispelled, or at least mitigated, by thinking in terms of global governance.

Finally, global justice must be approached in practical terms that address the contradictions and complexities of the present-day world. How can the cause of global justice be promoted given present realities? What role do international institutions play within the UN system and at a regional level? Can this institutional role be strengthened, and if so, in what respects? Should the path to humane governance be increasingly one of "deinstitutionalization," as with the downsizing operations that have been reconstituting the United Nations during the last several years? These inquiries find relevance in contexts in which the pursuit of global justice is a matter not of an imagined or desired future, but of an all-too-real present replete with dilemmas and risks.[34] A feature of global justice within the existing framework of world order is the pervasive need to find a balance between contradictory pressures; most prominent among these competing pressures are:

- Balancing claims of peace against claims of justice in a state's transition from an authoritarian past to a democratic present and future;
- Balancing claims of aggregate economic growth against claims of equity and environmental protection, especially in relation to the acutely disadvantaged;
- Balancing claims on behalf of a free and open market against claims in support of regulation in the public interest;
- Balancing claims on behalf of current human consumption against claims of fairness to future generations;
- Balancing claims on behalf of institutional efficiency, constitutional tradition, and democratic consensus against claims in support of unheard and marginalized voices;
- Balancing claims of geopolitical leaders to provide order against claims associated with legal and moral prohibitions on the use of nondefensive force;
- Balancing claims of respect for cultural diversity against claims associated with the implementation of a universally binding framework of international human rights.

CONCEPTUALIZING THE CHALLENGE

Global justice, no matter how it's conceived, seems distant from the realities of international life. Two complementary logics underpin the current system of world order: statist logic deriving from the Westphalian view of international society as constituted by territorial sovereign states, and market logic deriving from the moving forces of capital efficiency and minimal governmental regulation in an era of globalization. Increased opportunities for investment, growth, and trade are treated as the tests of a successful economic policy without raising questions about social harm.[35] Neither of these two logics of world order allows significant room for justice unless one gives credence to the rhetorical flourishes of political leaders. Indeed, the Westphalian state system has, as Ken Booth convincingly argues, disappointingly accommodated a series of severe "human wrongs" ever since its beginnings in 1648.[36] The laissez-faire orientation of the market has taken refuge in the lame conviction that, in due course, the invisible hand of economic growth would overcome economic hardship, a view almost completely lacking empirical support.[37]

The statist orientation has been associated primarily, especially in the last half-century, with realist thinking derived from Machiavelli and Hobbes, and restated for our time by many public figures, perhaps most influentially by George Kennan and Henry Kissinger. This approach views policy through the prism of national interests and scorns any serious effort to work toward human betterment or to overcome the anarchical character of international society.[38] There are, of course, many variations on the realist theme, but amid this diversity, coherence is maintained by a stress on the formative role played by power in the structuring of relations among states— still regarded as the main, if not sole international political actors.[39] As a group, realists are generally negative about the normative role of international institutions, seeking to pursue peace by way of countervailing power, and disregarding justice altogether except when humanitarian challenges induce philanthropic responses.[40] The main point here is that governments are dominated by realist modes of thinking, and this orientation is transferred to most of the personnel working on behalf of international institutions. Any discourse examining the prospects for global justice is treated by most realists as a waste of energy, or worse, a diverting manifestation of naïve or utopian thinking. Such a critique is regarded as especially necessary in the United States, which realists have always regarded as peculiarly vulnerable to woolly-headed idealistic schemes, a tendency that allegedly reached its most alarming proportions during the latter years of Woodrow Wilson's presidency.[41]

If we shift our attention to the market logic, the outlook is no more favorable with respect to the attainment of justice. The current version of market logic has, for two or more decades, been shaped by a seemingly coherent group of ideas variously labeled "neoliberalism," "rational economics," or "the Washington consensus." It is hazardous to generalize the content of these ideas, but their main thrust is to favor liberalization of the economy, privatization of ownership, a minimal regulatory role for government, a stress on the most efficient return on capital, and a conviction that poverty, social distress, and even environmental deterioration are best addressed through the invisible hand of rapid economic growth and the beneficence of the private sector.

This view of the market is reinforced by an "Internet ethos" that also favors minimizing the role of government and believes that the Internet, as a self-organizing system, requires no guidance to assure justice for the peoples of the world.[42] It needs to be understood that globalization as such, involving interconnectedness and global-scale technological innovations, especially in relation to information, does *not* entail an indifference to justice. This indifference arises from a set of ideas that could easily be reversed in a different political climate. Several recent events indicate that the political climate is becoming more receptive to concerns about justice. Examples include Tony Blair's advocacy of "the Third Way," the leftward slant of elections in several major European countries, and the rethinking of economic policy provoked by the depth and duration of the world economic crisis that started in Southeast Asia in mid-1997 and spread to such important countries as Japan, Russia, and Brazil.[43]

Nevertheless, the pursuit of global justice at this time is hampered by the strength of realism and neoliberalism, which continue to reflect the ideological orientation of policymaking elites in most parts of the world. The difficulty in pursuing global justice assumes three main forms: first, the trend toward the social disempowerment of the state, as evident in the ever greater emphasis on the promotion of finance and business and the diminishing focus on the priorities of organized labor and the challenges of homelessness and unemployment; second, the downward pressure on expenditures for public goods such as education and culture, and especially on global public goods associated with financing the United Nations and protecting the global commons against climate change and pollution; third, the libertarian outlook of minimal government (less taxes and regulation) and maximum individualism that seems to be predominant among the most influential developers of information technology.

The social disempowerment of the state follows from the impact of neoliberal ideas, reinforced by arguments about competitiveness in more closely linked regional and world markets. Because the state possesses the most powerful mobilizing capabilities, it will be difficult to envision addressing the justice claims of the poor and of economically disadvantaged societies without a political process that results in the social reempowerment of the state.

The reduced support for investment in public goods also derives from pressures to downsize the state, eliminate its inefficiencies, and marginalize its role in providing for such basic human needs as health, education, environmental protection, and culture. Internationally, this reluctance to support public goods has been manifested in part by the financial crisis of the United Nations, especially by the withholding for years by the United States of more than $1 billion in long-overdue UN dues. But beyond the current reluctance to support the United Nations is the even greater unwillingness to allow it to expand in ways that take advantage of the opportunities for more effective forms of governance that could include the active promotion of justice.

The libertarian outlook expresses the anarchistic spirit of the electronic frontier, where the Internet gives individuals the freedoms associated with the wild spaces of the cyberworld. Such an ethic reinforces and is reinforced by the enthusiasm for market guidance fostered by the business community. Both tend to stand together in their dislike of government as an interventionist instrument with respect to the economy or social relations. The Internet also reinforces the individualism and self-centeredness of capitalism by weakening bonds based on community and tradition and finds an ethos of social responsibility antithetical to its aims, especially in the form of government welfare. Part of the anarchistic outlook is an opposition to either the expansion of public-sector institutions or the creation of new institutions. Hence, at this time the Internet culture, despite some positive features, poses a new and formidable obstacle to the promotion of global justice.[44]

FIVE CONTEMPORARY DRAMAS: PURSUING GLOBAL JUSTICE

There are many specific concerns about the pursuit of global justice within the historical and structural constraints of world order as it is currently constituted and evolving. Such nonideal realities pose difficult choices between contending viewpoints as to the requirements and attainability of global justice. But these realities also confirm that the pursuit of justice is a matter of present relevance and cannot be relegated to the future. Decisions are controversial, and attentive citizens and responsible leaders make choices that disclose the character of global justice in concrete situations. In an important sense, global justice under present conditions of world order can be best understood as the effort to resolve a series of dilemmas, which are here illustrated by reference to five dramas.

In resolving a dilemma, it is always possible for those who believed that it should have been resolved differently to argue that the policy outcome was unjust or inappropriate. Global justice as a present dimension of world order is continuously in the process of gestation by way of reinforcement or repudiation of earlier decisions. As such, it can be seen as resembling the evolution of common law itself, or as a crucial feature of self-realization for a democratic polity. How such a polity resolves justice dilemmas significantly helps to establish its specific identity as a political system of a given character at a given time.

There is a special complexity about this process at the global level. In a political order that lacks a government, the dynamics of decision tend to be more dispersed and more difficult to interpret authoritatively. Many of the most important contributions to the pursuit of global justice are the result of actions taken at national levels of decision and may often involve assessment of the policy consequences for a particular state if it adheres to international standards of law and morality. In this regard, the voluntary adherence by a sovereign state to international legal standards may itself be understood as one embodiment of global justice.

Let us now view these general considerations in relation to the more specific dilemmas that seem to be of particular importance at this time with respect to the clarification of global justice.

Peace versus Justice in the Setting of Democratization

One of the most persistent problems of this period is how to reconcile conflicting goals in the aftermath of severe criminality on the part of a past governing process. The regime responsible for crimes against humanity or genocidal behavior has passed from the scene but remains to varying degrees at large, often as part of a bargain by which its impunity was "purchased" in exchange for its voluntary relinquishment of power. From its modern origins in the Nuremberg and Tokyo trials of surviving German and Japanese leaders after the Second World War, international law has progressed to the point where such behavior is increasingly subject to indictment, prosecution, and punishment in various appropriate circumstances.

But the character of appropriate circumstances is far from self-evident. It often involves a delicate balancing of opposed considerations favoring either peace, in the sense of nonviolent coexistence between former leaders (the alleged perpetrators) and emergent leaders (the would-be constitutionalists), or justice, in the sense of imposing accountability for past conduct. The current anguish and controversy concerning the role and effects of the Truth and Reconciliation Commission in South Africa are a vivid example of the always risky search for peace. The optimistic view is that foregoing criminal prosecution while documenting, acknowledging, and denouncing the criminality of apartheid will avoid incensing the perpetrators of these crimes and yet provide satisfaction and relief to those South Africans who were victims or closely associated with victims. The less hopeful view is that the commission process will lead to a double failure. Namely, that the perpetrators and their friends will remain incensed by their public humiliation, and the victims and their associates will feel that far too little has been achieved to close the book on such acute and pervasive cruelty and abuse.

What gives the issue its unavoidable character as a matter of justice is the perceived character of past behavior as constituting unforgivable crimes. From the perspective of minimum international standards of law and morality, these crimes are perhaps best categorized as "crimes against humanity" and "genocide."[45] And yet, if the cost of prosecution is seen as jeopardizing the transition to democracy or the peace of the community, the decision to grant impunity or amnesty seems understandable, even beneficial.

A poignant example of this dilemma has been presented prominently by the Pinochet controversy. In the fall of 1998, while former Chilean dictator Augusto Pinochet was in Britain for medical treatment, a Spanish court requested his extradition to face charges relating to crimes of state involving Spaniards who were in Chile during Pinochet's rule. Several other European countries also issued such requests. The Chilean government requested the release of General Pinochet and his return to Chile, arguing that the former leader was entitled to diplomatic immunity with respect to the behavior in question and that he was the object of criminal prosecutions in Chile. After complex deliberations, the English House of Lords indicated by a 3–2 vote that the government of Britain should accede to the request for extradition so that Pinochet's alleged responsibility for crimes against humanity could be prosecuted in Spain. Unfortunately, that vote subsequently has been set aside by the House of Lords for technical reasons, leaving the outcome uncertain once more. The House of Lords has assembled a new panel of judges to hear a second presentation of the case, which as of late 1999 has reinstated the propriety of the Spanish extradition request. In the end, the British courts upheld the contested finding that Pinochet is medically unfit to stand trial and should be returned to Chile.

Here, the complexity of justice assumes a very fundamental form. The essential dilemma is whether the final decision in Britain should be made by reference to international standards or whether deference should be accorded to the views of the Chilean government. It is the Chilean people who might well bear the burden of a regression to military rule or more probably to incidents of civil strife. At the same time, all of international society has an interest in the application of these international standards as part of a wider effort to establish an effective procedure to ensure the accountability of leaders for such criminality. In an important sense, grants of amnesty or impunity in such settings are always "Faustian bargains."[46] Yet even if the premise of unforgivable crime is accepted, given the suffering that a society has experienced, should not the decision of its democratically elected leaders prevail? But even if one posits this argument, the outcome may not be so evident. Perhaps the current leaders are making a pro forma show of seeking the return of Pinochet while making it clear through confidential diplomatic circles that their real preference is for him to face prosecution overseas. Should not the views of those who identify with the victims most directly be given great weight in reaching a decision? There is little doubt that vocal anti-Pinochet Chileans would welcome his prosecution while pro-Pinochet Chileans would decry it.

At this stage of international history, it seems clear that these types of issues faced by many societies during the last decade need to be resolved on a contextual basis. The people that have endured the crimes, and their representatives, should have the first opportunity to resolve the dilemma of peace and justice. If the subject matter spills over the borders of a given country, as was the case with the Pinochet controversy, then the balance of considerations assumes a far more complex form. The dynamics of global justice would benefit from the expanded opportunities for prosecution and the denial of claims of immunity. But would the dynamics of peace be obstructed by undermining the reliability of impunity bargains struck in the past? Would dictators hesitate to relinquish the reins of power knowing that they may be vulnerable to future prosecutions if they should venture beyond the borders of their own country?

Such difficult questions suggest two conclusions: first, that the contextual attributes in each instance should be thoroughly explored, and second, that the process of appraisal and controversy should be carefully nurtured to clarify the issues at stake.

Economic Growth versus Social Equity

During recent decades, economic policy has been increasingly shaped by neoliberal criteria that emphasize the primacy of capital efficiency in the allocation of resources. Part of this emphasis involves privatization and liberalization, in which social and economic functions shift from the public to the private sector. The intranational result is the partial social disempowerment of the state. The *inter*national result is the decline of direct development assistance and the general conditionality of loans administered by the World Bank and International Monetary Fund. In effect, these institutions mount pressure to assure that a governmental recipient of funds does not use public resources for poverty alleviation and social distress, but rather to build a high-growth economy.[47]

The ethical rationale buttressing such policies rests on variants of the invisible hand, by which the entire social spectrum automatically benefits, although not necessarily equally, from economic growth. In order to diminish the human suffering involved in achieving fiscal reform, there will need to be a greater willingness to take into balance social equity concerns against economistic goals.

The empirical evidence suggests growing inequality across a range of dimensions, a depiction well-summarized by Nancy Fraser. The search for justice, she says, occurs:

> ... in a world of exacerbated inequality—in income and property ownership; in access to paid work, education, health care, and leisure time; but also, more starkly, in caloric intake and exposure to environmental toxicity, and hence in life expectancy and rates of morbidity and mortality. Material inequality is on the rise in most of the world's countries—in the United States and in China, in Sweden and in India, in Russia and in Brazil. It is also increasingly global, most dramatically across the line that divides North from South.[48]

These trends have also been amply documented and summarized in the annual volumes of the UN Human Development Report. From this report emerge two important ideas that relate to the pursuit of global justice. First, the commitment to economic growth does improve the aggregate economic well-being of people in general, with overall reductions in various forms of impoverishment. Second, this process of growth also accentuates inequalities, making the rich richer and the poor poorer in every region of the world.[49]

Such observations occur under conditions of limited ideological alternatives. A socialist ethos—or even an international welfare program—does not currently seem politically viable. At the same time, there are increasing acknowledgments of the problem, perhaps most comprehensively at the Copenhagen Social Summit in 1995, which called for more concerted action to provide jobs, address poverty, and overcome other types of social insecurity.

A further set of developments challenges the ideological primacy of neoliberalism, calling for various modifications in the direction of some social reempowerment of the state. The first includes the rethinking under way within the Bretton Woods institutions—a reaction to the inability of structural adjustment to arrest the deterioration of living standards for a substantial number of countries experiencing financial crisis since 1997. Of particular concern are their efforts to condition bailout relief on structural adjustments that produce political turmoil and massive impoverishment, as witnessed most alarmingly in Indonesia.

The second development concerns the mandate implied by a series of European elections that appeared to repudiate neoliberal political orientations in favor of more social-democratic outlooks, articulated in the context of economic globalization as "the Third Way" or as a call for the establishment of social Europe. The notion of social Europe as the Third Way seeks to reaffirm the social commitments to the poor or jobless without repudiating the move toward a dynamic model of European economic integration. In effect, social Europe implies that the advantages of this new phase of capitalism do not have to eclipse the human achievements of the welfare state, the labor movement, and social democracy. The United Nations Development Program has been encouraging a similar approach, which it calls "pro-poor growth," and amounts to an affirmative-action strategy of capital investment that gives priority to those forms of investment that clearly benefit the poor.[50]

The global justice aspects of this growth/equity dilemma relate both to the duties to alleviate distress, which are specified as economic and social rights of the disadvantaged, and to the moral obligation to adopt policies that diminish inequalities between countries, regions, races, genders, and civilizations. These concerns are often considered in relation to the question of distributive justice and its applicability to a world of sovereign states.[51] These problems have recently highlighted the degree to which economic globalization, and its impact on national economic policy, have diminished the capacity and will of governments to be compassionate toward their own citizens.[52] International institutions play an important role in gathering information about the degrees of deprivation and inequality, and about the adaptation of resource allocation in response to equity concerns. The rethinking apparently under way within the Bretton Woods institutions may well point toward a new balance between a purely economic view of growth and a more normative concern with overcoming human suffering and inequality.

Claims of Present Generations versus Claims of Future Generations

In this period of extraordinarily rapid technological change, and increasingly evident environmental decay and depletion of resources, ever greater attention has been devoted to the justice claims of future generations.[53] International environmental treaty law has begun to acknowledge this obligation, and environmentalists have been urging a more rigorous application of "the precautionary principle" as one practical means of upholding the well-being of future generations. This principle urges that environmental risks be taken seriously as a guide to prudent behavior before conclusive scientific information is available to confirm the gravity of such risks.

This idea that global justice involves relations through time and space is gaining prominence. Global justice between spatial communities appears to be declining as a result of neoliberalism and globalization, as evidenced in the decline of foreign economic assistance in North-South relations. Global justice between temporal communities, however, actually seems to be increasing, as evidenced by various expressions of greater sensitivity to past injustices and future dangers.

The distinction between temporal and spatial communities is crucial. For centuries, the relations among territorially bounded sovereign entities called "states" ("spatial communities") preoccupied discussions of world order. More recently, this spatial focus has been attenuated by a rising concern about grievances from the past and worries about the life circumstances of future generations—that is, of "temporal communities."

There has also been an upsurge in efforts to rectify the injustices of the past, and in some instances, the rather distant past. Some of these efforts have involved substantive redress, although more often the results are largely symbolic. The recovery of Holocaust-era gold reserves from Swiss banks and of art treasures stolen by the Nazi regime constitutes instances of substantive redress. Instances of symbolic redress, on the other hand, include apologies by Japanese leaders for atrocities committed against China and Korea during its Imperial Era, by President Clinton to African societies for the cruelties of slavery, or by the Canadian government to indigenous peoples for their dispossession.

As with other dimensions of global justice, acceding to these claims and resolving historic grievances pose dilemmas that are not easily overcome. Present elites may resist circumscribing their own activities and may refuse to invoke a moral obligation to satisfy the needs of those currently afflicted.

A related and frequently posed argument is that technology almost certainly will, on balance, improve the lives of future generations by improving productivity and providing better medical attention. This contention has held true on a material level for almost two centuries when measured by such yardsticks of well-being as longevity and literacy. To the extent that this argument is accepted, the present generation is relieved of any duty to restrain its consumptive patterns. If, on the other hand, the risks to the future involve a heightened probability of catastrophic climate change and pollution, then technological optimism, even if justified in some respects, is mainly beside the point.

Resistance to redressing past grievances includes the insistence that the behavior in question occurred within a different framework of values, and that present generations have no direct responsibility for the actions of their forebears. There is also some opposition based on the view that even symbolic forms of redress are unhealthy expressions of collective guilt or undermine a societal sense of self-worth. How to weigh this balance is subject to sharply divergent viewpoints and is likely to be determined in the end by the play of political forces.

Many of the concerns about the future and unresolved past grievances call attention to the degree to which the pursuit of global justice involves the axis of time—an increasingly important focus for normative energies.[54] International institutions can play a role in giving concrete meaning—in the form of specific prohibitions or through protective measures—to either claims of forbearance in view of future risks of harm or grievances derived from the past. With particular regard to contested views surrounding past events, institutions that embody commissions of experts or moral authority figures can play a constructive role in the search for acceptable solutions.

Tradition, Consensus, and Political Order versus the Rights of the Marginalized

A major preoccupation of recent decades has been to develop a framework of law for overcoming several forms of noneconomic inequality. This effort has focused on the protection of human rights and involves overcoming certain systemic forms of injustice. The pursuit of global justice, then, is a matter of diminishing the levels of injustice associated with the inequalities of race, gender, religious belief, civilizational orientation, and age.

International institutions have played a crucial role in this process, generating authoritative norms by way of lawmaking treaties, declarations, and reports on practice. One of the most impressive achievements of the United Nations in its first half-century has been to provide the peoples of the world with the normative architecture of a comprehensive human rights system. Such a development has assumed great practical relevance because of three complementary developments: first, the rise of human rights–oriented transnational nongovernmental organizations (NGOs), which have used their access to information about violations to promote compliance; second, the effectiveness of human rights as an instrument of struggle in the resistance movements in Eastern Europe during the 1980s and the anti-apartheid campaign in South Africa; and third, the increased prominence of human rights in the foreign policy of some major states.

Further notable factors have also added to the overall effort to implement human rights as an element of global justice. Perhaps most dramatic of all has been the role of the European justice system. This system includes judicial remedies, a respected regional court, and the possibility that an individual can secure protection from abuses against her or his own government. The respect accorded this system and its substantive contributions suggest a model for other regions that has already been emulated to some degree in Latin America and to a modest extent in Africa, Asia, and the Middle East. Also helpful in some settings has been the reluctance of the World Bank and the IMF to extend support to countries with particularly poor human rights records.

This positive picture is not, unfortunately, the whole story. Geopolitical factors make the political reinforcement of human rights norms uneven, leading to perceptions of double standards and accusations of hypocrisy. Cultural practices may contradict human rights norms in ways that are exceedingly difficult to challenge effectively even if the territorial government acts in good faith. This is particularly true when long-entrenched religious beliefs oppose movements toward overcoming injustice, as in relation to the treatment of women.

In India, for instance, since independence the central government has formally and sincerely subscribed to secularism and international human rights standards, but has often seemed helpless at the level of implementation where such standards challenged fundamental cultural practices, such as those involving discrimination against women. This inability is especially manifest at the village level, where the national commitment to secularism has rarely made an impact on traditional Hindu culture. The control of the Indian government is now in the hands of a coalition led by the Bharatiya Janata Party (BJP), which has attempted to incorporate Hindu nationalism into its political agenda. Consequently, even the commitment to secularism is now open to doubt, further complicating the practice of overcoming discrimination against women. Specifically, where cultural norms and populist preferences strongly conflict with legal norms, it is difficult for the latter to prevail without a political struggle at the grassroots level.

The most pervasive forms of injustice are difficult to overcome because their existence is embedded in the deep structure of power and privilege. For example, male dominance of structures of authority and decision-making in all sectors of society is so pervasive that it is still treated as natural, despite important inroads made by feminism and the global human rights movement. Similarly, the modernist assumptions of society are so strongly held that efforts by indigenous peoples to retain their traditional ways of life are poorly understood and rarely appreciated beyond a small circle of sympathizers. In effect, established patterns—even if abusive—are very difficult to challenge effectively, especially by those at the margins of society, given their civilizational orientation and low social or economic status.

Some positive movement-based steps are being taken, however. Women and indigenous peoples have established their own networks and pressure groups that operate in institutional arenas throughout the world. The UN system has provided formal and informal arenas for both women and indigenous peoples to develop their own programs of action. Some concessions have been achieved by these transnational initiatives associated with an emergent global civil society. During the first half of the 1990s, such marginalized social forces made particularly good use of global conferences, under UN auspices, to put their grievances on the world policy agenda.[55] Indeed, these efforts were so successful that a statist backlash ensued, expressed in terms of budgetary concerns and the deriding of such global conferences as useless "spectacles." Cost cutting is often used by the established international order and its representatives as an excuse to mask the real concern over the threatening rise of transnational social forces. It has been widely noticed that the UN conferences provide such forces with increased political leverage and media access, thus eroding governmental control over policy outcomes with respect to such sensitive issues as abortion, the role of women, environmental regulation, and financial responsibility. As a result, these international institutional forums for political action are not nearly as likely to be available in the decade ahead, and this vehicle for the pursuit of global justice has been lost, at least temporarily.

This terrain is exceedingly complex and the results remain inconclusive. A normative framework exists that supports those struggling against varieties of acute inequality. Activists representing the main victim constituencies are organized as never before. At the same time, entrenched structures are difficult to reform in fundamental respects, and the interests of elites are generally aligned with the established order and its implicit assumptions about superiority and inferiority. This agenda of issues relating to cultural modes of inequality definitely deserves to be included in any contemporary inquiry into the pursuit of global justice. Such inclusion is virtually assured by the salience of such issues in the state-society relations of every country in the world.

Traditional Geopolitics versus the Legal Prohibition of International Aggression

A core goal associated with global justice has been minimizing the role of violence and warfare on all levels of political interaction, especially in the relations among states. There remains a fundamental disagreement about how such goals can be achieved given the structures and character of international society. The control of world politics remains firmly in the hands of realists—ideological descendants of Machiavelli—who believe that only countervailing power, combined with a credible will to use force if provoked, can maintain peace and stability in the world. Within this perspective, nuclear weaponry is considered an indispensable instrument of geopolitical management, dangerous only if these weapons fall into the wrong hands, but a generally constructive, stabilizing influence. On this basis, priority is accorded to antiproliferation efforts, and nuclear disarmament is perceived as politically unattractive and generally contributing to a less successfully managed world order.

The contrasting view has been that peace and justice in the world are best preserved by moving away from geopolitical management toward collective security, as embodied in the United Nations under the specific authority of the Security Council. The weakness of this challenge to realism is evident in the fact that the United Nations tends to incorporate the very ideas it opposes. The Security Council is itself a geopolitical instrument, giving each permanent member veto power, conducting its sensitive discussions in secret, and operating without any constraints that are not self-imposed. Consequently, the United Nations faithfully reflects prevailing patterns of geopolitics. It was largely gridlocked by the bipolar rivalry of the cold war and, subsequently, has been responsive primarily to the United States as the manager of unipolar geopolitics.[56]

The sharp ideological lines of debate are reductive, however, missing many valuable roles played by the United Nations. From time to time the United Nations does lend support to antiaggression norms and to closely related efforts to achieve other goals of global justice. The Security Council, partly in compensation for a failure of geopolitical will, established the war crimes tribunals in The Hague and in Arusha, Tanzania, to address the most severe wrongs associated with, respectively, the breakup of the former Yugoslavia and the genocidal outbreak in Rwanda. Furthermore, in mobilizing widespread support against Iraq's conquest of Kuwait in 1990, the United Nations managed to act effectively against Iraq's blatant aggression directed at another member of the organization.[57]

An important secondary arena of controversy involves responses to intranational conflicts that are causing great human suffering. The issue has surfaced in the past decade in relation to whether the United Nations should serve as an agency for humanitarian intervention, and if so, whether it can do so successfully. Here, the relevance of geopolitics becomes evident. International institutions cannot act effectively unless their undertakings converge with the strategic interests, as well as the normative sentiments, of the geopolitical managers. Such were the painful lessons of Somalia, Bosnia, and Rwanda.[58] There is also the legalist critique that relates global justice to adherence to international law. The original contract embedded in Article 2(7) of the UN Charter precludes intervention in domestic affairs of states. It can be maintained that such a constraint represents the limit of what can be expected from the United Nations given the persistence of geopolitical management of power and the consequent failure of the United Nations to command resources or independent peacekeeping capabilities.

So far as the nature of global justice is concerned in relation to uses of force, the core issues remain unresolved. An uneasy, suppressed tension exists between, on the one hand, legalist preferences for compliance with international law and for a gradual transfer of security functions to international institutions, and on the other, geopolitical preferences for configuring available power in such a manner as to discourage and punish antisocial behavior by irresponsible and evil political actors, pariah states, and terrorist movements.

TOWARD HUMANE GOVERNANCE

Global justice has so far been considered under the nonideal conditions of the established world order, which is evolving in the direction of some form of global governance. Whether this transition process, which appears to be superseding the Westphalian idea of territorial sovereignty, is leading humanity toward a beneficial form of global governance is unclear at present. Contradictory trends are evident.

It seems appropriate to end this chapter with a few indications of the positive prospects for reframing the pursuit of global justice. It needs to be emphasized that, at present, these prospects seem marginal to the main drift of change in the direction of a highly marketized, nonsustainable, and grossly unequal set of relations among the peoples of the world, with weak structures of legal authority and even weaker sentiments of human solidarity. Happily, however, our historical insight is often flawed, ignoring concealed forces. Such was the case with respect to the abrupt end of the cold war and the Soviet collapse, as well as the peaceful dismantling of apartheid in South Africa. We do not understand political reality well enough to be pessimistic, or for that matter, optimistic.

What is positive can be identified in summary form: (1) The gradual realization that warfare among major, technologically advanced states is an obsolete form of conflict resolution, particularly given the increasingly nonterritorial bases of wealth and power; (2) the emergence of transnational networks of activists motivated by a commitment to human rights, the environment, humanitarian diplomacy, economic well-being, and civilizational dialogue; (3) the widespread adherence to democratic ideals as the moral foundation of humane governance in all arenas of authority and decision, including support for a vision of cosmopolitan democracy as the next stage of constitutionalism; (4) the beginnings of an ethos of criminal account-ability that contains no exemptions for political leaders and is being imple-mented at the global level under the universal rubric of punishing anyone guilty of crimes against humanity and through the moves to establish a judi-cial institution of global character with such a mandate; and (5) the strong move toward integration at regional levels with accompanying shifts in allegiance away from the nation-state, moving outward in relation to species, civilization, and region, and inward toward local community identities.[59]

Whether these positive elements can be fashioned in such a way as to lead toward humane governance, and the equally ambitious realization of global justice, remains uncertain. What is more evident is that such an outcome will be far more likely if it engages the peoples of the world and their associations in the struggle to achieve specific human rights. In essence, the future will be what we as individual citizens make it.

To carry forward this line of inquiry requires a more detailed examina-tion of the surprising emergence of human rights as a prominent issue on the global policy agenda of major political actors. Indeed, the dynamics of globalization seem to be pushing transnational corporations in equally unex-pected directions, toward compliance with human rights and environmen-tal standards. Such insinuations of "stakeholder capitalism" need to be explored with critical reserve, especially when the exponents include in their ranks such notorious private-sector actors as Shell, British Petroleum, and Merck. The next chapter looks comprehensively at the emergence of human rights from the sinews of a statist world order.

A Half-Century of Human Rights   2

FIFTY YEARS OF BACKGROUND: A TENTATIVE BALANCE SHEET

Although human rights are affirmed in the United Nations Charter in very general language, their operative reality was not specified, and their overall role in international political life was deemed marginal in the aftermath of World War II.[1] This marginality existed in 1945 in the face of the vivid disclosures of the Nazi era, as well as the surfacing of a vague aura of guilt hovering over Western liberal democracies. This guilt was associated with their prolonged forbearance in relation to Nazi Germany so long as Hitler's atrocious crimes were directed at his own citizenry. Despite this mood, the foundation of world order continued to rest very much on the territorial logic of territorial states, in conjunction with the supportive doctrine of sovereignty and the ideology of nationalism.[2] A major implication of this logic was that the internal arrangements and policies of states were never properly subject to external accountability.[3] The UN Charter confirmed this statist feature of world order in Article 2(7) by reassuring its members that it lacked the authority to intervene in matters that were "essentially within the domestic jurisdiction" of states. This prohibition was subject only to qualification relating to the overriding responsibility of the UN acting under Chapter VII of the Charter to maintain international peace and security.

Even the original articulation of international human rights in the form of the Universal Declaration of Human Rights fifty years ago was not *initially* perceived to be a significant development. The norms affirmed were a comprehensive compilation of various legal and moral ideas about state-society-individual relationships. This enumeration of standards was at most conceived as an admonishment to governments, and more relevantly, as a kind of heterogeneous wish list cobbled together by representatives of liberal individualism and collectivist socialism. In effect, at birth the Declaration amounted to a rather innocuous and syncretist statement of consensus about desirable societal goals and future aspirations for humanity as a whole; the norms set forth were formulated as if self-regarding states in a world of gross material disparities did not exist. Also, it should be appreciated that by using the language of "declaration" and by avoiding all pretensions of implementation, a clear signal was given that the contents were not to be treated as necessarily authoritative and binding.[4]

Perhaps more damaging was the patent hypocrisy manifest in the issuance of the Universal Declaration. Many of the endorsing governments were at the time imposing control over their society in a manner that systematically ignored or repudiated the standards being affirmed by the Universal Declaration. And it was not only the Soviet Union and the countries under its sway that seemed resolutely opposed to upholding the main thrust of the Universal Declaration as it pertained to the rights of individuals in relation to the state. The participation of the colonial powers of Europe was also beset by contradiction, given their role at the time in holding most of the peoples of Asia and Africa under their dominion by means of oppressive rule. Furthermore, the military dictatorships that then dotted the political landscapes in Latin America never could have intended to take seriously a series of human rights standards, which if even loosely applied, would undermine their authoritarian style of rule. So from the outset of these moves fifty years ago to make the observance of human rights a matter of international law, there were strong grounds for skepticism as to whether to regard the development as nominal rather than substantive. Such a note of skepticism could not be avoided given the patterns of governance that existed around the world. Only the most naïve legalist could ignore the obvious rhetorical question: Why did oppressive governments agree to such an elaborate framework for human rights unless their leaders were convinced that the Universal Declaration was nothing more than a paper tiger?

In fact, the resistance to this process of internationalization of human rights is even more deeply rooted and pervasive than the considerations so far mentioned. A country like the United States, with its strong domestic constitutional and ideological commitment to human rights, has several awkward skeletons in its closet, including slavery, racial discrimination, and ethnocidal policies pursued against Native American people. Also, the United States Government has been notably laggard with respect to formal adherence to the very international legal framework that it invokes against others. It has generally viewed human rights standards as important for the countries of the South, but superfluous for the countries of the North, and certainly unnecessary with respect to the internal political life of the United

States. The confusingly one-sided message that has been sent by the most powerful state in the world is that human rights are conceived as almost exclusively an instrument of *foreign* policy. In effect, the United States acts as if human rights were a series of obligations binding on others. Such a view overlooks the reality of human rights, that their concerns focus on *domestic* life, that is, the relations of state and society within each country, including the United States.

Official spokespersons for China took evident satisfaction in pointing out several years ago that it was strange for Washington to present itself as the world champion of international human rights. After all, the record showed that China had ratified seventeen major human rights treaties while the United States had only managed to ratify fifteen. There are, in other words, strong sources of sovereignty-oriented resistance to the internationalization of human rights even on the part of major liberal democracies, based on the idea that a sovereign people should never confer any legal authority on an international body external to the state.[5] This subordination of human rights to the abstraction of sovereignty has been systematically challenged only within the comfortable confines of the European Union. In this setting, the commonality of outlook among the members and a longstanding alliance have produced a political community that upholds human rights in a form that anticipates their implementation by recourse to the European Commission of Human Rights and the European Court of Human Rights. Such a breakthrough in the *internationalization* of protection for human rights is conceptually irreconcilable with the Westphalian logic of world order.

European exceptionalism aside, for the rest of the world, regardless of its commitment to constitutional democracy as the foundation of domestic public order, the internationalization of human rights remains minimal, and its prospect is still to varying degrees problematic.[6] Not only do the political and juridical aspects of sovereignty and the prohibition of intervention get in the way, but there are a variety of other types of resistance that reflect the characteristics of state-society relations within each particular country. While adherence to the framework of international human rights is a widely shared sentiment around the world, one which definitely informs the conduct of diplomacy and the language of statecraft, resistance is evident in all parts of the world, though its nature varies from state to state, reflecting differences in history, culture, stage of development, domestic public order, and many other factors.

Additionally, it is important to take account of some influential general patterns of criticism directed at the claim that the norms of international human rights law deserve unconditional respect. For one thing, several anti-hegemonic discourses have been challenging the authoritativeness of human rights claims from a variety of perspectives. These critical discourses are par-

ticularly persuasive in the postcolonial circumstances of many countries of
the South. Political discourse in many former colonies frequently invokes
the history of prior Western colonial abuse and exploitation, including territorial intrusions under the auspices of international rules concerning
protection of foreign nationals and capitulary regimes exempting European
nationals from indigenous criminal law in non-Western countries during
the colonial era. This line of analysis contends that, despite the end of colonialism, this structure of dominance has been essentially maintained, assuming more indirect and disguised forms. These critical discourses argue
accordingly that the promotion of human rights needs to be understood primarily as yet another pretext for continued neocolonial intervention. In
effect, current patterns of intervention are allegedly being shaped by the realities of postcolonialism.[7] Furthermore, it is argued, along a quite independent line of reasoning, that adherence to international human rights standards
is not entirely warranted from either a substantive or procedural viewpoint.
If due account is taken of the facts surrounding the Western origins and
biases of international human rights standards, then their universal applicability is drawn into question.[8]

The most serious of all constraints bearing on the application of international human rights norms, however, is perhaps the one least brought to
light. It is, in essence, the staunchly realist orientation of the political elites
who have continued to control the shaping of foreign policy on behalf of
most states, and especially on behalf of those states that play the most active
geopolitical roles. The realist frame of reference entertains extremely serious, *principled* doubts about the relevance of law and morality to the proper
operation of the state system. Realism is not easily reconciled with the
human rights tradition unless such concerns are *pragmatically* invoked as an
instrument of foreign policy, and even then only in a selective and opportunistic manner.

Alleging human rights violations has become a useful means for realists
to indict foreign adversaries in a manner that generates media attention. In
this way, exposing human rights violations often helps to prepare the ground
for sanctions and other forms of hostile action. The realist outlook is reasonably forthright about subordinating any commitment to international
human rights to its strategic priorities, including patterns of alignment and
conflict. This deference to the interests of the state has often given human
rights a bad name in many circles, as their invocation and evasion by prominent governments seems opportunistic, and thereby lacking in substance and
values-driven convictions. In this manner, the human rights rhetoric used
by political leaders and diplomats causes an impression that is somewhat
similar to that created when a film substitutes dubbed voices in another language. A foreign language is superimposed on the soundtrack, but the lips
of the actors on the screen are out of sync, moving with the rhythms of the

film's original spoken language. In geopolitical terms, the superimposed language is that of human rights, but the lips of political authority are still moving according to the discordant logic of geopolitics. It is this core interaction between different approaches to the action and identity of the state that causes so much of the confusion and uncertainty about the significance of human rights, and its future prospects.[9] This is an unfortunate state of affairs, as it encourages the formation of misleading polar attitudes about the significance of human rights, pitting the exaggerated expectations of human rights activists against the cynical dismissal of power-wielders.

In many respects, the opposing faces of realist manipulation of human rights have both been exemplified by the approach taken by the Clinton Administration to its relationship with China.[10] So long as the issue of human rights made for good domestic ideological posturing within the United States, it seemed beneficial to highlight China's responsibility for the bloody crackdown of the democracy movement in Tiananmen Square in June 1989 and its overall miserable human rights record. But the attention of American political leaders began to shift in 1997 to China's role in the hoped-for recovery from the Asian fiscal crisis, and its role as an economic superpower and major trading partner. At that point it became desirable to downplay China's human rights abuses and focus instead on the benefits arising from what is now being called "cordial engagement," as opposed to the colder diplomatic approach that had been generally known as "constructive engagement."[11]

This shift in emphasis gave rise to extensive and often intemperate commentary in response to President Clinton's visit to China in June 1998. On the one side were those who felt bitterly disappointed by Clinton's moral capitulation, a viewpoint strongly expressed by the former Chinese political prisoner Wei Jingsheng: "America has become the leader of a full Western retreat from the human rights cause in China. Clinton's decision to go to Beijing at this time sends a very clear signal that he is more concerned with supporting the autocracy than with the democratic movement in China. The timing of the West's abandonment of China's democratic movement could not be worse."[12] The realist counterattack was equally vigorous and uncompromising. Charles Freeman, Jr., First Assistant Secretary of State for International Security Affairs, insisted that it was time to approach China from a strategic viewpoint rather than to persist with the feel-good human rights agenda: "[T]he administration accepted that it was going to have to deal seriously with China, that China was more than a theme park for the human rights advocates and the Dalai Lama's followers."[13] The unfortunate impression created by this remark was that the earlier insistence on human rights was an essentially frivolous way for the United States to approach a state of such size and importance as China. The moment had now arrived when the United States needed to abandon its foreign policy commitment in support of human rights in order to pursue its *real* interests, which meant a "mature" approach that was based on economic opportunity and the calculus of power relations in Asia.

Given the primacy of realist priorities, human rights activists are often disappointed by their recurrent inability to gain the commanding heights of policymaking, especially when strong strategic interests appear to point in an opposite direction. Policymakers are generally trying hard to diminish the impact of what they believe to be sentimental and ideological concerns that should not in most circumstances be given too much weight if the practice of international relations is going to proceed in a rational manner. Confusion arises because realists themselves "use" human rights from time to time to accentuate positions of hostility or to appease domestic pressure groups, raising expectations and then abandoning human rights concerns just as easily when strategic winds change direction. In these respects, the impact of the realist outlook in geopolitics produces results that are often confusing and uncertain. Realism has given human rights an important push from time to time, as occurred in the latter phases of the cold war, but realists are ever ready to shove human rights aside if the domestic mood changes or strategic interest points in a different direction. Realists contend that what is needed is a rational assessment of interests relating to wealth and power. In some respects, what is required for an understanding of both the achievements and limits of international human rights is a "Hindu sensibility," that is, a frame of mind that accepts contradiction as an inherent part of life—quite unlike the rigidly dualistic Western mind. The Hindu perspective is attractive because it is so much more comfortable in finding a measure of truth in both viewpoints.

The discussion has so far proceeded within the conventional framework of a statist world order, with the impetus for norms and their implementation coming from governmental and intergovernmental action. Such a focus on state action, however, tells far from the whole story of the emergence of human rights on the global agenda. This emergence owes much to the rise of transnational human rights activism, which deserves major credit for reviving the Universal Declaration. It is also relevant to note the gradual emergence of human rights as a major dimension of activity within the United Nations. The UN system is much more firmly committed to the promotion of human rights than it was in 1948, when the Universal Declaration was first made public. This rising curve of attention to human rights was dramatized by the 1993 UN Conference on Human Rights and Development held in Vienna, which was followed shortly by the creation of the new UN post of High Commissioner for Human Rights, an office now held by the former president of Ireland, Mary Robinson.

This background raises two main questions more than fifty years after the issuance of the Universal Declaration: Why did governments ever agree in the first place to subvert their own territorial sovereignty? And why, despite massive obstacles, has the field of international human rights evolved to the point where it is widely acknowledged to be of substantive importance and growing salience in the contexts of foreign policy and world order? It can be argued that governments initially accepted the Universal Declaration simply because they thought it would amount to nothing. This calculation turned out to be wrong, thanks to the unanticipated, voluntary activism of citizens' associations, the emergence of a global visual media, and the contending ideological claims of the superpowers in the various arenas of the cold war. Human rights became more politically potent than could have been anticipated fifty years ago.

At the outset of a new century, another question emerges concerning the future of human rights. Is it likely that the next fifty years are likely to witness the further inclusion of international human rights standards and implementing authority within both formal and informal structures of global governance? Current trends seem contradictory in many respects. Those who believe in the strengthening of international human rights can find encouraging signs in growing attention and institutionalization. Yet, by the same token, those who believe that self-interest and power are the persisting mainsprings of international relations can find confirmation in the opportunistic evasion of human rights considerations by political leaders and market forces.

In the next section of this chapter, the relation between international human rights and geopolitical priorities will be discussed with an eye toward a partial acceptance of their coexistence. A later section will then evaluate several of the main human rights initiatives of the last fifty years. On these bases, the final section of this chapter will offer tentative thoughts on the future of human rights, given the accelerating process of economic globalization.

GEOPOLITICS AND INTERNATIONAL HUMAN RIGHTS: UNRESOLVED AND UNRESOLVABLE?

As suggested earlier, there exist two main viewpoints about how best to interpret the international experience of the last fifty years with respect to human rights. The first viewpoint is normatively driven, perceiving the attention given to human rights as indicative of the growing importance of law and morality in the world. The second is power-driven, perceiving an essential continuity of geopolitics over time based on the power of sovereign states to wage war and to mobilize resources, and their tendency to suppress legal and moral considerations when their power is seriously challenged.

The first view, as might be expected, is generally satisfied with the progress made during the last fifty years in protecting international human rights. It finds support for its positive assessment in the large number of multilateral treaties devoted to human rights, the increased activity on behalf of human rights in various arenas of the United Nations and at regional levels, and the greater attention being given to questions of human rights in the media and on the part of policy-makers. Adherents of this rights-oriented view are, to be sure, frequently disappointed by what are usually explained as lapses in leadership or as unfortunate concessions to domestic pressure groups. There is no doubt on the part of those who endorse the first view that human rights will continue to increase in influence over time—and that it is desirable to subordinate other goals of foreign policy to this overriding effort to achieve full implementation of global human rights standards.

In contrast, the second view finds that geopolitical factors remain the decisive forces moving history. From this perspective, the greater visibility of human rights is heavily discounted merely as a new kind of window-dressing favored by the winners in the cold war, who have remained trapped within the confines of their own anticommunist propaganda. This view also holds that the promotion of values at the expense of strategic interests is a dangerous indulgence that is likely to intensify conflict among states without really helping the victims of human rights abuses. A rational foreign policy, according to this view, is based on calculations of gains and losses, not on a comparison of rights and wrongs, and if progress is to be made in the way governments treat individuals and groups within their borders, it will be as a result of internal struggle and reform.

These polar ways of thinking about the relations between human rights norms and geopolitics reflect a clash of preferences and worldviews, a clash that has been sharpened by the profound shifts in the world order in recent years.[14] It is possible that the promotion of human rights and realist geopolitics will increasingly converge in the future. It is also possible that one or the other will displace its rival, and become the uncontested view of how things do and should work in the relation of power to values.

But some sort of reconciliation is also possible. There are several political and ideological trends that hint at a partial reconciliation between geopolitics and human rights. The mass cross-border migration of refugees fleeing human rights catastrophes in strife-torn countries can be a major source of trouble for neighboring states. When the United States led the UN effort in 1995 to preserve the democratic process in Haiti and protect Haitians against the brutalities of the military junta, it was strongly motivated by its interest in curtailing the outflow of refugees, who were at the time unwelcome entrants to American society, and were threatening to provoke an angry domestic political reaction. The U.S. government had previously dealt with this problem by intercepting the refugees at sea and putting them in detention centers, but this, too, provoked a damaging political backlash among African Americans in and out of government. The Clinton administration did not want to alienate this constituency, and so it was faced with finding a policy that both avoided an influx of refugees from Haiti and showed compassion for victims of Haitian oppression. By installing a moderate civilian government in Haiti—essentially "imposing" democracy and human rights—the U.S. intervention had the intended effect of curtailing the outflow of Haitians, thereby overcoming Clinton's refugee dilemma.[15] Whether Haiti will accept this solution is subject to considerable doubt, especially given signs of social and economic deterioration, and the renewed threat of challenges from the militarist right wing. In this respect, what may appear as a reconciliation of geopolitics and human rights may turn out to be temporary and quite limited.

Still, many internal struggles around the world have produced similar massive refugee outflows that can be ended and reversed only by political moderation and stability, which usually entails an overall improvement in the human rights situation. This pattern also influenced the European and American decision to support NATO initiatives to end the war in Bosnia and to restore autonomy and human rights to Kosovo. In the case of the Balkan conflicts, part of the geopolitical motivation was an anxiety about the potential of the conflict to spread, potentially to NATO member states such as Greece and Turkey. Whether or not these concerns were well founded, a positive link was established between insisting upon human rights for the Kosovars and the geopolitical interest in avoiding a wider European conflict. It should be noted that such a geopolitical link is far from universally applicable in separatist conflicts, as the response to the situation in Tibet or Chechnya confirms. But it should also be appreciated that the protection of human rights now often provides a functional alternative to the sort of bloc stability that had been a feature of the cold war era—a stability often achieved at the expense of the well-being of oppressed peoples and nations.

The problems of internal chaos and strife have grown far more common since the fall of the Soviet Union and its satellite countries, as the unravelling of Yugoslavia most revealingly illustrated. This unravelling, if it occurs outside the domain of strategic interests, as in sub-Saharan Africa, is not likely to mount strong pressure for humanitarian diplomacy. Such is "the lesson of Mogadishu," the failed U.S./UN humanitarian intervention in Somalia during 1992–94. The unwillingness of the United States and the United Nations to take steps in the mid-1990s to avoid humanitarian disasters in Rwanda, Burundi, and Zaire/Congo—three regions with little perceived geopolitical importance—is also a revealing part of the increasingly intertwined relationship of human rights and geopolitics.

In summary, the polarization of human rights and geopolitics evident in the two standard positions is increasingly misleading. International developments have created important sectors of mutuality in which geopolitical incentives exist for the multinational implementation of human rights standards. At the same time, such a convergence should not be exaggerated or generalized. Everything depends on context, and the perceived interests of the major political actors. For example, the global geopolitical aversion to the balkanization of existing states frequently stymies legitimate independence movements, or legitimate pretexts for humanitarian intervention. Perhaps the most extreme example is the U.S./UN relationship to the internal situation in Iraq, where despite unprecedented intrusions on Iraqi sovereignty to ensure compliance with arms-control agreements, there has been no willingness to contest Saddam Hussein's oppressive rule for fear of fragmenting Iraq.[16]

Such geopolitical double standards are particularly obvious when comparing the international response to the conflicts in Bosnia and Kosovo to the response to human tragedies of great magnitude in Africa. It is only when geopolitical interests are at stake that a substantial international effort to protect the human rights of a deeply threatened citizenry is likely to be forthcoming.[17] The absence of geopolitical incentives is likely to result in a reduced international response. Such a complex interplay of human rights and geopolitics suggests the inappropriateness of the two prevailing views identified at the outset of this section, and the need for a third view that is more nuanced. This third view formulates the relationship on the basis of a partial and limited reconciliation of human rights and geopolitics.

HUMAN RIGHTS AND NEOLIBERALISM: CLOSING THE IDEOLOGICAL GAP

An ideological shift has been under way in recent years, one that strays from the dualistic approaches of the cold war. The traditional view in conservative political circles had been that non-Communist forms of authoritarian rule in the South were either the lesser of two evils or a necessary, if temporary, expedient in relation to the rivalry with the Soviet Union. The West, which operationally meant the United States, not only supported many such instances of repressive government on the basis of such reasoning, but actually relied upon interventionary diplomacy to disrupt or overthrow governments that appeared to be democratic. Covert operations were often relied upon to disguise this sponsorship of an antidemocratic "solution." Among the more notorious instances of antidemocratic intervention are the restoration to power of the Shah in Iran (1953), the overthrow of the Arbenz government in Guatemala (1954), and the efforts to destabilize the Allende government in Chile (1970–73).[18] Although it is conceptually possible for a benign autocrat to protect human rights more successfully than an incompetent or paralyzed democrat, it is usually the case that the displacement of democratic governance is accompanied by a dramatic deterioration in human rights. Such was certainly the case in the instances given above.

The new political ideology that has taken hold in the West since 1989 insists that only democratic forms of governance are fully legitimate—indeed with the assumption that human rights are inherent to democracy itself.[19] This advocacy of democracy is tied very closely to the endorsement of neoliberal ideas about state-society relations, especially the reliance on the market to guide economic priorities, the minimization of the social role of government, and the encouragement of maximum privatization of economic life. In neoliberalism's more progressive interpretations, however, there is a growing conviction that marketization is not enough. Indeed, this was the main theme of Bill Clinton's 1998 message directed at the Chinese people and their leaders, a message also meant to be heard back home by Congress and the media, which had been critical of his visit on human rights grounds. Clinton suggested to China that it would not achieve "the prosperity and social stability that it is seeking until it embraces greater individual freedoms."[20]

This linkage between the market and human rights had already started to influence world-order thinking during the Thatcher/Reagan era. The concept of "market-oriented constitutionalism" began to appear in the final documents of the annual economic summits of the Group of Seven. Such an outlook achieved a canonical form in the Charter of Paris for a New Europe, adopted at an important meeting of the Conference (later Organization) on Security and Cooperation in Europe in Paris on November 21, 1991.[21] This formulation signaled the ideological break between the mentality of the cold war and that of the dawning era of globalization.

Although an affirmation of human rights is integral to these neoliberal perspectives, it is only a part of the corpus of rights protected under international law. Human rights are understood to encompass exclusively the civil and political rights of the individual, with economic, social, and cultural rights being put aside. Indeed, the neoliberal repudiation of a socially activist government and of public-sector approaches to human well-being is an implicit rejection of many of the standards of human rights that are present in the Universal Declaration and the two Covenants. It is relevant to note that many of those provisions of the Declaration that are regarded as being of utmost importance in countries of the South are those that are treated as nonexistent by the North. The journalist William Pfaff has indicted the "unregulated capitalism," which is occurring under neoliberal banners of globalization, for its cruel and dangerous disregard of human well-being. He dismisses the invocation of democracy and human rights by neoliberal champions of globalization as a "complacent and unhistorical argument" that refuses to take account "of the moral nihilism of an unregulated capitalism," which is making livelihood and employment a "byproduct of the casino."[22]

It is too early to assess the full impact of economic globalization of a neoliberal character upon the pursuit of economic and social rights, and even in relation to civil and political rights. Until the Asian economic crisis of 1997 it seemed that globalization was bringing economic relief to tens of millions of previously impoverished peoples, and was providing a prospect for sustained economic improvement that would have a gradual spillover effect enhancing political and civil rights.[23] Geopolitically, as well, globalization seemed to be having a leveling effect, giving a global voice to any country that could claim to be economically dynamic.

Now it is more difficult to be so confident about the contributions of globalization. What the crisis managers both inside and outside the International Monetary Fund have done in reaction to the Asian financial crisis is exactly what one would expect: namely, to prescribe neoliberal medicines in varying dosages, which means in the short run a hardening of the life circumstances of the poorer sectors of society and a placement of the burden of adjustment costs during the process of recovery on those least able to bear it. It was reported in July 1998 that half of the Indonesian population has fallen back into a condition of destitution, and that some villagers are eating insects in order to survive.[24] The IMF approach is also spreading the neoliberal model of governance as a substitute for the now discredited Asian model of capitalist development. The Asian model, which itself had many diversities, included a larger role for the state in actively promoting employment, welfare, and antipoverty efforts. Unfortunately, it also created the conditions for the flourishing of crony capitalism. To the extent that the text of the Universal Declaration authoritatively identifies the scope of human rights, neoliberal ideology amounts to a drastic foreshortening with no legal or moral mandate. Human rights are narrowed to the point where only civil and political rights are affirmed. In the more general normative language of the day, "individual freedom" and "democracy" are asserted as beneficial, and indeed necessary, to the attainment of economic success via the market. By implication, moves to uphold social and economic rights by direct action are seen as generally dangerous to the maintenance of civil and political rights because of their tendency to consolidate power in the state and to undermine individualism.

In conclusion, the relationship between the realization of human rights and the ideological orientation of neoliberal globalization is ambiguous in conception and behavioral effects. To the extent that neoliberal perspectives are antiauthoritarian, they tend to encourage the implementation of human rights in state-society relations, especially through the argument that economic development will be frustrated if such rights are not upheld. However, the neoliberal outlook ruptures a sense of human solidarity within a given political community, and effectively rejects any commitment of responsibility to those members who are economically and socially disadvantaged. And in times of difficulties this weakening of community bonds tends to impose the most difficult burdens of adjustment on those least able to bear them, especially the under- and unemployed. As such, it represents a de facto narrowing of the broad scope of human rights as initially specified by the Universal Declaration, and carried forward in the International Covenant on Economic, Social, and Cultural Rights.[25]

A NOTE ON THE UNIVERSAL DECLARATION AND CIVILIZATIONAL VALUES

The evolution of human rights as a self-conscious tradition was principally associated with Western patterns of thought and practice, although formulated as if metaphysically grounded on principles of universal validity. There were many echoes and parallel ideas in scriptures and philosophical writings of other civilizations, but no coherent and consistent reliance on a rhetoric of rights. The appearance of the Universal Declaration fifty years ago coincided with the strident humanist claims of the West, which had recently prevailed in the struggle against fascism and still retained a large measure of control over non-Western civilizations. As such, the Declaration was never effectively challenged as being overly Western, and therefore not "universal," in origins and outlook. This challenge came much later, preceded by non-Western preoccupations with winning the various anticolonial struggles and then engaging in the daunting tasks of statebuilding and economic development. To the extent that a challenge was asserted at all, it was largely indirect and implicit, premised on the idea that human rights (and democracy) were not a priority for newly independent societies confronting massive poverty and underdevelopment. It was often argued that order, more than freedom, was the precondition for sustained economic development, which in turn was necessary if massive poverty was to be reduced in the face of a rapidly expanding population.

Whatever cleavage there was concerning human rights, it was regarded as essentially intra-Western, pitting the liberalism of individualist rights against the Marxist stress on social or collective rights. The Universal Declaration provides a framing of human rights that encompasses both traditions, allowing each side to stress its own ideological interpretation. This division was acknowledged to a greater extent during the second major stage of evolution, when the two human rights Covenants delineated two basic types of human rights: political and civil on one side and economic, social, and cultural on the other. The West, led by the United States, made it quite clear, especially from the time in the early 1980s when it went on the offensive in support of private capital and the market ethos, that it was committed to upholding the first Covenant, which would provide the basis for legitimate governance at the level of the state, but nothing more. At the same time, its diplomats were increasingly outspoken in their insistence that the second Covenant was virtually irrelevant within the context of international law. Thus, disguised beneath the original universal framing was the ideological debate that was carried on during the cold war years about the nature of human rights. In any event, the debate was always a bit one-sided, as the Soviet bloc suppressed its population economically as well as politically. In this fundamental sense, Soviet ideological postures had little to do with the country's policies and practices. In the end, the debate over rights quickly faded into oblivion with the fall of the Berlin Wall in 1989 and the general discrediting of socialist thinking.

Serious challenges to universalist claims (that is, affecting real practices and policies) began to emanate from a global network of indigenous peoples who became internationally active in the 1970s. Their profound grievances about the evolving international law of human rights assumed salience with the formation of the Informal Working Group of Indigenous Populations, a project of the Sub-Commission on the Prevention of Discrimination and Protection of Minorities of the UN Human Rights Commission. The sessions of the Working Group made it clear that indigenous peoples, despite their many differences one from another, were agreed that their worldviews and circumstances had been simply left out of consideration when the Universal Declaration was drafted. The Declaration had proceeded from the alien assumptions of modern and modernizing societies and did not speak to the conditions and needs of peoples intent on preserving traditional ways of life in the face of modernity. In addition, the efforts of the International Labor Office to remedy this failure to address the human rights of indigenous peoples, while helpful, were insufficient. The ILO did sponsor a comprehensive framework for rights of indigenous peoples in its Convention No. 169 (1989), which was a giant step forward when compared to the shamelessly paternalistic and assimilatist formulations of Convention No. 107 (1957).[26]

What has emerged from the more authentic undertaking by indigenous peoples acting for themselves is a document crafted by representatives of indigenous peoples over a period of more than a decade: the Draft Declaration on the Rights of Indigenous Peoples (1994). This document, long in the making, is built around the idea of indigenous peoples as distinct and separate from other peoples, yet equal and fully entitled to claim a right of self-determination.[27] This Declaration is locked in controversy within the United Nations system, and its future is in doubt. Whether such a document can survive intergovernmental scrutiny, especially with respect to the claimed right of self-determination, seems uncertain even after more than six years of consideration within the UN system. It is also far from clear that the network of indigenous peoples will go along with a sanitized version of what their lengthy deliberations produced, especially if the symbolic and substantively crucial affirmation of the right of self-determination is removed or curtailed. What is not in doubt is the continued claim that the 1948 Universal Declaration utterly failed to encompass the circumstances and worldviews of indigenous peoples, and that it never considered their participation in the norm-creating processes as essential to establish the claim of universality. In this regard, the challenge to universality comes from a vertical, nongeographical perspective as well as from a horizontal, spatial perspective. Indigenous peoples, seeking to have the right to a separate existence based on their traditional patterns of organization and governance, do not necessarily share the foundational secularist, modernist, and statist assumptions of the human rights mainstream. At the very least, they insist that the traditionalist alternative be legitimized, and to the extent necessary, safeguarded. Such a concern is far from symbolic, as such peoples are being displaced and their lands plundered in many parts of the world—perhaps most flagrantly in Amazonia and South Asia. The importance that indigenous peoples attach to self-determination is bound up with their claims of autonomy and with the history of their encounters with settlers intent on destroying them and their way of life.

The intercivilizational critique of human rights that has gained the most notoriety has been on the part of former European colonies. These critiques are associated both with the norms and with their implementation, especially by coercive or interventionary means. The critiques attack both the cultural relativism of the human rights debate (that the Universal Declaration is distinctively Western and as such is inconsistent with the beliefs and values of non-Western civilization) and Western postcolonial geopolitics (that human rights are a new pretext for intervention and encroachment upon sovereign rights).[28] The West, in turn, counters that the claims of Islamic exceptionalism and Asian values are largely diversionary efforts by brutal and arbitrary governments to evade fundamental responsibilities to their own peoples, and that they represent very cynical efforts to excuse authoritarian abuses that are condemned by the moral teachings of all civilizations.[29] There is also a tendency to suggest that civilizational objections to human rights standards can be reconciled with the claimed universalism of the Universal Declaration if interventionary implementation is avoided and ample space is provided for societal interpretation. Such a trend has been understood in the West as a reluctant affirmation of the authenticity of the international human rights tradition, and as evidence of the power of the human rights idea.[30]

Widespread public attention to these issues was raised by the clamor in the Muslim world surrounding the publication of Salman Rushdie's *Satanic Verses*, especially the *fatwa* issued in 1989 by Iran's Ayatollah Khomeini, which imposed a death sentence on Rushdie, a British subject. The *fatwa* has been revoked, but to this day a large reward still awaits an assassin of Rushdie. The controversy brought a number of issues to the fore. The first involves the imposition of a death sentence without trial or defense upon an absent individual over whom the sentencing party had no authority. The second involves the use of religion to provide the basis for condemning and restricting the distribution of a literary work, and justifying the punishment of its author. And the third involves differing views about protecting freedom of expression in the face of community sensitivities. These are complex matters, but the potential for international conflict arising from apparent differences based on civilizational outlook became apparent. Suddenly, the way seemed open for dangerously inflammatory views and the outbreak of culture wars; dire predictions ensued, including Samuel Huntington's view of an impending "clash of civilizations." On further reflection, however, it became evident that there were almost as many differences within Islam as there were between Islam and the West; as Edward Said has so persuasively written, all civilizations and cultures exhibit an extraordinary heterogeneity.[31] In other words, there are certainly differences in beliefs and values that can be given a civilizational expression, but such differences are not consistent enough across civilizational boundaries to be by themselves the basis of a new geopolitics, especially given the strength of global market forces and their tendency to establish a global countercivilization.

What may turn out to be the case is that the further elaboration and implementation of human rights will take on a regional character. In part, this follows the European example, but it also parallels the rise of regionalism in relation to economic and security relations. It is also a reaction to the decline of the United Nations, although so far this overall decline has not affected the UN role in relation to human rights, which has actually increased in the 1990s. To the extent that regional human rights initiatives are advanced, a part of the rationale will be, as it is in Europe, based on shared values and traditions. In this sense, the cultural critique of the Universal Declaration might in the near future become less polemical and take on a more substantive and specific character. Of course, in such a setting, intraregional differences are likely to gain greater attention, especially in Asia, where the diversities are so evident.

It bears mentioning that the most vocal commitments to "Asian Values" were concurrent with "the Asian economic miracle." The successful achievement of sustained economic growth in an atmosphere of political stability apparently gave Asian leaders the confidence to fend off international criticism with civilizational arguments, and to accuse the West of arrogance, pointing out the adverse social consequences of decadence and permissiveness. The Asian crisis, which shows no signs of an early abatement, has seemingly diverted attention from the cultural dimensions of Asia's relations with the West.

The Universal Declaration has definitely survived the civilizational critique mounted against the claim that the international human rights tradition deserves adherence in all parts of the world. At the same time, the Western origins and evolution of the tradition have exposed some important weaknesses. Undoubtedly, the claims of inadequacy brought to light by the efforts of indigenous peoples will persist. Controversy over implementation will undoubtedly continue to raise concerns about whether human rights are a vehicle for intervention or whether opposition to intervention is a pretext for shielding abusive behavior from international accountability. If the Universal Declaration had been drafted in 1998 rather than 1948 it would likely have exhibited far greater sensitivity to cultural diversity and to the relations between politics and religion, and perhaps less empathy for the economically and socially disadvantaged. And so the Universal Declaration has entered the next century, having been somewhat bypassed by historical developments, yet it still commands such widespread respect by governments and civil society as to remain authoritative in relation to the substance of international human rights standards.

ACHIEVEMENTS, PROSPECTS, AND PRIORITIES

The Universal Declaration was celebrated in 1998, the fiftieth anniversary of its drafting, partly because its text was the foundation for the worldwide human rights movement, but also because of its own textual reality, but also because it initiated a process that has had an extraordinary cumulative impact on the role of human rights in international political life in the course of the last half-century. This cumulative impact has exhibited ebbs and flows, and has reflected considerable selectivity in emphasis, as well as a vulnerability to the foreign policy agenda of major geopolitical actors. Nevertheless, the achievements have been impressive:

(1) *Changing the discourse of international relations*: To a considerable extent, invoking human rights standards has come to replace moralizing in statecraft. As such, it has been effective in establishing an objective, shared set of standards as the foundation for legitimate resistance by civil society to abuses of power by the state, and for the display of international concern within the United Nations and elsewhere. The parameters of this human rights discourse are not yet firmly established. Still, as compared to a half-century ago, this transnational discourse has challenged the idea of sovereignty in crucial respects. The outcome of this challenge is not yet clear, and the results are quite uneven at this point. The internationalization of human rights is one aspect of globalization and nascent global governance, which are still at an early stage of evolution. And yet, even at this point, this discourse on human rights has altered the language of diplomacy. In so doing, it has also narrowed the gaps between state and society, and between state

and world, by providing a common normative currency that is exchanged by government, international institutions, and civil society.

(2) *The elaboration of normative architecture*: Starting with the Universal Declaration, there has been a steady stream of international lawmaking treaties that have elaborated human rights standards in many areas of international life, and which have started to move the process from lawmaking to implementation. The most dramatic step in this direction was the transformation of the Universal Declaration into treaty form by way of the two Covenants in 1966. Because these Covenants included reporting requirements, the monitoring of compliance was formally brought within the scope of activity assigned to the UN Economic and Social Council. Subsequently, many additional human rights treaties were negotiated, signed, and ratified, widely enough, in fact, to qualify as customary international law. These include the Convention on the Status of Refugees (1951), the Convention on the Political Rights of Women (1953), the International Convention on the Elimination of all Forms of Racial Discrimination (1966), the Convention Against Torture and Other Cruel Inhuman or Degrading Treatment or Punishment (1984), and the Convention on the Rights of the Child (1989). In addition, there have been many declarations endorsed by the UN General Assembly that have added a further dimension to the human rights discourse. Among the most important of these are the Declaration on the Granting of Independence to Colonial Countries and Peoples (1960), the Universal Declaration on the Eradication of Hunger and Malnutrition (1974), the Declaration on the Elimination of All Forms of Intolerance Based on Religion or Belief (1981), the Declaration on the Right to Development (1986), the Declaration of the Rights of Persons Belonging to National or Ethnic Minorities (1992), and the Declaration on the Elimination of Violence Against Women (1993). In addition, there have been a series of very important regional initiatives with respect to the establishment of human rights standards and procedures, most significantly in Europe, but also in Latin America, in Africa, and in Asia.

(3) *Enhancing the role of human rights within the UN system*: While references to human rights within the UN Charter are minimal, over the years the United Nations has come to play a more and more significant part in developing human rights standards and providing an institutional capacity for monitoring compliance and censuring serious violations.[32] The UN Conference on Human Rights and Development in 1993 was a milestone in this regard; it provided an arena in which civil society could assert its particular concerns about the abused circumstances of women and indigenous peoples. One outcome of this event was the mandate to establish a High Commissioner for Human Rights, ensuring both budgetary support and agenda salience for human rights within the UN, despite downsizing pressures.

(4) *Historical struggles against oppressive circumstances*: On several dramatic occasions human rights have been at the very center of popular struggles for emancipation from oppressive circumstances. These occasions also exhibited the remarkable effects of popular movements for change in civil society converging with strong international support for the implementation of human rights. The most striking instances of this convergence are the anticolonial struggles of the Asian and African nations, the movements for freedom and rights in the countries of Eastern Europe and the Soviet Union during the 1980s, and, of course, the antiapartheid campaign in South Africa. In each case, a significant internal political dynamic was reinforced symbolically and diplomatically by international action based on fundamental human rights.

(5) *The engagement of civil society*: From the outset the effectiveness of human rights within the United Nations and elsewhere has reflected the importance of transnational and indigenous human rights associations. These associations regarded the realization of human rights as a political project with legal backing and the strongest possible moral support. The voices of civil society were also filling a vacuum created by realist patterns of statecraft that often wanted to give lip service to human rights while restricting the relevance of the human rights discourse to the channels of hostile propaganda. In many respects, the growth of global civil society was based on grassroots human rights activism, which originated in the Western democracies but gradually spread to all parts of the world.

(6) *Extensions to the humanitarian law of war and crimes against humanity*: Increasingly, the domain of human rights has been extended to include extreme behavior—an effort to encompass what Ken Booth has termed "human wrongs."[33] This dynamic has resulted in, among other things, the establishment of ad hoc tribunals charged with the indictment and prosecution of individuals charged with crimes against humanity and genocide in the former Yugoslavia and Rwanda. This revival of the effort begun after World War II, with the trials of surviving German and Japanese leaders, has also led to a strong movement to establish an independent international criminal court that would be generally available to deal with accusations of extreme abuses of human rights. The struggle to criminalize extreme abuse has produced a coalition of governments committed to this type of global reform, along with supportive elements in civil society that have mounted a massive global campaign. It has also produced a geopolitical backlash that has united several powerful states in resistance, including the United States, China, and France.

Looking forward to later in this century, it seems safe to predict that human rights will continue to provide a focus for normative energy within global civil society, in the UN system, and in the foreign policy of leading states. At the same time, the friction between realist orientations toward statecraft and the commitment to international human rights is likely to persist for the foreseeable future, producing inconsistent expressions of concern and allegations of double standards. It is also certain that efforts at implementation will continue to clash with claims of sovereign rights and arguments against interventionary techniques to advance human rights.

It is likely that those following the human rights debate in the near future can expert to see mixed results. The two major civic campaigns currently under way are the treaty banning antipersonnel landmines and the establishment of an international criminal court. Both involve innovative coalitions of like-minded governments, and both have generated geopolitical resistance. Their outcome will provide short-run litmus tests of the relative potency of the global human rights constituency, but these results are likely to be provisional. The past fifty years demonstrates, above all else, that the great human rights victories have occurred when grassroots activism converges with geopolitical opportunism in a context of favorable historical circumstances. It also demonstrates that the biggest frustrations and disappointments with respect to human rights are associated with the absence of civic momentum and the presence of geopolitical resistance.

As with many matters of global policy, the orientation of the American government plays a very influential role in relation to human rights. The first two years of the Carter presidency played an immense role in raising human rights to a high place in the global policy agenda by making human rights a primary foreign policy goal. This emphasis had extremely important secondary effects, such as encouraging greater risk-taking by opposition movements in oppressive societies and giving human rights a stronger voice in national bureaucracies, including that of the U.S. Government.

The Universal Declaration continues to provide an inspirational foundation for human rights, although its substantive authority seems to have been mainly transferred to subsequent documents with more specific focus and a more obligatory status. The as yet unrealized utopian provisions of the Universal Declaration, such as the promise of a universal standard of living sufficient to meet basic human needs, are likely to remain important reminders of the work that remains to be done.[34] The achievements in human rights over the course of the last fifty years are extraordinary, but the obstacles to full realization seem as insurmountable as ever.

Outside of the European Union, and with the exception of some concrete measures to prevent genocide, the prospects for international enforcement of human rights standards remain remote. Effective implementation on a consistent basis is likely to depend for the foreseeable future upon internalizing the enforcement process—that is, taking human rights seriously at home, which is the focus of the next chapter. Such seriousness depends both on a citizenry that is committed to a human rights culture and a government that is willing to apply human rights standards as rigorously within its own borders as it is in its foreign policy.

Taking Human Rights Seriously at Home 3

One of the great paradoxes of the progress of human rights thinking is that many prominent governments that adopt human rights treaties or bills of rights, basically believe that human rights are only relevant for other countries. Human rights are treated as above all as an instrument of foreign policy. This is evidently the case for the United Kingdom, where the Foreign Office is responsible for monitoring compliance with the European Convention on Human Rights and the International Covenant on Civil and Political Rights. It is particularly the case in the United States, which often likes to lead an international crusade on behalf of human rights while taking grave offense at any suggestion that some of its domestic practices raise human rights concerns. If the issue of human rights is featured in American political discourse, it is as a stick with which to beat other states that have fallen foul of the State Department or are regarded as adversaries that threaten U.S. strategic interests.

Even human rights groups in the United States have been reluctant to focus their energies on domestic human rights problems, or even on domestic events of close U.S. allies—Israel being the most obvious example. As with so many other issues, a seriousness about human rights must start from the proposition that human rights begin at home, that is, where infractions are most sensitive and hurtful.

A strong human rights culture is the necessary underpinning of an effective regime of human rights. Such a culture cannot take hold unless the political culture is supportive of human rights. But moving beyond the context of formal legal institutions and instruments, and even beyond the framework of constitutional democracy, it is increasingly obvious that one has to be concerned about the deformed, even dangerous, dimensions of political culture. And if democracy, as it is generally understood, is society's means of translating the will of the citizenry into prevailing policy, how does one find a sufficient counterweight to distortions in the political culture that are antipathetic, for instance, to minority rights at home or other peoples' rights abroad?

The emergence of a framework for assessing political behavior on an international level has been one of the great achievements of international society in the last half-century. It ranks in historic significance—and overlaps to some extent—with decolonization and the South African anti-apartheid campaign. In other words, the development of a moral, legal, and spiritual sense of solidarity among all peoples on issues of human rights, despite the ideological divisions of the cold war and the North-South divide, remains a powerful and useful normative architecture on which to build brighter prospects for a humane future. It is in part an unwitting achievement. The modern human rights movement after 1945 revealed a certain guilt among liberal democracies that they had done so little about Nazi atrocities, and that they had viewed the Nazi experience as essentially a domestic affair.

Still, these liberal democracies took no serious responsibility for the people displaced by what was happening in Germany. As is well known, refugees were turned away despite the desperation of their circumstances. The guilty conscience of these governments, reinforced by public opinion, gave rise to the political climate that allowed the Universal Declaration of Human Rights to be formulated. But this great instrument was conceived with the tacit understanding that it would never amount to very much. The modesty of objectives was signaled by calling the document of rights a "declaration," rather than a treaty, the latter being legally binding. In a world of sovereign states, international human rights, to the extent that they are taken seriously, are inherently subversive of sovereignty. As long as their implementation remains at the level of rhetoric, they amount to little more than a convenient moral banner. But if human rights become a real standard of assessment for the behavior of governments, they introduce a major qualification to the self-protective doctrine of non-intervention among states.

Two sets of factors gave the idea of human rights a political force that the founding states almost certainly did not anticipate. The first was the degree to which cold war rivalry allowed the issue of human rights to serve as a convenient way of castigating the ideological adversary. Both sides in the cold war emphasized those failings of their rivals that they felt exhibited their own superiority. The West emphasized individual freedom and the Soviet bloc the provision of collective rights and the degree to which social and economic responsibilities were more seriously accepted by socialist states than by their capitalist adversaries. So human rights were invoked by important states, partly out of conviction, but mainly as an instrument of propaganda. These ideological exchanges did, however, give human rights an unexpected political salience. The second development was the emergence of nongovernmental organizations, civil initiatives, and transnational social forces that did take seriously the international standards embodied in the Universal Declaration and pushed for their elaboration in the two UN Covenants—on civil and political, and on economic, social, and cultural rights—and in other international instruments. These treaties conferred legitimacy on human rights standards, which were then supervised by UN committees and could be invoked by activist groups. Governments found themselves in the awkward position of having to account for their failures to live up to standards that they had themselves articulated and affirmed.

An additional dimension of this international momentum involved the growing tendency of resistance movements to invoke human rights to legitimate their own struggles. This was to some degree true in the anticolonial movements, especially with respect to the right of self-determination. But it was perhaps most dramatically evident in the citizens' movements of Eastern and Central Europe during the 1980s. The Helsinki process played a crucial role through the Conference of Security and Cooperation in Europe (CSCE), with its "human rights dimension," in delegitimizing the puppet regimes and giving the social forces that were seeking reform a confidence that what they were doing domestically had been mandated by these international standards.[1] In a sense, then, one of the roles that the international human rights developments have played is to legitimize political resistance to oppression wherever it occurs in the world. It has been very important to resistance movements to have this kind of foundation for their political project, having their goals sanctified by law and based on a universal standard. The human rights framework has provided a ground for the politics of resistance, of opposition, and of struggle.

This post-1945 development of human rights is quite remarkable, considering the degree to which states have a shared interest in not having their internal behavior subject to external scrutiny. This reluctance has been very evident, for instance, in the manner in which the United Nations has handled the right of self-determination. Even during the height of the cold war, East and West were able to agree that the exercise of the right of self-determination must never shatter existing sovereign states. In other words, self-determination was acceptable during the process of decolonization, but not, say, in the context of Chechnya or the post-Soviet states, or in the context of Yugoslavia, Indonesia, and East Timor, or for the Kurdish insurgency in Iraq and Turkey. In these contexts, states were very clear that the rights of peoples had to be subordinated to the overriding interest of states in maintaining their territorial integrity, regardless of the human rights implications. Since 1989, the scope of the right of self-determination has become more ambiguous and remains unresolved. Practice has been quite inconsistent with the law as set forth in authoritative UN General Assembly resolutions, which deny validity to any claim of self-determination that is state-shattering. Yet recent international practice has acknowledged a whole series of new states emerging from within sovereign territorial units. The emerging nations of the former Soviet Union and former Yugoslavia have claimed a right of self-determination and their claims have been accepted.

Within this changing context, the highly innovative notion of the Democratic Audit can be seen as a way of carrying the human rights movement forward to a fourth stage. The Democratic Audit is a specifically British initiative to monitor and evaluate acts, domestic laws, administrative acts, and judicial decisions by reference to international human rights standards. I write "fourth stage" because the Italian political philosopher Norberto Bobbio has traced the evolution of human rights through three significant stages in *The Age of Rights*.[2] A first philosophical stage can be traced to the earliest reflections on the human condition in the writings of the Roman stoics.[3] They were concerned about the degree to which there is a human family and human solidarity, and they sought to justify treating all humans as equal and deserving of treatment worthy of their intrinsic dignity. This philosophical tradition, always marginal to the way politics was practiced, then entered a very forceful second stage during the American and French Revolutions, which proclaimed as a matter of national political resolve the commitment, albeit flawed, to give citizens certain basic rights. So these revolutionary movements provided the modern inspiration for translating the philosophical ideas about human dignity into legal form and political practice.

The third stage, of course, has been the transformation of these revolutionary ideals from their national settings into international, legal instruments. The process of discussing and creating those instruments has spread an awareness of human rights to the entire world and has enlisted, at least at the level of rhetoric, support for the idea that all societies must adhere to human rights to be legitimately governed. This normative consensus, of course, breaks down as soon as one considers the implementation of these international standards. It remains difficult for Westerners fully to appreciate the degree to which external pressure to uphold human rights is perceived in various parts of the world as a new pretext for interventionary diplomacy.

Intervention on behalf of human rights resembles the Mississippi River, it only flows from North to South. Human rights activism that is associated with the foreign policy of big states and particularly the United States, is therefore seen as a postcolonial kind of interventionary politics that uses the banner of human rights, often to the detriment of people in the target societies. Not only do these important states in the North invoke human rights, it is argued, but they invoke human rights as a pretext to interfere in foreign societies in ways that oppress people. The United States, for instance, has justified many of its interventions in Central America on the grounds that it was promoting democracy and human rights. In the case of Nicaragua, for instance, the U.S. State Department grounded its objection to the Sandinista government on the failure of the Sandinistas to grant adequate democratic space to the political opposition. This position was argued even though the Sandinista government was probably the best human rights government that Nicaragua ever had and the most impressive government in the region. But since Nicaragua's neighbors in Central America were allies of the United States, their dreadful human rights records were ignored. At the very moment that the United States was waging a "low-intensity" war against Nicaragua, killing many Nicaraguan people and sabotaging their livelihoods, the repressive military regimes in countries like Honduras and Guatemala were receiving large-scale military and economic support. So there is a problematic side to the enthusiasm for human rights once it gets entwined with geopolitics. The alleged promotion of human rights can be a way of undermining the sovereignty and independence of weaker countries. They can be exploited as a shield, validating intervention in other countries that is carried out for geopolitical purposes.

This complexity, then, suggests the great importance of the fourth stage of the evolution of a human rights culture and an international human rights regime—the internalization of human rights standards by indigenous action within a particular society, and especially within countries that are either practitioners of intervention or immune to interventionary pressures. Until an effort at serious internalization by the citizens of countries throughout the world actually takes place, the impact of international standards is likely to be uneven and sporadic, both domestically and globally. One needs, in other words, a continuing political struggle on the ground to realize human rights. It is for this reason that the Democratic Audit possesses such immense potential. It should be noted, however, that the extension of the Democratic Audit idea to other societies needs to be undertaken on their terms rather than in mimicry of the process that has gone on in the United Kingdom. In other words, the project is a bit like Italian wine that does not travel well; it has to be invented anew in each society. There are two ways of thinking about the Democratic Audit: one is as a liberal project with the political language that has been used in its operations in Britain; the other is as a process of internalizing human rights within the state-society relationship. In this second vision, the citizenry and the popular sector of societies must develop their own forms of internalization, their own political language, and their own means to collect and disseminate relevant information. In Malaysia, for example, an organization called the Just World Trust, or simply JUST, is very much concerned with the internalization of international standards of human rights. But it is equally concerned with the international structures that interfere with the capacities of some countries to fulfill human rights claims. For instance, it calls attention to the effects of the World Bank and IMF structural adjustment programs, which are difficult to reconcile with efforts to promote economic and social rights in a variety of heavily burdened countries in the South.

In the fourth stage, then, it is the spirit of the Democratic Audit that counts and that must be replicated as much as possible. It is very important that there be a strong participatory dimension to the way in which this internalization of international standards occurs. Helena Kennedy, a prominent British human rights advocate and lawyer, has, for instance, spoken persuasively about the participatory nature of the adoption of a Bill of Rights in Canada. Part of the strength of the emerging human rights culture in that country results from the consultative process in Canada, which gave people a sense that they were participating in the creation of the norms. Of course, the insistence on universality remains politically important on a global scale. But the universality debate in human rights has been insensitive to the fact that even if the standards that have emerged are universally valid in their core claims, the process by which they have been established has not been universal. They reflect primarily Western experience, and it was largely Western political minds that were responsible for drafting and advocating human rights instruments. Even if such instruments are given some kind of formal endorsement nationally, that endorsement does not create the strong political and moral "bonding" that is necessary to make human rights really take hold in a domestic political culture. In my view, popular participation in the process by which norms evolve is of great relevance to whether legitimacy is actually achieved. An ethos of participation and consultation needs to be at the very core of an effort to extend and build a human rights culture. Victims of human rights abuses, in particular, need to share in this process. This absence of meaningful participation in the norm-creation process by non-Western countries definitely limits the force of the international human rights standards as applied outside the West.

We can observe the consequences of nonparticipation very clearly in the case of indigenous peoples even while acknowledging that no single perspective can represent the range of outlooks encompassed by such peoples. They have generally not participated in the framing of international human rights instruments. Yet indigenous peoples have a distinctive perspective that bears on the content of human rights. The most fundamental concern of indigenous peoples is with maintaining their traditional way of life, which adds a new dimension to the concept of self-determination. What human rights and self-determination mean to various indigenous peoples was not at all reflected in the Universal Declaration or the Covenants, which are drafted on the assumption of protecting individuals living in modern societies. When the International Labor Organization attempted in 1957 to rectify this gap by drafting a convention especially tailored to indigenous peoples, it did so in a paternalistic spirit. This well-meaning body set about drafting a convention that would give indigenous peoples the opportunity of access on a nondiscriminatory basis to the benefits enjoyed by society at large. In other words, the ILO promulgated an assimilationist view of indigenous peoples' rights, one that was entirely at odds with what the overwhelming majority of their leaders and people wanted. As soon as indigenous peoples had their own arena in Geneva (Working Group on Indigenous Populations) for formulating their own human rights agenda, they found existing human rights instruments so inappropriate that they spent a decade writing their own draft declaration on the rights of indigenous peoples. Their declaration is now being scrutinized by various organs within the United Nations. Whether or not this declaration becomes international law, the whole experience confirms the view human rights cannot be solely concerned with substantive standards, but must be attentive to process, especially to the participation of vulnerable constituencies in the dynamics of norm-creation.

This emphasis on popular participation as a key element to the legitimacy of human rights standards has a bearing on current debates about Islam and the West. Islamic countries have been systematically excluded from participating in important arenas of authority, not only in relation to human rights but generally in international society. As a result, international standards have a very questionable purchase on moral reality for the Islamic world, being generally, yet not invariably, understood as hypocritical and alien Western efforts to perpetuate their influence in the postcolonial era.

Also essential to this debate is the complicated relationship between democracy and human rights. On one level, democracy itself is a human right, and is so stated, at least in basic terms, in Article 21 of the Universal Declaration of Human Rights. But one can observe a political culture in democratic societies that is often downright hostile to the implementation of human rights. There is, then, a tension between political democracy and respect for human rights. This tension is visible now in the United States—the so-called war against immigrants, to give just one example. Elements of American society are sending politicians the signal that anything they do to deprive immigrants, legal and illegal, of rights is politically rewarding. Majoritarian sentiment is leading opportunistic politicians far more than any ideological convictions they may have. This very serious problem is aggravated by the impact of economic globalization on workers and on the moral and social fabric of the society they live in. There is a search for scapegoats that singles out (among others) those who would enter political space without the credentials of citizenship.

With a similar logic, American and other societies are often ready to reward politicians who use force against foreign countries in violation of international law. This is a human rights question because, in effect, politicians are encouraged to challenge the right to life of people in other societies. Two salient examples of this type of political opportunism come to mind. The Israeli attacks on southern Lebanon in the run-up to the 1996 Israeli election were mainly motivated not by the threats of terrorism (the government line) but by then Prime Minister Shimon Perez's desire to appear tough in the face of hostile neighbors. It was a failed attempt, as it turned out, at the expense of innocent civilians in Lebanon. It was a political failure because too few in the Israeli electorate were persuaded by this kind of political demonstration to back the more peaceminded Labor Party.

Bill Clinton pursued the same strategy in 1996, when he ordered U.S. missile strikes against Iraq prior to the presidential elections. It appears that Clinton, too, sought to demonstrate to the American people that he is tough enough to use force against the enemies of the United States. This particular military action drew attention to the impact of high-tech warfare on human rights. The new technologies of war allow a country like the United States, or Israel for that matter, to use force against a foreign society with almost no human risks to its own people. It is a one-sided imposition of violence that darkly echoes the structure of torture. At a political level, society becomes complicit in the torture, and, indeed, by tacitly approving its leader's aggression, provided that no American lives are lost. Another expression of the problematic side of democracy was evident in the recent Bosnian elections. The ritual of voting, which is a quintessential democratic practice, was essentially used by outside forces to disguise and validate ethnic cleansing. In a sense, the democratic rituals were used to whitewash past abuses, to eliminate external responsibility, and even to impose an aura of respectability on leaders who were guilty of crimes against humanity.

There is a problem with the affirmation of political democracy in a culture that values violence against foreign societies or that is prejudiced against asylum-seekers and refugees, as in both the United States and much of Western Europe now. Recognizing this inherent problem is not tantamount to rejecting democratic constitutional forms; it simply reflects a desire to maintain a critical awareness of the limitations of democracy. These critical comments on the operation of political democracy are not unrelated to the criticisms of democracy that have been prevalent through the ages and that have sometime led morally sensitive observers, as in ancient Athens, to reject democracy as a system of governance.[4]

There remains another, often overlooked, international trend that is antagonistic to human rights throughout the world. Economic globalization within a neoliberalist framework has already had a negative impact on the pursuit of human rights. The constant ideological pressures, which seek to entrust social responsibility to the private sector and to encourage the transfer of responsibilities away from government and toward the market, draw into question the capacity of a contemporary government to administer a compassionate state. The problems are most cruelly felt in developing, or rather nondeveloping, countries, but every state in the world has to face the question: Can we afford to be compassionate toward our own people under the discipline of global capital? Or to put it a different way: Can Sweden still be Sweden? The fact is that even Sweden has had to accommodate the pressures of the global market rolling back some of the country's most impressive social welfare achievements. This "rolling back of the state" has essentially been endorsed by both main political parties and by the political mainstream in Sweden. The same is true in the United Kingdom, where the Labor Party, so-called New Labor, has essentially subscribed in many crucial respects to the political economy of its Tory adversary. Even the Democratic Party in the United States appears to have succumbed. To put it in general terms, governments are now generally unable and unwilling to promote economic and social rights as goals of official policy. Political leaders have given primacy to market forces, which are directly opposed to the imperatives of the economic and social rights, which in turn are the key to popular participation and political equality in our societies. A crisis is waiting to be born, or perhaps, to erupt.

How to proceed, given this general assessment? First, in addition to internalizing human rights and democratic aspirations in the spirit of the Democratic Audit, the political left must adopt a more critical perspective on the problematic aspects of political democracy, even in moderate societies like the United Kingdom. We must also devote far more thought to extending our understanding of the prospects for a human rights culture under the increasing pressures of economic globalization, which may be creating a set of economic practices and attitudes that is diametrically opposed to helping the most vulnerable sectors of society. For anyone who believes that the essence of the human rights is to protect the vulnerable, and that the identity of those vulnerable people changes as society evolves, the existing mixture of globalization and neoliberalism poses a very serious threat to human rights, particularly in an atmosphere that implies the absence of alternatives. At this moment, there seems to be no viable alternative to a neoliberal reliance on market forces and the logic of capital.

Therefore, there is a compelling need to adopt a wider frame of reference in the consideration of how to make a human rights culture a viable part of political life in countries throughout the world. Dialogue within and among the major world civilizations needs to be carried on in a way that involves far more deference to the experience and perspectives of non-Western participants on the world scene. In this regard, it is crucial to appreciate that human rights can be advanced only by reference to the particular conditions and challenges that exist in different societies and to the specific sensitivities of time and place. Such sensitivity is the most effective way of extending human rights to the South.

Finally, it is clear that military intervention to implement human rights should be avoided, particularly when that intervention does not have the backing of international institutions. The use of human rights as a foreign policy tool is almost always wrong. John Vincent once said, in reference to human rights, that coercion is only legitimate for the protection of the self, not for the enlightenment of the other. He drew a crucial distinction between the advocacy of human rights and the discussion of violations and interventionary practice in the domain of geopolitics.[5] The former is desirable in international politics, whereas the latter is not. Human rights in the end have to be implemented by the domestic efforts of peoples living in widely varying circumstances, although these efforts can be supported by the pressures of human rights groups and the activities of the United Nations.

While these conclusions are more global in perspective than they are country-specific, the two dimensions are interconnected and ultimately they reinforce each other. In this respect the Democratic Audit exercise is crucial because it situates the struggle for human rights within the indigenous capabilities of a particular country seeking to improve the quality of its own political life. Basically, this is how international standards can be best carried forward most effectively at this stage. Bodies like the European Court, the UN Human Rights Committee, the ILO, and a host of external nongovernmental organizations are required, of course, to facilitate the global and regional pursuit of human rights, particularly in generating information, awareness, and informed criticism, and by developing further norms and procedures. But to the extent that coercion is needed to overcome failures and prevent abuses of human rights, real progress has to arise from the organized political efforts of citizens directed at their own governments. In this critical regard, now that an international legal framework for the promotion of human rights exists, the challenge of implementation needs to be understood as a new priority of domestic policy, and not, as has often been the case, an ornament of foreign policy.

Indeed, there are numerous opportunities, outside the realm of geopolitical convenience, to promote international compliance with human rights norms. Such opportunities have already raised questions about the outer limits of territorial sovereignty in an increasingly globalized world. International law continues to uphold deference to the sovereign state, but as the next chapter suggests, an emergent tension between respect for sovereignty and the duty to promote compliance with human rights is beginning to appear in both doctrine and practice.

Moving Toward Implementation 4

I have no doubt that a major challenge for the UN in the future will be to find the right balance in the desperate situations that will arise between respecting sovereignty and maintaining peace and the security of mankind. The view has become increasingly accepted that the principle of nonintervention in matters that are within the domestic jurisdiction of states cannot be regarded as a protective barrier behind which human rights can be systematically violated with impunity.

—Javier Perez de Cuellar[1]

The injection of international military force to impose a resolution on a bitter conflict is likely to be a slippery slope, and is probably an ineffective instrument. . . . The international system—in the guise of the society of states—has not been normatively successful after 350 years. . . . In terms of spreading the good life, Westphalia is another of the West's failures.

—Ken Booth[2]

POINTS OF DEPARTURE

If the doctrine of sovereignty could be erased from the minds of political leaders, would it reduce those forms of human suffering associated with extreme governmental failure? Would such an erasure strengthen sentiments of human solidarity upon which an ethos of collective responsibility and individual accountability depends? This still dominant image of sovereignty is essentially negative, a prerogative to resist claims and encroachments that emanate from outside international boundaries—the right to say no. Such a view of sovereignty is especially prevalent among sub-Saharan African countries that look back on their pre-independence past in sorrow and anger because of the harms generally perceived to have resulted from the predatory interventions that lay at the core of the colonial experience. With this image still uppermost in political consciousness, the acquisition of independence, and with it, sovereign rights, was most often and influentially understood as an inversion of colonialism. Instead of complete domination from *outside* the country those countries sought the unencumbered freedom to act *inside* borders.[3]

But the predicaments of postcolonial Africa are quite different from those of colonial Africa. If following the lines of normative reasoning that flow from the American and French Revolutions, then sovereignty inheres ultimately not in the state, but in the citizenry, and is associated with the rights of peoples, although it may be exercised by their representatives. Such international moral, legal, and political ideas as the right of self-determination and the right of development are direct expressions of this understanding of sovereignty, but such an understanding has not yet formally conditioned the interplay between state, society, and the organized international community.

Under present circumstances the maturing of sovereignty as the foundation of the contemporary state calls for a more balanced, complex view of this foundational idea that continues to provide the ideological underpinning of world order. The growth of human rights and the emergence of a norm of democratic entitlement support a view that the state is itself the subject of obligations as well as rights, and that these obligations may be implemented both by a politics of resistance on the part of citizens and by a process of humanitarian intervention by the international community.[4] This conditioning of sovereignty is further developed in relation to the capacity of a state to carry out governmental functions. When the state fails to provide governance, other political actors are needed to protect a vulnerable citizenry from the perils of chaos and civil strife, as well as from unleashed forces of ethnic and religious extremism. This is particularly true in much of Africa, where the intermediate structures of civil society are very weak, offering little protection in the event that government institutions collapse.

At this stage, sovereignty means different things to different political actors:

- Sovereignty continues to serve governments as a shield against intervention and accountability; thus, a government may invoke the postcolonial claim that outside intervention to help the citizenry in situations of humanitarian emergency is not valid unless the state has first upheld its sovereign rights by giving or denying consent.
- Sovereignty may also be extended to justify humanitarian intervention by the United Nations or other political actors intent on mitigating human suffering in circumstances where the state has partially or totally collapsed.
- Sovereignty may also be used to encompass plural political frameworks that reflect differing degrees of autonomy and independence within the structure of the state.[5]
- Sovereignty can also foster social contracts linking states to international institutions by building, on the one hand, mutual bonds of deference and respect and, on the other, a mutual respect for nonintervention norms—an undertaking by governing authorities to protect the peoples within their domain against the ravages of humanitarian emergencies that threaten peace and security.[6] And if there is a failure to address these needs, then the gov-

ernment loses its representative rights with respect to sovereignty, and those rights are temporarily exercised by other actors, whether transnational humanitarian relief organizations or intergovernmental institutions. The state, once governance is restored, is entitled, of course, to represent its people, and deserves considerable, but not absolute, deference with respect to internal public order under normal circumstances.[7]

Aside from doctrinal confusion, manipulation, and uncertainty, there is a clear trend away from the idea of unconditional sovereignty and toward a conception of responsible sovereignty, namely, that governmental legitimacy depends upon adherence to minimum humanitarian norms and on a capacity to act effectively to protect citizens from acute threats to their security and well-being that derive from adverse territorial conditions. As with other fundamental norms and principles, sovereignty evolves in relation to practice and to shifts in community expectations. These shifts are the principal concern of this chapter.

For all its complexities, sovereignty continues to provide the agreed basis for political order in international life, as it has for several centuries. For better or worse, sovereignty, as a matter of rights and obligations, is universally affirmed as an unconditional pillar of contemporary world order.[8] Sovereignty is part of the historical baggage of several centuries of global political development and cannot be eliminated from an inquiry into a state's responsibility and accountability for acts committed under its authority. At the same time, the content and influence of sovereignty are political matters that reflect changes in the character of international society and the play of forces that define the present historical situation. There is no intrinsic or conceptual reason why effective procedures for responsibility and accountability should not be reconciled with a coherent, reconstructed conception of sovereignty. Furthermore, it is not possible to maintain persuasively that a single conception of sovereignty currently enjoys an authoritative status.

Still, those members of international society that are indifferent to the occurrence of human suffering or skeptical about the capacity or willingness of outsiders to take on ethical challenges continue to invoke sovereignty as a rationalization for inaction, or they simply disregard it in order to validate interventionary diplomacy. From their perspective, contentions about responsibility and accountability are thus disregarded as inappropriate, either because they engender false hopes, or worse, encourage dangerous and unsuccessful policies that then inhibit future responses.

In some respects, then, sovereignty as a political reality is less significant than the various political debates being carried on beneath the banner of sovereignty these days, debates that are of great relevance to the struggle to protect human society from various forms of extreme governmental failure.

A CONCEPTUAL INTRODUCTION

Sovereignty has been treated as a prime attribute of statehood, and state-hood is the essential qualification for full membership in international society, including membership in most important international organizations and full participation in diplomatic activities. The idea of sovereignty is enshrined in the United Nations Charter and embedded in international law in a variety of correlated doctrines: among them, the sovereign equality of states, nonintervention in domestic jurisdiction, and sovereign immunity. The idea of sovereignty is linked closely to a state-centric world order system generally associated with the legacy of the Peace of Westphalia in 1648, a legacy that has become a defining feature of the modern world.[9]

But as the clarity of statism recedes in an era of globalization, the essential character of sovereignty becomes more and more elusive and subject to renegotiation by the play of political forces, moral attitudes, and prevailing perceptions. As the postmodern political context takes shape, the association between sovereignty and territoriality is definitely weakened, although by no means defunct. The persisting importance of boundaries in relation to the control over the flow of people, ideas, and things is a reminder that the territorial dimensions of sovereignty are still paramount. What is new, however, is that sovereignty can no longer be reduced to territoriality; it now includes elements of normativity (human rights, humane governance, human dignity) and functionality (nonterritorial centers of authority and control).[10]

Thus, the existence of sovereignty remains firmly established, but its behavioral implications are in flux. There exist, as a matter of international law, significant commitments to uphold human rights and to refrain from practices that would appear to be genocidal in character or qualify as crimes against humanity. Additionally, in widely endorsed treaties such as the Genocide Convention and the Hague Conventions on the Law of War, states have accepted responsibility for implementing the standards agreed upon despite their intrusion upon the territorial authority of governments. These treaty obligations are now regarded as so fundamental as to be generally binding on all states by virtue of customary international law. Furthermore, since the governments of sovereign states are deemed to have accepted the obligation to uphold international law, accountability to the organized international community formally exists. After World War II, and recently in relation to the events of the 1990s in Bosnia and Rwanda, international war crimes tribunals have been established by governments acting through the UN Security Council, and though criticized for various shortcomings, they have generally been accepted as valid legal initiatives. These accountability procedures have explicitly ruled out defenses based on statist prerogatives, whether in the form of superior orders or the immunity of leaders acting on behalf of a state. Sovereignty has been *legally* interpreted in a manner that accommodates claims of responsibility and accountability. Both ruler and servants can indeed do wrong. Sovereignty is no longer absolute, but conditional and subject to a myriad of qualifications.

Legal accommodation, however, needs to be distinguished from *political* accommodation, and it is here that the apparent tension between geopolitical realities and wider patterns of responsibility and accountability exposes the fearful inadequacy of international society. Stronger states are unwilling even to pay the relatively modest costs of implementation for the initiatives that they have sponsored, except in those special circumstances where their strategic interests are deeply engaged. Weaker states are reluctant to trust strong states to act in a benign fashion, and suspect hegemonic motives. Oppressive states hypocritically rely on sovereignty as a shield to avoid responsibility and accountability. Strange coalitions emerge among governments that are essentially indifferent to these forms of human suffering and governments whose abusive conduct is responsible for such suffering, either as perpetrator or as enfeebled protector. In such an atmosphere, the efforts to construct an ethos of responsible sovereignty are subordinated to the earlier statist reductive understanding of sovereignty as territorial supremacy.

This double pattern of inaction and resistance is especially manifest in relation to the recent African experience. The strong states outside of Africa now lack the political will to uphold canons of responsible government and to impose accountability for gross abuses of human rights and crimes of state, while the weaker states within Africa, sensitive to their own memories of the colonial era and to their postcolonial encounters with geopolitics, are reluctant to solicit or approve of intervention as a means to mitigate the human suffering that arises from extreme governmental failure.

Such a regional reality for Africa is reinforced by bad examples in the wider global arena. Countries that subscribe to and promote an ethos of human rights are, nevertheless, often unwilling to commit themselves to procedures of accountability in relation to their own behavior. For instance, current proposals to establish an international criminal court have been framed in such a way as to ensure that no action takes place without prior approval from the UN Security Council, whose five permanent members can veto any decision that threatens themselves and their allies. Stronger states are unwilling to see the discipline of international law applied to their own behavior on matters of vital interests, insisting on the retention of unilateral discretion to act without subsequent accountability to the wider society of states.[11] In this respect, there has been no *geopolitical* reconciliation between sovereign rights and the responsibility for upholding international law—and thus no globally effective procedures to ensure the accountability of those individuals accused of gross violations of international law, regardless of whether their country is strong or weak, or whether it has won or lost a war. As the next section attempts to clarify, the idea of sovereignty inevitably and dynamically reflects the unresolved tensions between the juridical world of *equal* states and the geopolitical world of *unequal* states. Unfortunately, the universal affirmation of human rights as applicable to governance at all levels of social organization, including that of the state, is no assurance whatsoever of effective or consistent implementation, even in circumstances of gross, even catastrophic human rights violations.

THE EVOLUTION OF SOVEREIGNTY

The idea of sovereignty is not static; it has evolved to reflect fundamental changes in political life. Sovereignty originated as a powerful conception in late-medieval Europe, initially to validate the claims of kings to consolidate power within the boundaries of emergent states, and thereby supersede feudal claims of local autonomy. In a fundamental sense, the king was the dominant feudal lord who provided order among principalities, overcoming often chaotic and dangerous internal conditions. As such, the locus of sovereignty was initially associated with royal absolutism, with an imposed system of governance providing the framework for order and development. Furthermore, the king tended to claim a divine right to rule as the basis for his authority, which could not be questioned by any competing source of internal or external authority. What is relevant about these origins of sovereignty is the unconditional character of the authority embodied in the state, and the developing notion of a territory delimited by boundaries.

One challenge against sovereignty imposed from the outset by such formative political theorists as Hobbes and Locke was the right to resist tyrannical rule. From the time of the Magna Carta onward, constitutional limitations on sovereignty as the absolute authority of the ruler were the outcome of successful social struggle. An important additional step in this process occurred during the American and French Revolutions, especially the latter, in which a Rousseauist view of sovereignty takes hold: sovereignty is associated with the nation, and the nation with the people, and the people with the existence of inalienable rights. From this time forward, the power of the state was not coincident with its internal legitimacy, the latter depending on various inconsistent ideological notions. After the Napoleonic Wars the countries of Europe briefly maintained a right of intervention to restore legitimate rule as measured by dynastic criteria; later, Marxist ideas of class conflict associated the legitimate state with one dominated by the proletariat. What is important is that disputes about the nature of legitimate authority were closely related to resistance movements and interventionary claims, culminating in the middle of this century with the anticolonial movement that brought independence to the peoples of Africa and Asia. By stages this movement was endorsed by the United Nations, undermining the legitimacy of colonial claims to rule and thereby validating emancipatory efforts.[12] The UN role in supporting the antiapartheid campaign extended this notion of illegitimate rule to settler states that governed on the basis of racial claims of superiority. Such support built a consensus around the idea that official doctrines of racial discrimination violated minimum standards of conduct applicable to all governments and thus substantially eroded the legal basis for respect of sovereign rights as exclusively territorial. The more recent project of insisting that the political legitimacy of a state depends on its adoption of market-oriented constitutionalism is an extension of the effort by dominant states and market forces to impose a restrictive version of governmental entitlement on *all* states.[13]

This twin heritage of sovereignty helps explain the peculiar nature of contemporary disputes about its applicability: it represented both a consolidation of governmental power and a grant of authority to the state and its citizenry. The governing process of a sovereign state implies a logic of hierarchy in relation to other *internal* claimants, especially relying on monopoly control with respect to authority to use force. Sovereignty also provided a foundation for *external* relations with regard to other sovereign entities. The external applicability of sovereignty rested on a logic of equality among sovereign states. International law incorporated this duality as fundamental to its role in regulating relations among states.

Yet, as has been evident all along, there are crucial gaps between the legal postulates of hierarchy and equality and the operational reality of international life. In many circumstances governments could not effectively subordinate all competing internal centers of power and authority. In international relations, from the outset, inequalities in size, resources, and military capabilities undermined supposedly mutual relationships that were intended to govern the conduct of states toward each other. As a result, the formal doctrine of sovereignty has always operated, to some extent, as a legal fiction, given the gap between its formal dimensions and the empirical realities.

This gap has been more and more evident in recent decades because the rise of human rights as a parallel doctrine embodied in international law highlights the ambiguity of sovereignty as a source of governmental authority and a guideline for behavior. Part of the ambiguity is based on the view that internal sovereignty implies capacity as well as will, and that in the setting of Africa, many of the independent states were, in effect, born as "quasi-states" because of their inability to exercise governmental authority in an effective or legitimate fashion.[14] Another part of this argument is that the failure by a state to uphold the human rights of its people, or in some readings, to institutionalize democracy, suspends or restricts territorial sovereignty and validates interventionary claims, even if asserted without the backing of international institutions. Putting this argument in its most contemporary, postmodern form the claim is that international society has a responsibility to address humanitarian emergencies, to ensure compliance with human rights, and to guarantee the operation of constitutional democracy by imposing sanctions and even by recourse to armed intervention.

Not all observers are prepared to scrap territorial sovereignty as a basis for international order, however. Even such normatively engaged realists as Hedley Bull, Inis Claude, John Vincent, and Adam Roberts are wary of any vindication of interventionary claims. Adam Roberts recently expressed this view: "However imperfectly observed, the presumption against military intervention, including even humanitarian intervention, has not served badly as an ordering principle in international relations."[15] What is meant here is that those with the capacity to intervene are generally not to be trusted in terms of the purity of their alleged motivation, and that such intervention has often compounded the suffering it was meant to stop. Furthermore, this argument holds, interventionary diplomacy in recent international practice tends to intensify both the scale and duration of conflict and is rarely effective as a transformative instrument, even when the intervening side has a wide margin of military superiority. The U.S. experience in Vietnam, partly justified at the time as a defense of freedom and democracy, illustrated vividly the hypocrisy of such normative claims, the huge risks of escalation that can arise from such intervention, and the inability of the intervenor to translate military superiority into a desired political outcome. In effect, say realists like Roberts, there is no consistently responsible and effective *external* agency to achieve implementation of normative sovereignty. Such implementations can be achieved only through the dynamics of *internal resistance*, that is, by the dynamics of self-determination.

Other observers, however, are less rigid; they take a cautious evolutionary view that sees a series of encouraging signs pointing to the creation of a more reliable basis for responsibility and accountability in relation to extreme governmental failure. The record is not consistent, and the evolutionary path is by no means linear or free from contradiction, but several developments offer some encouragement for the emergence of normative sovereignty as a counterpoint to the traditions of territorial sovereignty:

- the acceptance of human rights standards as universally applicable, and the articulation of these standards and their embodiment in international treaties;
- the endorsement of the right of self-determination on behalf of peoples subject to colonial rule, and the support for their independence struggles, including the antiapartheid campaign;
- the extension in the European Community of procedures for the implementation of human rights standards by introducing an external procedure of assessment;

- the imposition of criminal liability on leaders of Germany and Japan after World War II, the incorporation into international law of the Nuremberg Principles, and the establishment of an international tribunal to prosecute individuals accused of war crimes in both the Balkan and Rwandan conflicts in the 1990s;
- the protective zone established in northern Iraq to protect the Kurdish people against the oppressive policies of the Iraqi government in the aftermath of the Gulf War;
- the effort to alleviate the suffering of the people of Somalia as a result of the breakdown of governmental authority and the outbreak of severe interclan violence;
- the restoration to power of the elected civilian government of Haiti and the removal from authority of a brutal military junta that had seized power;
- the imposition of peace in Bosnia, which included an effort to end the suffering of the people, to insist on accountability for those guilty of war crimes, and to commit the future political leadership to respect human rights and constitutional procedures, including elections;
- the role of the globalized media in mobilizing sentiments of human solidarity in response to occasions of extreme governmental failure and humanitarian emergency ("The CNN factor");
- the rise and spread of transnational humanitarian initiatives and private-sector social forces dedicated to the alleviation of human suffering regardless of territorial locus.

It is not the contention here that these developments are without serious flaws and inconsistencies when considered separately and objectively. It is also the case that important structural regional and global impediments persist in relation to the establishment of effective regimes of international responsibility and accountability. These impediments are especially serious in sub-Saharan Africa since the end of the cold war. The perceived geopolitical stakes are too low in many instances to support a framework based on normative sovereignty, and the result has been a tragic wavering between deformed claims of territorial sovereignty and destructive instances of pure chaos.[16] What is certain is only that there are enough encouraging developments to make the project of responsibility and accountability, the essence of normative sovereignty, worthy of continued commitment, despite the bleakness of immediate prospects. Also, such developments complicate any simple assessment of the impact of sovereign rights and tend to reinforce skeptical conclusions about humanitarian intervention from above and to encourage generally positive conclusions about humanitarian intervention from below.[17] Of course, there are no panaceas on the normative horizons, and the international reactions to recent tragedies in Africa give little ground for believing that even the modest and ambiguous achievements of the early

1990s can be maintained in the face of a series of adverse developments—among them the widely alleged mission failures in Somalia and Bosnia, the refusal to heed pleas for modest increases in UN peacekeeping capabilities in Rwanda and Burundi, the failure to act in response to the refugee crisis in Congo, the diminished reputation of the United Nations as agent of international responsibility, and the general failure of support for global public initiatives (as partly evidenced by the UN financial crisis). Normative sovereignty, unlike territorial sovereignty, depends on a supportive infrastructure of institutional capabilities and transnational initiatives.

CONTEMPORARY THEMES

In the present world order there exists a complex normative tension between claimants invoking alleged sovereign rights of territorial supremacy and claimants relying upon purported humanitarian concerns that challenge the discretion and capacity of governmental authority to act appropriately within the boundaries of a state. A closely related tension arises in the event of a collapse of governmental authority, which exposes the civilian population of a country to the consequences of official inaction in the form of chaos, disease, famine, and civic violence. Under such conditions, despite the persistence of the formal attributes of statehood, including representation in the United Nations, do normal sovereign rights persist? Where there is no effective operative government, can the international community mandate interventionary action, without any indigenous consent, for the sake of the distressed population? If the international community fails to act can regional actors, neighboring states, or great powers respond unilaterally? In addressing these questions a distinction should be made between situations involving an abusive government and situations in which governments have collapsed altogether. Both circumstances have been prevalent in the recent African political experience, giving these questions urgent political and normative, and not merely conceptual, relevance.

Indeed, it is misleading to treat these world order challenges as if they were purely legal questions involving the identification of the proper limits on sovereign rights. What seems evident is that a strong moral basis exists for external action to mitigate those instances of acute human suffering that a territorial government is unwilling or unable to alleviate. The critical variable is the intensity and benevolence of the political interests of potential external intervenors. It is only when there is a congruence of moral and political factors that a given instance of intervention will be perceived as legitimate by a substantial body of world public opinion, and it is only when there is a sufficient congruence of legal and political factors that the intervention is likely to be effective in achieving its goals. In other words, the doctrine of sovereignty as such does not present itself as a decisive obstacle in international refusals to respond to various humanitarian crises; rather, it is the weakness of political motivation on the part of critical actors that remains the main explanatory variable.

This conceptual effort to sort out the issues associated with humanitarian emergencies induced by governmental failure must contend with two further sets of conditions. First of all, an unresolved internal struggle among various factions or regions to reconstitute governmental authority frequently gives rise to the perception that external actors, whether under the auspices of the United Nations or not, are taking sides. This pattern complicated, and some say doomed, the latter phases of the Somalia operation in 1993–94.[18] Second, external actors have been accused of reconstituting governmental authority in a manner that confers benefits on them, a process that seemed to occur in Kuwait after the Gulf War, when lucrative construction contracts were awarded to foreign firms from the main intervening states. In both instances, it can be seen that sovereignty, in its negative aspects, is not necessarily suspended by governmental failure. Rather, what is suspended is the governmental capacity of a sovereign state to give or withhold consent in relation to an interventionary response. International law provides no alternative way to assess the will of the citizenry in the target society. Prevailing international morality is generally respectful toward territorial sovereignty. This conditions international humanitarian initiatives to alleviate suffering. International statist morality implies a political effort to respect the dynamics of self-determination. This respect is supposed to exist under conditions of governmental collapse, and to the extent possible, even in exceptional circumstances that mandate recourse to humanitarian intervention.[19]

The complexities of humanitarian intervention have been particularly visible in numerous instances in Africa. As the colonial order unraveled, the cold war temporarily endowed African countries with strategic importance as relatively distant arenas within which to test the will and capabilities of the two opposed superpowers; the continent became a geopolitical battleground in these years, with often tragic consequences. Starting with the Congo in 1960, superpower rivalry for influence in the political orientation of African governments led both to open conflict and to high-stakes games in which economic assistance and other positive inducements became contingent on geopolitical alignment. Among these "positive inducements" were tacit agreements on the part of superpowers to ignore human rights violations. Another inducement was to stabilize governmental authority even if corrupt and oppressive, to help defuse popular unrest by providing emergency relief. With the end of the cold war, political turmoil and economic distress in Africa lost most of its strategic relevance, and to the extent that it challenged the north at all, it was primarily as a matter of humanitarian concern. True, there was concern about the spread of Islamic extremism in

Africa, especially as the government in Sudan began to project an anti-Western image and was alleged to be giving support to international terrorist activities. But the main impact of Africa on public and elites alike since the end of the cold war has been humanitarian, a question of whether and how much should be done to assist large numbers of people in circumstances of acute distress. These humanitarian challenges have occasionally been translated into modest policy responses when public pressure was effectively mounted and the risks of deeper involvement did not seem too high. Somalia, for example, was an intervention mainly prompted by humanitarian concerns, and deliberately kept modest in scope to avoid costlier and less predictable results. The death of eighteen American servicemen in June 1993, however, essentially ended the illusion that effective humanitarian interventions in Africa could be cheaply organized and easily contained.

It is important to realize that respect for sovereignty figured little in the minds of external actors in the various humanitarian crises in Africa, except when it was invoked as a reminder that interfering in unresolved struggles for political control of an African state may well trigger violent resistance. Thus being sensitive to sovereign rights is a prudential means to stay clear of interventionary quagmires even in settings of collapsed governments. Such sensitivity was particularly evident in American foreign policy during the Bush years and during the Clinton presidency after late 1993, when the decision was made to terminate UN operations in Somalia. The same observation applies to the role of the United Nations in such situations, given the directive of Article 2(7); this provision, in essence, is based less on an abstract belief in the inviolability of state sovereignty than it is on the practical understanding that member states are not inclined to act *altruistically* to resolve the internal traumas of foreign countries. The domestic jurisdiction idea is thus both a reassurance to weak states that their sovereignty will be respected by the United Nations, and a limitation on the responsibility undertaken by strong states to uphold international peace and security.

This generalization was confirmed by the inaction in both Bosnia and Rwanda, despite exceptional moral and legal justifications for UN protective action. In this regard, there are ample conceptual means to restrict the nonintervention norm, but such means will not be relied upon unless geopolitical conditions for intervention on a significant scale are also present. My analysis of the contemporary scene is that such conditions were often, although not invariably, satisfied during the cold war years, but not generally since then. Sovereignty has in effect become a banner under which potential intervenors can call attention to the high stakes of intervention—its costs too high, its risks too great, and its gains, if any, marginal. If the society is a state, even in a condition of domestic anarchy, any humanitarian undertaking risks being regarded as "interventionary" and hostile to the plans of one group or another to exert its own form of governance. In other words, without a relevant form of effective consent, entry onto the territory of a foreign state may generate resistance, however selfless the motivation of the intervenors.

Contemporary public consciousness of humanitarian intervention has over the years been shaped by a number of perceived "lessons." The U.S. government remains a critical world leader in relation to almost all humanitarian challenges that require large-scale external action, and its outlook has been colored by a number of distinctly negative experiences. In this regard, the Vietnam War, although by now relatively remote in time, remains a restraining influence, especially in military circles; it is reinforced by the failed attempt at state-building in Lebanon in 1982–83 and by the disappointing outcomes of peacekeeping missions in Somalia and Bosnia. Against this record of perceived failure, as a matter of domestic understanding, the "success" stories seem trivial and controversial (Grenada, Panama, El Salvador, Haiti). American collective memory is largely shaped by these failures, as the negative outcomes are vivid and painful, while the positive results have a low-profile character that is of minimal interest to the media or to the political fortunes of policymakers. Abstention seems less politically dangerous in these settings than does risky proactive interventionism. Such an assessment expresses the inward turn of governmental policy in the new global setting. Such an inward turn, a new mode of partial isolationism, is taking place in the face of globalization, partly as a compensation for the internationalization of foreign economic policy, which has certain adverse territorial effects.[20] For their part, the people who are the intended beneficiaries of humanitarian intervention have learned that resistance is possible and, if tactically appropriate, likely to be effective even in the face of massive military superiority. In this regard, the era of cheap intervention (so-called "gunboat diplomacy") is a misleading and inapplicable image of intervention, one that formed prior to nationalist mobilizations in the countries of the South. Under most contemporary conditions, the instrumental role of intervention is quite problematic, although the imposition of an external presence in Haiti during the last several years may provide a contemporary limit case.[21]

It is not quite accurate, however, to disregard sovereignty altogether as a factor. The mobilization of resistance to intervention can draw upon the historical memories of subordinated peoples. General Aidid did this effectively in response to the efforts by the United Nations to restore normal government-society relations in Somalia. In effect, the invocation of sovereignty in the setting of an ex-colony or weak state rests on the strong conviction that outsiders should give virtually unconditional respect to its political independence and territorial integrity even in the absence of a functioning government. The coalition that was led by the United States in the Gulf War achieved a political consensus partly by maintaining a rigid, and in many respects unfortunate, distinction between restoring Kuwait's sovereign rights and challenging internal public order in Iraq. If the latter had been part of the UN mandate the precedent would have been threatening to coalition members from the Middle East, especially Syria. In other words, given strategic priorities, deference to sovereign rights may irresponsibly shield oppressive governments and their leaders from accountability, despite the great suffering that is being inflicted on the citizenry of a given country.[22]

It seems remiss to discuss the impact of sovereignty without considering the complex and elusive impact of globalization, an imprecise designation that variously denotes the increased interconnectedness of all aspects of international life, especially pertaining to business operations, finance markets, and the electronic transmission of information. Metaphors such as "a global village" and "a borderless world" express the belief that sovereignty as a marker of significance has been superseded in important domains of transnational relations.[23] As a result the state has lost some of its power and authority, but without any corresponding relocation of responsibility and accountability.[24] Indeed, the decline of sovereignty does not necessarily occasion a stronger sense of regional or global community, and without such sentiments globalization is not likely to contribute to more concerted efforts to address human suffering caused by extreme governmental failures, especially if such failures are not encroaching upon short-run market opportunities. Indeed, the priority of market considerations has induced tolerance for governmental abuse in some instances, particularly in the strong growth economies in the Asia/Pacific region. It is possible, however, that territorial backlash organized by the victims of globalization may eventually encourage the strengthening of wider frameworks of responsibility and accountability, as when Jacques Chirac briefly abandoned his neoliberal precepts and started talking about "social Europe" in response to disruptive strikes in France during December 1995. Such political language discloses a challenge to neoliberal attitudes, which are, in principle, reluctant to endow institutions of governance with any social responsibilities for ensuring the minimal conditions of human decency. Sovereignty, then, needs to be conceptualized in two different, principal formats: first, as a deference to established governmental authority in a state, and second, as a possible basis for endorsing or repudiating intervention by outside states or other political actors that claim to be serving humanitarian goals.

THE PROBLEM OF AGENCY

To protect humanity from governmental failure is a difficult challenge in a world order that combines globalization, geopolitics, a realist calculus of interests, a lapse in political leadership, and an absence of reliable and competent international institutions at a regional or global level. These difficulties present themselves currently in their most acute form in Africa, where oppression, corruption, poverty, and disorder are prevalent in several countries. There is no short-run prospect for any dramatic improvement in the capacities of international society to offer effective protection to those being victimized, but modest improvements are possible even in the unfavorable current atmosphere.

A reformist outlook weighted toward the promotion of the human dignity of all persons and peoples needs to begin with the problem of agency; of binding actors capable of rendering help in some form to those in the most vulnerable situations. For much of the history of the statist world order, the problem of agency was conflated with the doctrine of sovereignty. Only the territorial government was empowered to uphold the well-being of the people subject to its authority, and governments were conceived to be, as Hedley Bull put it, "local agents of the world common good."[25] This idea of agency was supposedly guided in prior centuries by the directive authority of natural law as interpreted and mediated through the conscience of the absolute leader, a moralistic fiction in many circumstances. With the secularization of political authority, the rise of positivist notions of law, this form of agency was connected with rule of law, including the duty to implement international law internally, a duty given specific substance in the last half-century by the development of the international law of human rights. In the present context, however, such agency is useless or worse, since so much human suffering today is largely the result of either the collapse of government or its oppressive relationship to its own population. Naturally, it is the objective of international law to ensure that governments, to the extent possible, do become agents of the public good within their territorial domains, but whether this is even possible for governments confronting massive poverty and natural disaster in an era of globalization is far from self-evident.[26] What is evident is the need for additional forms of agency.

In most respects, the most congenial type of agency for African countries would seem to be in the shape of autonomous regional initiatives that avoid any impression of dependence on the former colonial powers or the West. The Organization of African Unity has, on occasion, been usefully invoked, as in the early stages of civil strife in Liberia, but its resources and capabilities are very limited, and it is often difficult to shape a political consensus, especially if the call is for some degree of intervention. Even in Europe, where regionalism is far more established, the breakup of Yugoslavia posed challenges that were unmet even in the face of the widely publicized atrocities of ethnic cleansing. The agency of regional institutions in relation to governmental failure is marginal in the current framework, although promising in the middle term, as the basis for a meaningful normative community in which sentiments of empathy and solidarity can be developed as a potential basis for effective agency in the future.

To some degree the same observations apply to the agency of the United Nations. The United Nations under certain favorable conditions can be an effective agent of response to governmental failure, but it is dependent for its effectiveness upon financial and diplomatic support from leading member states, especially the United States. This support wanes and waxes depending on the perception of geopolitical interests at stake, the orientation of political leadership in the leading countries, the outlook of public opinion, and the solvency and credibility of the United Nations as an impartial and effective actor. Somalia is seen as the turning point in the most recent phase of UN efforts, not only representing the most ambitious effort to respond to governmental failure but also revealing the limits to such response. The joint U.S./UN effort since 1995 to rescue the people of Haiti has been fashioned in the shadow of the Somalia failure, and has succeeded up to this point, although the depth of commitment has not been tested and the response was encouraged by a very specific geopolitical dilemma confronting Washington—the inability to contain the politically unacceptable outflow of Haitian refugees to the United States. In many respects, it is the United Nations that could be empowered to endow international society with responsibility and accountability in response to governmental failure, but realizing this potential depends on a changed political atmosphere in which much greater support exists for financing global public goods and freeing the organization from geopolitical control. Such support would require a reinterpretation of the neoliberal consensus, either by an adjustment in market calculations as to the adverse effects of inaction or by applying countervailing pressures sufficient to produce influential transnational civil initiatives in the area of human rights and economic development.[27]

A promising yet problematic solution to the agency problem in certain settings is to employ what William Charles Maynes has dubbed "benign realpolitik." In effect, such a view relies upon the interventionary capacities of powerful global and regional actors. The United States in Central America and the Caribbean, France in Francophone Africa, Russia in its "near abroad," India in relation to its smaller neighbors—all constitute such normative spheres of influence that have been active in recent years. This pattern of benign geopolitics is attractive because it reflects the presence of real interests in addressing a particular instance of governmental failure, but it is problematic because geopolitical motivations are likely to include elements of self-interest that are often insensitive or opposed to the well-being of peoples in the target society. This pattern was evident in Somalia in 1993, when the Somali population was alienated by the reckless disregard of civilian life through reliance on high-tech, indiscriminate weaponry in Mogadishu, or in 1989 in Panama, when the U.S. intervention to restore democratic governance was carried out in a manner that produced heavy casualties among the civilian population and seemed crudely insensitive to the sovereign rights of Panama as an independent country. Yet Panama was a case of partial governmental failure, an illegally annulled election, that might have justified intervention. The motives and means of the United States, however, caused widespread criticism, not least from Panamanians. The United States relied on a hegemonic style of intervention that exhibited little deference to the sovereign right of the Panamanian people to choose their own future. It is such behavior that leads governments of the South to insist on sovereignty as grounds for opposing all forms of interventionary diplomacy and to reject the contention that geopolitics can ever be benign.

Another source of agency, one with a very different pedigree, is the transnational humanitarian social entity. High on sensitivity to territorial well-being but low in capabilities relative to the scale of the challenge, medical groups and relief organizations have performed heroically under dangerous conditions, often acting in conflict zones where outside state actors would arouse opposition. This type of agency, possibly coordinated with international institutions, could offer the best prospect of satisfying the seemingly irreconcilable needs for effectiveness and legitimacy, but it, too, is far from unproblematic, as repeated attacks on relief workers shows. The underlying problem is broadly political and contextual. Transnational relief efforts may be linked, or at least seen to be linked, to outside or internal political forces, and thus become regarded as friend or enemy under conditions of extreme insecurity and antagonism. The result is a territorial backlash or a deliberate effort to scare off such humanitarian initiatives as an aspect of the unresolved political struggle.

A final source of relevant agency arises from domestic initiatives of civil society, grassroots and local activism that addresses the human suffering that attends governmental failure and collapse. This sort of protective reaction is beneficial, but is often hampered by woefully inadequate resources and by either an oppressive government or by oppositional activity that is seeking to isolate portions of the population from protection in its struggle to gain political control. In many countries of the South, especially in Africa and the Middle East, there is little tradition of such civil initiatives, although extended family and kinship patterns, along with religious organizations, perform many functions in these societies related to the mitigation of suffering.

This brief survey of alternative sources of agency helps us understand the difficulty of generating satisfactory responses to governmental failure, especially in Africa, given the decline of the strategic relevance of the countries involved and considering the overall trend in political arenas toward decline in support for global public goods. Additionally, to the extent that human suffering is embedded in unresolved political conflict, any sort of effective intervention seeking to restore normalcy is exceedingly difficult to carry out from a logistical viewpoint, and this difficulty needs to be borne in mind in each instance to avoid framing responses in a manner that discredits a particular source of agency. Such a pattern of deficient framing is one way to understand the diminished reputation in the 1990s of the United Nations as a locus of international responsibility for governmental failure.

A CONCLUDING NOTE

The question of sovereignty remains central, problematic, and controversial in relation to the dynamics of humanitarian intervention. There is a growing belief that sovereignty is not a bar to nonmilitary forms of intervention if authorized by an appropriate international institution or centered around the activities of independent transnational humanitarian initiatives. In a context of severe government oppression or collapse, however, a new series of problems comes to light. Is the concept of sovereignty still applicable when there is no longer a legitimate or effective locus of governmental authority? Does sovereignty depend on the existence of a legitimate and effective government? Or is sovereignty a set of rights embodied in civil society and associated with the authority of a people or peoples to pursue self-determination within their international boundaries without external interference? Or is sovereignty a relative legal term that depends on a balance between, on the one hand, rights of political independence and, on the other, the duties of national institutions to uphold human rights and humane, democratic governance?

What is called for is a reconceptualization of sovereignty that takes due account of changing world order trends. Such a move is difficult, since sovereignty and statehood remain fused in the collective political memory by the anticolonial struggle. A misleading impression may have been created, especially in Africa, that sovereignty is a status, once and for all, and not a process, evolving to incorporate responsibilities of states as well as rights.

The debate over sovereignty and humanitarian intervention is faced with a number of disturbing developments. First, there has been a decline in the interest of global political actors in sustaining the viability of poor or troubled states, reflecting a negative outcome of the cold war. Second, there has been a further decline in the interest of global political actors in the destiny of states that are not seen as attractive markets for investment, production, and consumption—a consequence of the prevailing neoliberal economic climate. Third, recent years have witnessed an increase in civic trauma in fragile or poor states arising from population pressures, migrations, macroeconomic adjustment programs, environmental degradation, reductions in economic assistance, and natural disasters. Fourth, weak states are increasingly susceptible to the growth of extremist and secessionist politics based on exclusivist identities—a phenomenon that has seen its worst manifestations in Rwanda, Burundi, Liberia, and Sudan, and in other sites of ethnic strife, massacres, crimes against humanity, and genocide. Finally, there is a marked decline in support for large-scale and ambitious humanitarian operations carried out under the auspices of the United Nations.

Promoting responsible sovereignty in this setting is a daunting, yet necessary, challenge. There is growing support for the idea that sovereignty is a two-way street, one endowed with rights but also with responsibilities. Preaching responsible sovereignty in the difficult circumstances confronting much of Africa is a profound undertaking at the end of this century, particularly so for those who favor the implementation of human rights and international law in those very societies that are the scene of the most gruesome humanitarian emergencies.

Such support for human rights cannot be separated from patterns of domination in world politics, entrenched geopolitical conventions that make non-Western countries particularly suspicious about Western enthusiasm for interventionary initiatives. To many developing countries, such Western moves to implement human rights recall the abuses of the colonial era, and even the Crusades—that is, moralizing intrusions on non-Western civilizations for the sake of naked exploitation. Of course, the controversy here is subtle and varies from context to context. The anxiety about renewed forms of Western domination is genuine, but it may also be relied upon by an authoritarian and abusive government to insulate itself from democratizing pressures being mounted by its own citizenry. The next chapter seeks to comprehend the often heard criticism that the human rights discourse is merely an expression of Western ideological hegemony. It seems important for those of us in the West to listen more sympathetically to such criticism, and not immediately step forward with a series of facile refutations of the indictment.[28]

Patterns of Global Dominance and Non-Western Attitudes Toward Human Rights   5

PRELIMINARY OBSERVATIONS

One of the most harmful features of Western-style global dominance is the perpetual rediscovery of its own perceived innocence. No amount of abuse and exploitation, however catastrophic its consequences for the non-Western victims, seems able to erode this sense of innocence. The United States seems especially immune to second thoughts or self-criticism. It retains its sense of self as the last best hope of humanity, as "the city on the hill," "the new Jerusalem"—all expressions of noble intentions and high expectations. Yet despite the dispossession of the indigenous peoples of North America, despite slavery and its aftermath, despite Hiroshima and Vietnam, this self-proclaimed innocence remains untarnished. This basic self-affirmation seems equally oblivious to the domestic scandals of homelessness, urban decay, and high homicide rates that continue to afflict American society. Americans, leaders and citizens alike, believe they have much to teach, and little to learn, especially on matters of human rights. There are those, of course, who call attention to past or present wrongdoings, yet their voices are seldom heard, and even more seldom heeded.

Such a pattern of cultural denial is enforced both from above and from below. A recent controversy involving the Smithsonian Museum in Washington, D.C., is particularly revealing. Museum curators were planning an exhibition concerning the American use of the atomic bomb against Japan at the end of World War II. Evidence contained in the exhibition cast doubt after fifty years on the official claims of "military necessity." It showed the suffering and devastation caused by the explosions and radiation, and it prompted visitors to question whether the real motives behind the attack were not hatred of and revenge against Japan and intimidation of the Soviet Union. After veterans groups protested, politicians responded, and the Smithsonian exhibit was effectively cancelled; instead of the original material, the show now consisted only of the surviving fuselage of the plane that delivered the first atomic bomb, unaccompanied by commentary or pictures of the human consequences.

Such a deep-seated reluctance to confront openly the legacy of human rights violations within the history of the United States is indicative of the larger, global obstacles facing progressive policymakers, scholars, and activists attempting to be heard amid the strident voices of Western dominance. Indeed, it is very difficult to become disengaged from the distorting misconceptions that are part of the deep structures of conventional Western discourse on human rights, as these structures are often hidden below the level of consciousness. If we are to extricate ourselves from such deep structures, it is crucial to understand and open the mind to three important premises:

1. *Responsibilities* must be conceived as correlative to *rights*. Such a premise would be well served by the drafting of a Universal Declaration of Human Responsibilities as an indispensable companion to the Universal Declaration of Human Rights. The Western discourse on human rights works within the invisible boundaries of self-expression and resistance to authority (the individualist ethos that gives rise to consumer absolutism and all forms of permissiveness), and without any sense of responsibility to the well-being and needs of the community. The notion of protecting the individual is a great advance over its absolutist antecedents, but it needs to be balanced by the acknowledgment that the individual is embedded within a community. The importance of placing limits upon human assertiveness at all levels of social organization is overlooked if the stress is placed only on the protection of individuals.

2. Secularism is not always a necessary precondition for a tolerant society. In other words, a secure environment for human rights is not necessarily inconsistent with the embodiment of religious conviction in public policy and political leadership. The current situation in Malaysia, for example, illustrates the extent to which the governance of a country can be both Islamic *and* tolerant. The character of the Malaysian state, though not without flaws, is thus a challenge to the contemporary belief structure of Western human rights discourse, which holds that the fusion of religious and political authority always undermines tolerance of different races, religions, and nationalities. Conventional Western discourse refuses to acknowledge that Islam may encourage the leadership of a country to exhibit tolerance toward non-Islamic minorities, rather than being a ground for repression and intolerance. Of course, any degree of historical consciousness would confirm that the past record of interreligious and interethnic tolerance in the Muslim

world far exceeds that in the West, perhaps most spectacularly with respect to anti-Semitism.

3. Nongovernmental organizations are not necessarily geopolitically neutral. This last premise contradicts the widespread belief that all NGOs are counter-hegemonic, democratizing forces. The fact is that, by and large, the Western NGO approach shares the statist view that the programmatic content of human rights consists only of political and civil rights and cannot be meaningfully extended to economic and social rights, despite the fact that both categories of rights are treated as equivalent under international law, and despite the greater relevance of economic and social rights to the lives of most people on the planet.

These three premises are just a starting point, however, in reformulating a human rights discourse. It is time for the West to realize that unless rights are balanced by a framework of responsibilities, "freedoms" are likely to degenerate into societal decadence. To be dedicated to forms of secularism that ignore a spiritual sense of human identity is to deprive our political and moral imaginations of the only reliable basis for overcoming the contradictions of modernism.

It should also be emphasized that such premises should not be embraced uncritically. Rather, they should enable us to see the discourse on human rights from *without* in order to appreciate its limitations and distortions. Such a view from without does not involve any suspension of critical assessment; nor should it be used to exonerate arbitrary or oppressive leadership. It does, however, put the focus more directly on Western contributions to human suffering as a consequence of its role in constructing and maintaining dominance structures.

This view from without, which is in effect a reflection in the mirror of Asian thought and practice, encourages Western self-criticism. It prompts observers to see broader patterns of global dominance—the distortions of priorities, the long-term deprivations and the deformations of cultural identity being produced in non-Western societies by Western modes of popular culture and consumerism. A government may reasonably have to infringe upon freedom of expression to protect a country from such baleful influences.

WESTERN SOCIAL REALITY AS A DIMENSION OF GLOBAL DOMINATION

The West is no longer a geographic space; today, it exists largely in a non-territorial and mostly nonaccountable global market that represent the new locus of geopolitics and that sets the agenda in matters of political economy for even the most powerful states by establishing the priorities for global policy, especially on matters of peace and security. In this regard, upholding Western control over oil supplies in the Gulf was deemed worth a major war, but protecting Bosnia or Rwanda from genocide merited only the meekest gestures of concern, and protecting the Chechens from Russian aggression failed to occasion even a note of condemnation. The impact of this ascendancy of market forces is to reduce the sense of alternatives available to leaders at the level of the state. At risk, in particular, are compassionate approaches to poverty and social vulnerability. The globalized market produces a narrowing of the political space available to the governments of the West. This is true even for the most powerful states.

The imperative of competitiveness drives down wages, weakens safety measures, and also rolls back welfare. Particularly revealing in this period is the collapse of "social democracy" as a more compassionate alternative to market-oriented politics. Whether it is the French "socialism" of Mitterrand, the tilt toward Wall Street by "the new Democrats" in the Clinton administration, the realignment of the British Labour Party and the Japanese Socialist Party, or the move away from the welfare state in Scandinavia, the story is the same. It is evident that social democracy must now submit to the market rather than pursue its own program of action; it seems as if politics is becoming capital-driven rather than people-driven. It is a structural story. And it is one that renders elections and political parties less and less consequential, creating a crisis for constitutional democracy in the West. Until these global market forces can be regulated on the basis of human, and environmental priorities, the dynamics of trade, investment, and growth are likely to gravely jeopardize the mission of human rights to protect those who are most at risk economically, socially, politically, and culturally.

This set of circumstances is aggravated by the degree to which the human rights discourse in the West continues to maintain a dangerous, outmoded deference to the autonomy of market forces and refuses to challenge the consequences of secularism in its postmodern forms, with its strong connections to consumerism and its propagation of a mood of despair. In the most minimal sense this means that the West refuses to acknowledge that homelessness, permanent joblessness, urban squalor, drug culture, crime, and the commercialization of violence are more than mere law and order problems—they represent a human rights crisis. The UN Social Development Summit, held in Copenhagen in March 1995, was a response to this neglect and was designed to insert these concerns back into the political agenda of states, and to reshape the human rights agenda in light of these developments. Unfortunately, the summit was severely constrained by the political need to win the support of governments, which limited an all-out attack on the role of global market forces in the worst patterns of social abuse.

As mentioned earlier, Western social reality is alienated from its own criminal past to an alarming degree, and is therefore encompassed by it. This is especially true of the United States, whose postal service recently revealed plans to issue a stamp commemorating the fiftieth anniversary of Hiroshima and Nagasaki, with the brazen caption "atomic bombs that saved lives." Japanese protests led to a White House decision to rescind the stamp, yet the effectiveness of Japanese pressure primarily reflected Japan's role as major trading partner and as a crucial member of the Group of Seven. President Clinton's request that the U.S. Postal Service cancel the stamp did not arise because the U.S. government was suddenly willing to confront the criminality of Hiroshima and Nagasaki, or even to challenge the post–cold war military utility of nuclear missiles. We can imagine the sense of indignation and outrage that would follow in the U.S. if Germany issued a stamp interpreting its concentration camps in a self-serving way—possibly a picture of Auschwitz with the caption "overcoming the humiliation of Versailles." But is it so different? This criminality of the West includes the genocidal ordeal of indigenous peoples who stood in the way of colonial conquerors; it extends to the horrifying reliance on slavery as the basis of economic development in the New World; and it relates to the deprivations and humiliations of the colonial era, to the continuing exploitation of the poor, and to the ecological plunder of the planet.

An aspect of this refusal by the West to perceive its own role in generating abuses arises from a pervasive misconception that human rights are mainly for others, especially those in the South. Whether it is a matter of government policy or academic literature, the Western, and particularly American, emphasis is on human rights as an instrument of foreign policy, not as a corrective to domestic shortcomings. Recently this has made human rights a central dimension of debates associated with intervention in Haiti and elsewhere, and of inquiries into whether the humanitarian cause is a worthwhile basis for foreign policy. This self-righteous diplomacy is producing a new crusader mentality that underpins the advocacy of humanitarian intervention, the geographic axis of which runs always North to South, with no contemplation that perhaps there are circumstances of abuse that might validate South-to-North forms of intervention. At the same time, where the cause is perceived as mainly humanitarian, as in Bosnia or Chechnya, there is little willingness to take the necessary steps toward implementation.

There is a peculiarly distorting tendency in the current controversies over whether to exclude human rights concerns from economic interactions between the West and the countries of Asia. The source of the distortion is, once again, the self-perceived innocence of the West, which remains oblivious to its own historical role in the region. For example, the U.S. government's self-appointed role as the natural agent for the promotion of human rights in China and Indonesia is hardly credible, given the legacy of abuse. The postcolonial approach has delivered a clear message to Asian countries: adopt Western-style economic growth as your number-one priority, even at the expense of human rights. Revealingly, the predatory capitalism of East Asia was frequently called "a miracle," a description that blatantly overlooks the extent to which management-worker relations in Asia recall the worst excesses of early capitalism in the West (pre-Marx, pre–labor movement, pre–safety regulations and before minimum age and wage laws). This observation does not mean to deny that the economic development of the last few decades for the countries in this region has been remarkable, and even beneficial for many people. The fact is, however, that amid the rampant private-sector growth, those who are vulnerable still need protection. The good will and sense of responsibility of entrepreneurs is not enough. Only vigilance by government and democratic social forces can create a balance between the logic of the market and the ethos of humane social conditions. The regional and global scale of the market requires that this balance be struck at an international level so that all societies within a given region can compete on the basis of common ground rules.

This relative play of forces can be explored by comparing U.S. policy toward China with that toward Haiti. With China, as was predictable, global market forces have deterred the U.S. government from pushing too hard on human rights, since China is a trading partner of increasing importance. Yet, when U.S. intellectual property rights were at risk, then even a trade war was threatened to induce Chinese cooperation.

In relation to Haiti, market forces contributed differently to the formation of policy. The logic of American policy went something like this: If we must intervene to restore Jean-Bertrand Aristide in order to stop the flow of unwanted Haitian refugees into the United States, then we will do so in a manner that doesn't revive his populist program for the Haitian poor. Notwithstanding the almost 80 percent electoral mandate Aristide's program received from the citizens of Haiti, we will make Aristide swallow the IMF economic austerity pill and adopt an approach to development that makes it impossible to implement economic policies designed to mitigate poverty. To be sure that Aristide has no second thoughts, we will not dismantle or disarm the brutal paramilitary organization FRAPH, in case they need to step in again if Aristide should return to a politics based on a vision of social justice.

Despite such gross contradictions in Western policy, all is not bleak. There have been signs that this domineering, selective, and hypocritical approach to human rights in the West is being powerfully challenged both by social forces within these countries and by those without. Some recent instances are encouraging. For example, indigenous peoples in North and South America displayed a new strength in 1992 by derailing plans to celebrate the five-hundredth anniversary of Columbus' arrival—and subsequent plunder of—the new world. Also, women have emerged as a global emancipatory force, managing to reshape the agenda and outcome at the UN Conference on Population and Development held in Cairo in 1994, and exhibiting some possibilities for the emergence of global democracy. Women's groups made clear that improving overall social conditions for women—especially in the education of young girls—was more critical by far than promoting birth control in the battle to control population growth.

CONCLUSIONS

It is now more critical than ever to embark upon a fundamental rethinking of the Western human rights paradigm. An important aspect of such a rethinking is to establish the connection between a regulatory framework of global and regional market forces and the safeguarding of human rights in the social and economic realm. What is needed is a global vision of the future, in which the tolerance, even the celebration, of diversity combines with a reconstruction of the social and cultural order so as to endow the individual and collective identity of humanity with spiritual significance. Finally, the interplay of different cultural and religious traditions suggests the importance of multicivilizational dialogue involving the participation of various viewpoints, especially those with non-Western orientations. The world does not need a wholesale merging of different cultures and civilizations; rather, it simply needs to foster a new level of respect and reconciliation between and among its ever changing and ever diverse peoples and nations.

Against the background of those opening chapters, we turn now to consider a series of substantive concerns that have given rise to controversy about the proper limits of particular human rights norms. Many of these substantive concerns relate to the closely linked issues of self-determination, indigenous peoples, and humanitarian intervention.

PART 2

Substantive Dilemmas

Revisiting the Right of Self-Determination 6

What makes the right of self-determination such a difficult topic at this stage is that its exercise involves a clash of fundamental world order principles. On the one side is the basic geopolitical norm that the existing array of states is close to the maximum that can be accommodated within accepted diplomatic frameworks. Any significant further fragmentation of existing states is widely seen as producing an unwieldy and inefficient world order compared with present arrangements for global and regional governance. There is also the fear that nurturing the dream of statehood for the several thousand distinct peoples in the world will provide ample fuel for strife.

On the other side is the sense that all peoples should be treated equally, and that since some peoples have the benefit of statehood, others should be entitled to it as well. Proponents of this view also argue that involuntary patterns of state-society relations are basically inconsistent with the drive to spread human rights and democracy to all persons on the planet. In this regard, the right of self-determination has been a powerful mobilizing instrument with which to resist involuntary governance. A qualification of this strain of resistance, however, is the realization that the achievement of self-determination on the part of one group of people all too often entails the denial of that same right to another group of people.

The resolution of these opposed lines of concerns in specific situations requires a delicate balance of political, legal, and moral forces. The patterns of denial and attainment are bound to be arbitrary, reflecting the vagaries of geopolitical priorities and constraints more often than the relative weight of equitable argument. The plight of the Kurds in both Turkey and Iraq illustrates the geopolitical impulse on the part of major powers both to encourage restive peoples when it seems strategically convenient and to safeguard the integrity of existing states, even if that integrity depends on extreme forms of coercion over long periods of time.

Given such harsh truths, the most challenging question is whether tools can be provided to mitigate strife, and to provide parties with the means to reach compromises that accommodate the basic goals of both sides. Compromise is not always possible, or even appropriate, and then the outcome is likely to be shaped by a contest of wills often accompanied by severe and protracted violence. Resolution, in the end, usually results either from mutual exhaustion or from political/military domination.

THE RIGHT OF SELF-DETERMINATION IN THE CONTEMPORARY CONTEXT

The right of self-determination has at least two distinct embodiments in international law. One is the straightforward and generally uncontested assertion that self-determination is the underpinning for all individual claims for the legal protection of human rights—an assertion expressed expressed in Article 1 of both the Covenant on Civil and Political Rights and the Covenant on Economic, Social and Cultural Rights.[1] The other embodiment has always been controversial in application and, more recently, even in concept. It involves the wide range of claims of independence and sovereignty—or at least the right to exert effective control over one's collective destiny—on the part of myriad ethnic groups around the world. It is this second, geopolitical dimension of self-determination that is the focus of inquiry in this chapter, although some consideration will be given to the human rights dimension as well.

Aside from the collapse of communism in Europe and Russia, perhaps the most astonishing feature of the past decade and a half has been the remarkable success of secessionist political movements and the subsequent emergence of a series of new sovereign states. Attention to issues of self-determination has also been raised by a number of unsuccessful, and often bloody, attempts at autonomy and statehood. That these events have been framed as struggles for self-determination has both strained prior conceptual boundaries and created an increasingly awkward gap between doctrinal and experiential accounts of self-determination, resulting, as might be expected, in controversy and confusion.

Such strains have been particularly acute during the traumatic disintegration of the Soviet Union and Yugoslavia in the early 1990s—both violent ruptures arising from contradictory claims of self-determination put forward by antagonistic and previously suppressed nationalisms. These ruptures were most severe in the wars fought over the shape of political arrangements in Croatia and Bosnia, as well as in several of the former Soviet republics. Before these conflicts, a consensus had held in international society that the right of self-determination was a matter to be resolved within existing international boundaries no matter how ethnically artificial or nationalistically oppressive. This consensus was generally upheld, despite several prominent secessionist challenges in sub-Saharan Africa, throughout the post-1945 decades of decolonization. International law doctrine, as will be discussed, generally confirmed this political and moral consensus that the "self" in self-determination was meant to signify in all circumstances the people, as located within the boundaries of the *existing* states constituting international society. Self-determination was meant to apply only at the level of the state, and not intended to give rights at the level of fractions of one state. The only acceptable exceptions to this legal norm of limitation were in situations of secession by agreement, that is, a voluntary arrangement agreed upon by the government of the existing state and representatives of the secessionist movement. This exception can be illustrated by the instance of Czechoslovakia voluntarily splitting in two, resulting in the Czech Republic and Slovakia. Canada and Quebec have also proceeded on the basis that a voluntary accommodation of competing claims would resolve the encounter between the federal government of Canada and the potentially secessionist province of Quebec. Such accommodation includes the apparent willingness of both sides to respect referenda that have on several occasions sought to assess the wishes of the provincial population with respect to the future of Quebec, and its relationship to the rest of Canada.

There have been several forces converging in the past decade to erode, and possibly undermine, this always fragile and somewhat arbitrary doctrinal clarity about the right of self-determination. There was, first of all, a broad moral and political sympathy in the West for the Baltic peoples that had been forcibly annexed by the Soviet Union in a way that extinguished their external status as states. As the Gorbachev leadership softened the Soviet approach to imposed control over satellite states, the resurgence of Baltic nationalism succeeded in reestablishing the independent states of Latvia, Estonia, and Lithuania. In one sense, this particular outcome could be perceived and presented in non-threatening terms as merely *reestablishing* the sovereign rights of existing states that had temporarily been suppressed by Soviet "illegal" annexation; thus their reemergence as independent entities would not genuinely represent an expansion of the right of self-determination. But from another angle the newfound statehood of the Baltic nations could not be explained in such simple terms. After all, the prior unity of the Soviet Union was being successfully challenged on many additional, more ambiguous fronts by a range of nationalist movements, whose assertions of self-determination called for new and separate states. What made political independence for the Baltic states relatively unproblematic was the fact that, unlike most of the other constituent republics, the Baltic countries had enjoyed a degree of autonomy in the Soviet era, and indeed had been independent states during the years preceding World War II. The rash of independence movements that followed, however, seemed of a more state-shattering character leading to an intrastate collision of national and ethnic ambitions that produced civil violence of considerable ferocity, especially in Georgia, Azerbaijan, Armenia, and Tadjikistan. In this type of nationalist claim for self-determination, the threatened minority tends to opt either for the old order, with its tendency to suppress all subordinate nationalisms, or for an additional cycle of self-determination that shifts adherents to a more congenial and less vulnerable circumstance. Then, ironically, it is the original claimant of self-determination that changes roles, and is now protective of territorial unity and sovereignty as reconfigured at the level of the former federal units, resisting further fragmentation implicit in claims of self-determination based on ethnic or religious identity.

First-order self-determination refers to the struggle of a people to overcome alien rule, and achieve political independence within internationally agreed boundaries. Decolonization epitomizes first-order self-determination. Second-order self-determination involves an analogous move toward independence for a distinct people within internally established boundaries, as in the case of "states" or "republics" belonging to a federal system. The achievement of self-determination by the republics encompassed by the Soviet Union or former Yugoslavia are apt examples. Third-order self-determination refers to a subunit of either a unitary state or of a member of a federal system. Chechnya and Kosovo are illustrative. It is also possible to regard the self-determination claims of indigenous peoples as forming an additional, special category, referred to by this classificatory scheme as fourth-order self-determination.

Second-order types of self-determination generally involve claims by constituent peoples, trapped within *new* sovereign boundaries, who seek assurances of self-determination and autonomy, and of protection against discrimination and denials of identity under the new political arrangement. This second cycle of self-determination can be seen either as a legitimate move toward self-preservation on the part of national minorities within a fledgling state, or as an opportunistic reaction on the part of restive secessionists intent on exploiting the fragility of the new state. Unlike independence movements of the first order, these claims of self-determination cannot invoke the federal boundaries of the former state, although the geographical extent of their claim may be equally clear—say, as a sub-federal administrative unit in the original federal state. The suppression of these second-order movements is often bloody, as was the case in Chechnya. There, Moscow refused to countenance any territorial dismemberment of Russia, despite having recently celebrated its own independence from the Soviet Union.

Why, then, should former federal boundaries count for so much and the administrative boundaries or endangered circumstances of distinct peoples count for so little in the debate over the right of self-determination? If part of the rationale for self-determination is the promotion of human rights, are not people who are confined in a single unitary state often the most at risk of systematic oppression? Are their human rights justification for asserting a claim of statehood not equally strong? The events in Chechnya and Kosovo brought these contradictions to light with particular poignancy. Why should the claims of the Chechnyans or Kosovars count for so much less than those of the people of Georgia and Azerbaijan?

The arbitrariness of the doctrinal approach arises because the basis for claiming the right of self-determination is similar in each of these settings, but the validation of the claim is routine only at the level of the internal state unit even if this entity enjoyed neither international status nor substantive autonomy in the prior federal setup. Under some circumstances, especially during the last several years, validation of self-determination claims has been extended to the *internal* federal units. This still leaves out in the cold those peoples who qualify as "nations," and yet are trapped *within* these internal boundaries. Of course, international law and statecraft are wrestling with the dilemma of accommodating major historical convulsions while holding the line against the fragmentation of the state system into unmanageably small states whose overall number could make diplomacy ever more cumbersome.

What the Soviet experience suggested, and the Yugoslav sequel confirmed, is that claims of self-determination in situations of ethnic, religious, and national diversity can provide occasions for bitter, bloody fights for nationhood. Slovenia has avoided such a bloody fate largely because its former boundaries encompassed a generally homogeneous population, in contrast to those of Croatia and Bosnia. Thus the challenge to traditional doctrine is not necessarily attributable to state-shattering alone, but to the particular mix of factors weighting the balance between the inviolability of existing state boundaries and claims of autonomy and independence. Both Slovenia and Slovakia emerged as states by relatively peaceful means, if amid controversy and in war-threatening situations. What seems most inflamed and threatening is state-shattering in circumstances of heterogeneous populations, especially if substantial minorities feel freshly and more menacingly entrapped. Such peoples can be manipulated by leaders who perceive the breakup of the prior federal state as a rare window of opportunity to realize dreams of nationhood and to redress historical oppression, real or perceived. It is difficult to evaluate these concerns, which involve a volatile mixture of the genuine and the opportunistic. The tragic, still unresolved, fates of Bosnia and Kosovo exemplify the sort of ordeal that can follow the assertion and subsequent denial of overlapping, contradictory claims of self-determination.

The outright rejection of such claims rarely provides a solution. Conflicts in Chechnya, Kashmir, Tibet, and in the Kurdish territories of Iraq and Turkey are all situations in which the legal and political ideal of territorial unity causes moral havoc and social, economic, and cultural injustice resulting in great suffering and endless strife for these entrapped peoples. A strict, doctrinal interpretation of international law seems to sanction such oppression by repudiating alien rule only at the level of the state. The obligation to respect human rights, if met, would nonetheless offer a measure of protection to all persons, thereby presumably weakening the impulse to insist on secession. These legalistic accounts suppress contrary practices, as when they regard de facto attainment of independence as "fact" rather than "law," a jural fiction that formalistically reconciles doctrine with experience, but at the expense of relevance. Worse still, the validation of successful claims tends to reward recourse to violence by separatist or antiseparatist movements and provides no procedure by which to assess separatist controversies on a case-by-case basis from the standpoint of nonviolence or the justice of the cause.

Not all claims possess the same moral and political weight. For instance, a separatist claim in a deeply divided societal unit is far more likely to produce disaster than is a separatist claim on the part of a homogeneous unit. But even here there are no clear categories. If the former federal unit is itself divided between two ethnic, religious identities, then the pursuit of self-determination by the dominant group can encourage a two-stage process of "ethnic cleansing" on both sides—the first to ensure a clear identity for the new polity and the second to pave the way for a separatist, reactive claim on behalf of the weaker group. In the former federal context, both identities were to an extent subordinated, and their tension with one another nonexistent or trivial. Such a pattern definitely emerged with respect to the political evolution of Bosnia.

There are other exceptions, as well, to the standard legal solution: for example, limiting the right of self-determination to the level of the state unless the fission of an existing state is amicably arranged. This means that other types of political evolution that seek independence for a given people are not treated as proper instances of self-determination, but must somehow be either accommodated within existing state structures or be handled extralegally as political facts. It also means that the struggle of indigenous peoples for their own right of self-determination, as acknowledged in international law, is in deep jeopardy despite being enshrined in Articles 3 and 31 of the 1994 Draft Declaration on the Rights of Indigenous Peoples. It is in jeopardy partly because it would not be formally reconcilable with the UN-era conceptualization of self-determination, despite the colonialist background in many instances, which is quite unreasonably ignored because the geographic scope of indigenous communities does not correspond with coherent colonial units. This resistance is reinforced by political worries that endowing indigenous peoples with such a right of self-determination could validate extreme scenarios of fragmentation, given the several thousand distinct peoples on the planet. Such an extreme scenario is often put forward as a justification for resisting the formal acknowledgment of a right of self-determination on behalf of indigenous peoples. This is so even though it is widely appreciated that the real goals of such indigenous claimants is almost always "autonomy" and symbolic sovereignty in an economically, politically, and culturally meaningful form. Such "nations" have no aspiration to become separate states in the international sense, and it would not be a viable project from a practical perspective.

But the impasse persists because representatives of indigenous peoples insist on the full dignity of their status as a people, and this dignity has become irreversibly fused now with an unconditional, first-class right of self-determination, which in turn implies a theoretical option to claim sovereignty and political independence. Such a posture is then interpreted by those in control of modern society as a threat, if not a plan, to break up existing states into fragments, and is stubbornly resisted, thus keeping relations between states and indigenous peoples in perpetual limbo. In the background are other anxieties, including the idea that endowing indigenous peoples with rights of self-determination will encourage other ethnic communities to mount comparable claims.

In fact, several recent international meetings have aired explicit suggestions that self-determination be closed down as a *collective* legal, political, and moral right, that its relevance in the postcolonial setting be limited to its human rights role of ensuring equitable treatment within existing state structures of authority. Such an approach urges claimants to abandon the discourse of self-determination in favor of seeking specific constituent rights concerning resources, self-government, and territorial delimitation.

Proposals to disallow any further claims of self-determination generally falls on deaf ears, or worse, engenders a hostile response that aggravates discord. In some ways it recalls the early North-South environmental dialogues in which the newly independent countries felt they were being told to forego affluence to avoid causing further pollution of the planet. At this stage, it is too late to put the genie of self-determination back in its colonialist bottle. Too many additional claims have now been validated, and too large a meaning has been invested in the language of self-determination. It is too late for a rhetorical, or even a doctrinal, retreat. The symbolic battle lines have been indissolubly drawn.

For these reasons the Liechtenstein Proposals on Self-Administration offers an approach that is especially apropos. These Liechtenstein Proposals are an initiative at the United Nations sponsored by the micro-state of Liechtenstein. Liechtenstein has also provided the resources for a continuing research project established at Princeton University in 1995, Liechtenstein Research Program on Self-Determination, under the direction of

Wolfgang Danzprechgruber. The Liechtenstein framework validates extensions of rights of self-determination but associates its normal application with self-administration. As such, it allows symbolic flexibility while avoiding state-shattering substantial application. Of course, there are some possible traps: the convention can be seen as an empty symbolic gesture that effectively deprives self-determination of its content, or it can be seen as a call to open the floodgates of expanded self-determination without providing any reliable checks and balances.

Against this background of controversy, the next section of this chapter will trace the evolution of the right of self-determination within the domain of international law, including responses to the two sets of recent challenges mounted by noncolonial separatist claims in Europe and Asia and by the international movement on behalf of indigenous peoples. It briefly suggests, on this basis, the problematic challenges posed by the Kurdish dilemma in the Middle East and by the conflicting enactments of self-determination by indigenous peoples and Quebec separatists in Canada.

SELF-DETERMINATION AND INTERNATIONAL LAW: HISTORICAL BACKGROUND

The right of self-determination emerged as a serious element in international life during the latter stages of World War I. It emerged in two forms that prefigured, in their essence, the ideological rivalry between East and West that decades later ripened into the cold war. The more radical, but less overtly influential, proposal was articulated by Lenin prior to the Bolshevik Revolution. Lenin, writing in a revolutionary vein, proclaimed self-determination as an indispensable condition for peace in the world, and he intended it to apply unconditionally to the non-European peoples being held in the grasp of the colonial order. In Lenin's words, "the liberation of all colonies, the liberation of all dependent, oppressed, and nonsovereign peoples" is necessary for the maintenance of international peace.[2]

The more moderate version of the right of self-determination, the one more prominently associated with the subsequent development of the right, is, of course, that associated with Woodrow Wilson. It was articulated most influentially in Wilson's Fourteen Points, a policy put forward as an authoritative statement of the U.S. approach to the peace process in 1918. Wilson intended the principle of self-determination to apply immediately and unconditionally to the peoples of Europe, with particular reference to those peoples who formerly had been ruled by the Ottoman Empire, and to a lesser extent by the Austro-Hungarian Empire. Wilson did also intend, in an ambiguous and half-hearted manner, self-determination to have some uncertain and eventual application in non-European settings. Wilson's fifth point embodies this aspect of his approach: "A free, open-minded, and absolutely impartial adjustment of all colonial claims, based upon a strict observance of the principle that in determining all such questions of sovereignty the interests of the populations concerned must have equal weight with the equitable claims of the government whose title is to be determined." The American secretary of state at the time, Robert Lansing, definitely sensed that it might become difficult to resist the wider implications of such a formulation of self-determination, and made an effort to distinguish Wilson's views from those of Lenin. Lansing insisted that Wilson's advocacy be understood as applying only to the promotion of self-government *within* the colonial order, not to the dissolution of the order itself, a prospect that Lansing (and Wilson) believed would be dangerous for "the stability of the future world."[3] This restrictive view was also expressed by Wilson's steadfast refusal at Versailles to meet with representatives, including a young Ho Chi Minh, of anticolonial movements of national independence.

In effect, as we now know, the Wilsonian restrictive version of self-determination prevailed at first. The legitimacy of colonial rule was not challenged until decades after World War I, and the victorious colonial powers acquired considerable control over additional peoples by way of the Mandates system established in connection with the creation of the League of Nations. This was a means of lawfully incorporating the former colonial peoples of the losing side in World War I into the remaining colonial empires. The Mandates system rested on a variable fiction, depending on practice and the classification given to a particular mandate. The administering states were accountable to the League for the well-being of the colonized peoples as part of a "sacred trust of civilization," as this latter idea was expressed in Article 22 of the Covenant of the League of Nations. The operational authority, then, effectively rested with the colonial power, and the paternalistic language stressing the duty to promote well-being often meant little in practice. True, there was a commitment to work toward independence for mandated peoples, and there was a sharp set of differences in legal conception between the three classes of mandates. Class A mandates were viewed as temporary, with the clear expectation that they would be replaced over time by political independence for the mandated peoples. Operationally, it seems evident that the mandates system was a holding operation, delaying decolonization to varying degrees, depending supposedly on the relative capacity of a given society for self-rule. Yet the system also set in motion a process of self-assertion that led eventually in every instance to political independence and full statehood.

In retrospect, it seems evident that the Wilsonian top-down approach to self-determination was of limited application. The Leninist approach, although never designated as such, gradually caught on as a rationale for the extension of the ethos of anticolonial nationalism that was to sweep across the planet in the aftermath of World War II. In its essence, despite the efforts to craft a conception of self-determination that does not disturb the established order, the idea itself is subversive to the legitimacy of all political arrangements between distinct peoples that do not flow from genuine and continuing consent. It is this subversive feature that has been working its way through the history of international relations during the latter part of this century. It gives a variable and expanding content to the right of self-determination, whether the right is considered in relation to the identity of its claimants or to the extent of substantive claims being advanced.

As World War II came to an end there was a repetition of the split between Leninist and Wilsonian views, but it was not labeled in those terms. The Soviet Union supported those tendencies in international society that were challenging the colonial order. The European powers, though weakened to various degrees by the devastation of war, remained committed to retaining their colonies, by force if necessary. The United States positioned itself in the middle, allied with the European colonial powers in strategic and ideological respects, yet normatively sympathetic, in part because of its own historical legacy, to the claims of peoples seeking independence. The UN Charter embodied this compromise in its specification of guiding principles, especially in the language of Article 1(2): "To develop friendly relations among nations based on respect for the principle of equal rights and self-determination of peoples. . . ."[4] Note that the Charter deliberately refers to self-determination as a "principle" rather than a "right." It is only later, in both human rights and decolonization settings, that UN official terminology confirms that peoples enjoy a *right* of self-determination. Arguably, this is an inconsequential distinction in the substantive context of international law. To the extent that a principle exists and is actualized, it implies the existence of rights and duties to ensure its application, or at least encompasses the prospect that such rights will, as appropriate, be specified and realized.

The limits envisioned for the application of the principle of self-determination by the United Nations are also illuminated in Chapter XI of the Charter, which addresses "Non-Self-Governing Territories." Article 73 asserts that the well-being of a territory's inhabitants is "paramount," but implementation is essentially left in the hands of the administering state. In all instances this vested legal authority is a European or North American state (with the exception of South Africa). Article 73(b) expresses a central commitment to encourage territories "to develop self-government," but not necessarily national independence. Article 76(b), however, does anticipate "advancement of the inhabitants of the trust territories, and their progressive development towards self-government or independence as may be appropriate to the particular circumstance of each territory and its peoples and the freely expressed wishes of the peoples concerned." Still, the normative content is ambiguous, due partly to the vague language. The tone is paternalistic with respect to administration, yet subversive if considered in relation to the expected aspirations of subordinated peoples. This trust concept, as introduced into UN operations, is relevant to the rights and circumstances of dependent peoples, but it is not meant to have any relevance to the legal circumstances of indigenous peoples. Such peoples have never been granted, nor have their representatives claimed, a trust status as understood in the UN Charter. Their core claim is to possess an inalienable status of nationhood as understood within their civilizational world picture, which is not statist and does not associate identity with clearly demarcated boundaries in space.

The right of self-determination has matured along three distinct, often overlapping, and sometimes uneven and confusing paths: that of morality, of politics, and of law. The incorporation of self-determination into international law has consistently lagged behind advocacy based on aspirations of justice (moral considerations) and on political movements and their results (political considerations). This century has witnessed an ebb and flow in global attention to self-determination, but there has also been a discernable movement toward its legal acknowledgment and its application across an expanded spectrum of circumstances. Three root factors have helped fuel this expansion:

1. the weakening of the capacity of the European colonial powers as a result of the two world wars;
2. the rise of an ideology of nationalism, reinforced by the basic democratic perspective that governing arrangements, to be legitimate, should be genuinely consensual and participatory in relation to their citizenry;
3. the unconditional ideological, diplomatic support extended to anticolonial struggles by the Soviet Union and its satellites after 1945, and the concern by the United States that the West would lose out geopolitically in the Third World if it tied its destiny indefinitely to the defense of the colonial order.

Against this background, the evolving dynamics of decolonization gradually deepened the acknowledgment of a right of self-determination. The great moment of acceptance within the United Nations came with the adoption of the famous Declaration on the Granting of Independence to Colonial Peoples in the form of a General Assembly Resolution in 1960.[5] The thinking expressed in Resolution 1514 remains important in understanding the most recent postcolonial phases of the struggle to apply the right of self-determination. The resolution does not attempt to clarify the specific legal content of the right, nor does it identify the circumstances of its application and their outer limits.[6] Indeed, one source of difficulty is that the generality of the resolution's language can be read to support a wide range of aspirants seeking political independence, even though leading governments understood the language more narrowly—that is, in relation to colonial rule of formal character.

The preamble of the Declaration sets forth a litany of considerations that came by 1960 to express the content of the anticolonial movement. The preamble recognizes "that the peoples of the world ardently desire the end of colonialism in all its manifestations," and that "the process of liberation is irresistible and irreversible and that . . . an end must be put to colonialism." Of particular relevance to current concerns about the scope of the right of self-determination is the fact that this Declaration incorporates a potentially far broader ethos than merely that of anticolonialism, one that encompasses "all dependent peoples" and rests in such peoples permanent sovereignty over "natural wealth and resources."[7]

The approach taken by the 1960 Declaration is instructive, both in terms of its attempt to confirm the right of self-determination in relation to colonialism and to deny some forms of wider application. It is important to keep in mind the relationship of this right to the parallel set of claims associated with the territorial integrity of existing and emerging sovereign states. Operative provision (2) reads:

> All peoples have the right of self-determination; by virtue of that right they freely determine their political status and freely pursue their economic, social and cultural development.

Provision (3) adds that "[i]nadequacy of political, economic, social or educational preparedness should never serve as a pretext for delaying independence." These affirmations are then qualified by the now familiar deference to the territorial integrity of existing states contained in provision (6):

> Any attempt at the partial or total disruption of the national unity and the territorial integrity of a country is incompatible with the purposes and principles of the Charter of the United Nations.

This approach to self-determination culminated in the influential Declaration of Principles Concerning Friendly Relations Among States, adopted as General Assembly Resolution 2625 in 1970.[8] This authoritative formulation significantly accepted the principle of self-determination (linked to the notion of "equal rights of peoples") as a constitutive norm of international order in the cold war era, giving it moral, political, and legal stature all at once.

This approach was endorsed by Africa during the peak decade of decolonization, the 1960s, via the Organization of African Unity. In a 1964 resolution, and with frequent reiteration thereafter, the organization agreed that colonial frontiers, even if arbitrary and unjust, were to provide the only acceptable basis for delimiting sovereign states in Africa as colonial entities achieved independence. In effect, the African consensus on self-determination was intended to deny ethnic/tribal claimants any right of secession in the midst of decolonization, thereby validating an approach that could be given a more legalistic explanation by reference to the Roman principle of *uti possidetis*. Then professor Rosalyn Higgins, commenting on this development, argues not that the OAU approach provides direct legal authority for *uti possidetis*, but that it reflects the African acceptance of "an underlying norm—that of commitment to territorial integrity and international stability."[9] The OAU's fear was that the moment of independence would open up the continent to devastating civil strife, possibly producing a pattern of ethnically oriented states that had little chance of coping with the challenges of modernity.

But, as Higgins recognizes, matters are not so simple. Self-determination as a right came also to be an anchoring norm for human rights in noncolonial settings. In attempting to resolve the tension, Higgins invokes the words of Professor Georges Abi-Saab, the distinguished Judge Ad Hoc of Mali: "Without stability of frontiers, the exercise of self-determination is in reality a mirage. Turmoil is not conducive to human rights."[10] But such an assertion, without further elaboration, doesn't resolve a fundamental question: The stability of *which* frontiers?

In some settings, it seems evident that only by perpetuating colonial boundaries can turmoil be overcome, and stability restored. Yet the effort to maintain such boundaries will often depend upon a systematic denial of human rights, as has been the experience of Tibet or East Timor (a Portuguese colony, incorporated by force into Indonesia shortly after its independence in 1975). What may have seemed convincing in Africa as decolonization was taking place now seems selectively problematic thirty years later when severe ethnic tension produces genocidal onslaughts. The confusion is compounded by the fact that, as has been asserted in this chapter, the contours of the right of self-determination have never been and are not now fixed in the concrete of rigid legal doctrine. The right has been continuously evolving conceptually and experientially in response to the pressure of events, geopolitical priorities, and the prevailing moral and political climate. This combination of factors tends to produce a confusing pattern of historically conditioned precedents, leaving considerable room for widely disparate interpretations bearing on legal doctrine.

Expressing the potency of the anti-apartheid movement and the general revulsion against racism, the 1970 Declaration on Friendly Relations goes further than Resolution 1514, expanding the scope of self-determination in a manner not earlier anticipated. The language used in the Declaration is again instructive with respect to understanding the expansionist evolution of the right of self-determination, and the impossibility of pinning down the acceptable limits of a plausible legal claim. The principle of territorial integrity is reasserted, but, significantly, in a more conditional form. The Declaration insists that nothing about the right of self-determination "shall be construed as authorizing or encouraging any action which would dismember or impair, totally or in part, the territorial integrity or political unity of sovereign and independent States conducting themselves in compliance with the principle of equal rights and self-determination of peoples . . . and thus possessed of a government representing the whole people belonging to the territory without distinction as to race, creed or color." What is notable here is the generality of the language, which ensures a potential receptivity to and loopholes for self-determination claims that are not strictly reconcilable with the previously inviolable imperatives of territorial integrity and political unity. That is, what if a given state is not "conducting [itself] in compliance with the principle of equal rights," and what if the government cannot be said to be "representing the whole people . . . without distinction as to race, creed or color"?

There had always been a second rather bewildering dimension to the struggle of self-determination: not the collective struggle for national independence, but individual and group quests for human rights. In this latter setting the exercise of the right of self-determination did not normally imply, as it did in the anticolonial context, an insistence on the potential exercise of sovereign rights associated with statehood. Such a distinction has led to discussions of "internal" self-determination, that is, the protection of minority rights, and the avoidance of discriminatory and exclusionary policies based on race and religion. As applied in group settings, internal self-determination involved the linking of movements for cultural and political autonomy for distinct peoples with the right of self-determination.[11] But again, even this constrained view of self-determination cannot be derived from the plain meaning of the shared Article 1 of the two Covenants on human rights, which affirm the right without placing any limitations on its exercise. Nor can the scope of the right be convincingly restricted to Article 27 of the Covenant on Civil and Political Rights, which declares that individuals belonging to "ethnic, religious or linguistic minorities" shall "not be denied the right, in community with the other members of the group, to enjoy their own culture, to profess and practice their own religion, or to use their own language."

Suppose that, after decades of repression and suffering, a people demand secession as a foundation for exercising their right of self-determination. Can we say conclusively, on the basis of international legal doctrine and practice, that such a demand is inherently unacceptable? The position of this chapter is that we cannot reach such an invariable conclusion, but must assess the merits of such a claim in its particular context, and the outcome will almost always be controversial. An international assessment is likely to reflect some compromise between the capacity to assert the claim effectively and its seeming legal and moral merit. There is a misleading sense of definiteness about the content of legal guidelines offered by those who continue to rely upon a cautious and literal reading of the Friendly Relations Declaration that ignores international practice that gives a less definite sense of the limits pertaining to self-determination. Similarly misleading is reliance on some of the rather tangential findings and assertions of the International Court of Justice, especially in *The Western Sahara Case*.[12]

In this regard, this chapter adopts a view close to the position of Judge Hardy Dillard, especially as expressed in his oft-quoted phrase appearing in his Separate Opinion in *Western Sahara*: "It is for the people to determine the destiny of the territory and not the territory the destiny of the people."[13] Professor Higgins criticizes Dillard's orientation here by showing clearly that the court only confirmed the relevance of the right of self-determination once it concluded that Western Sahara should be regarded as a Spanish colonial possession of separate identity and not belonging within the sovereign domain of either Morocco or Mauritania. Such an assessment is persuasive within the four corners of the dispute about the delimitation of Western Sahara, but Judge Dillard is both accurate and prophetic with respect to the most appropriate legal comprehension of the variable content of the right of self-determination.

In the international law literature on self-determination two main tendencies are at odds. The first is to hold the line against expanding the right of self-determination by insisting on a restrictive view of rights that must defer to the persisting relevance of territorial unity of existing states. As such, an unconditional limitation on the exercise of the right of self-determination is retained to preclude all claims with state-shattering effects. The second tendency acknowledges and, to varying degrees, validates recent state-shattering practice in a reformulated legal approach. It concedes that the character and scope of the right is more unsettled than ever, but is nevertheless expansionary at this point, evolving and contracting in response to patterns of practice. One element of this practice is the acceptance or rejection of new entities by the international community. This latter view takes due note of the degree to which diplomatic recognition and admission to the United Nations has been granted to federal units formerly encompassed as nonsovereign components of the Soviet Union and Yugoslavia.[14]

Professor Higgins, in her continuing adherence to the more restrictive view of self-determination, writes that the long struggle to establish the right as law "now faces a new danger: that of being all things to all men."[15] Yet the whole history of the right of self-determination is, for better and worse, the story of adaptation to the evolving struggles of peoples attempting to achieve effective control over their own destinies, especially in reaction to circumstances that are discriminatory and oppressive. For a period states agreed that self-determination would not have secessionist implications except in colonial settings, and even here, it was more a matter of changed status, and only secessionist in relation to the colonial empire.

This attitude was acceptable to the Soviet Union, which appreciated the explosive danger of encouraging either captive nationalities within its sovereign boundaries or the various captive peoples restive within its East European satellite countries to assert independence. At the same time, as already suggested, the former colonial peoples were in general agreement that opening up for revision the colonial boundaries could contribute to political disarray and widespread warfare, especially in Africa and parts of Asia. The large-scale bloodshed accompanying the secession of Pakistan from India, and then Bangladesh from Pakistan, lends credence to the view that altering colonial borders would be extremely destabilizing. Furthermore, the United States and other countries in the Western Hemisphere were aware that indigenous peoples within their boundaries continued to insist on their status as sovereign nations, and these countries were reluctant to give any encouragement to such longings. There was thus a political and moral consensus among the governments that shaped the legal conception of the right of self-determination during the cold war, but it was a historically conditioned conception that has weakened its hold on the political imagination in the period since 1989. A decade later, however, there may be a return to a tighter view of self-determination. This reversion can be observed in the NATO responses to the Kosovo conflict: NATO supported moves for autonomy and human rights, but withheld wholesale approval of secession from the former Yugoslavia.

In the last five years, the practice of states, the transnational assertiveness of indigenous peoples, and the moral force of groups' rights in various situations have expanded the scope of the legal right of self-determination, bringing its operational content closer to Judge Dillard's view than to various positivist attempts to deny self-determination any broad legal status. The more flexible international law approach, which is sensitive to context and the trends in official practice, gives a more realistic picture of the relevance of law to current discussions of self-determination than does its restrictive counterpart, which purports a clarity and rigidity that seems increasingly out of touch with the ways in which self-determination claims have been validated by diplomatic recognition, UN admissions procedures, and geopolitical priorities. The flexible approach, to be sure, is not immune to criticism, but to deny the complexity of the situation is to attempt by legalistic sleight-of-hand to contain self-determination in the doctrinal box of a statist world. It is high time to realize that such a world has been definitively eroded. To pretend otherwise is to place an unacceptable strain on the descriptive and prescriptive character of international law. Such artificial clarity also conceals the need for a politically effective way to recapture the genie of self-determination, by way of establishing new legal guidelines that reflect recent patterns of international practice and opinion. The political outcome of high-profile situations such as Kosovo and Chechnya will for a period reshape our sense of the scope of the right of self-determination. In effect, the balance of internal and external forces either will manage to defeat secessionist claims or will succumb to them.

1989 TO THE PRESENT: DOCTRINE VERSUS PRACTICE

The striking feature of recent practice is both its extension of the right of self-determination beyond earlier conceptions and the variability of arrangements satisfying particular claims of self-determination. In effect, earlier doctrinal conceptions are no longer descriptive of practice, but neither is it accurate to equate every movement for self-determination with secessionist ambitions. In this section, this pattern of state-shattering practice is depicted in relation to doctrinal efforts to avoid the legal implications of such practice, to avoid treating rights-expanding realities as legal precedents, and ultimately to limit the applicability of self-determination as a collective right of people.

International practice up until 1989 had emphasized the UN consensus of an emergent right of self-determination for peoples held under colonial, alien, or racist rule, a right to be exercised in a manner that did not challenge prior *external* boundaries. Even in this period, the secession in 1972 of East Pakistan from Pakistan to form Bangladesh, in the wake of atrocities perpetrated by the armies of the central government, was widely approved as a beneficial response, and Bangladesh was quickly recognized by other states. Not long afterward, Bangladesh became a UN member, even though its emergence altered the external boundaries of the former Pakistan and generated a second sovereign state. Such an outcome was substantively an exercise of the right of self-determination by the peoples involved even if it was not so described at the time. The quest for a national homeland by the Palestinians, the various Kurdish national movements, and the struggles for independence by ethnic groups in the former Soviet Union should all be regarded as efforts to assert rights of self-determination. It should be kept in mind that a claim of self-determination can be satisfied either internally through a variety of autonomy arrangements or externally by the establishment of a new state. A movement dedicated to exercising its right of self-determination may "succeed" even if political independence is not claimed and even if no attempt is made to join international institutions or to establish distinct diplomatic relations. There is no assured or necessary link between the right of self-determination and a particular outcome. As the longstanding political debate over the future of Puerto Rico has illustrated, the majority of a particular people may under certain conditions reject the option of independence and favor remaining in a subordinated status within a larger political entity even if that status evolved out of a colonialist background.

The disintegration of the Soviet Union and Yugoslavia in 1991 gave birth to a series of new, sovereign states that sought diplomatic recognition and full membership in international institutions. In effect, these emergent states shattered the territorial unity of the former federated entities, and ostensibly departed from UN guidelines, which prescribed the exercise of the right of self-determination only *within* existing states, not at the level of the federal units that together constitute a state. This recent practice is a significant confirmation of the extent to which the effective political outcomes that are consistent with a geopolitical consensus and are welcomed by important countries produce *legal* results incompatible with earlier conceptions of legal doctrine. Community responses to such state-shattering practice is registered by way of recognition and admission to international institutions, and such admission has a legitimizing effect quite inconsistent with earlier efforts to reject self-determination claims of a state-shattering variety even if their cause seemed morally justified. At the same time, the implications of these political movements are extremely threatening to established political arrangements, especially to the extent that there is opened a Pandora's Box of microethnic claims to self-determination. This combination of factors generates pressure to avoid treating secessionist results as precedent-setting in situations that have yielded new states by diminishing the territorial domain of a former state. This tension between practice and doctrinal preference has been clearly evident in the opinions of the Badinter Commission, which was established by the European Community to evaluate the legal consequences of the disintegration of Yugoslavia, and in a commissioned report submitted to the Quebec Assembly by five distinguished international law specialists to assess the effects of Quebec's possible accession to sovereignty should its separatist movement succeed. Both of these efforts to formulate doctrinal contours of the right of self-determination in the face of actual and potential expansionist practice have produced confused and unconvincing legal analyses that are exceedingly vulnerable to technical and political critical reaction. Such efforts at reconciliation have not put the issues to rest, but rather have called further attention to the challenge.

A prime example of this confusion is the work of the Badinter Commission established by the European Community in 1991 as part of its effort to minimize and contain the violent conflict attending the breakup of Yugoslavia. The Commission was composed of five presidents of constitutional tribunals in European countries and was headed by Robert Badinter, president of the French Constitutional Council. This Arbitration Commission, or Badinter Commission, as it came to be known, lacked legal authority but was given an advisory role in relation to the ongoing peace diplomacy; despite its name it had no arbitration functions. Lord Carrington, president at the time of the International Conference on Yugoslavia, put several questions to the Commission, as did the Government of Serbia.[16]

In Opinion No. 2 the Commission addressed self-determination in the context of Serbian claims on behalf of Serbian ethnic minorities in Croatia and Bosnia, concluding that although the right of self-determination is not spelled out "... it is well established that, whatever the circumstances, the right to self-determination must not involve changes to existing frontiers at the time of independence (*uti possidetis juris*) except where the States concerned agree otherwise." In its tersely worded opinion the commission says that Serbs are entitled to full protection as "minorities," and that the right of self-determination is a matter of human rights, allowing Serbs if they so wish, to insist that their distinct national identity be respected by Bosnia and Croatia.

The commission never discussed the crucial issue—the desire of a minority to become a nation—and thus seems to miss the main point. The right of self-determination is a collective right of a people, and the scope of that right is determined by a mixture of contexts (the threat of atrocities, say, or discrimination, or the fear of both) by geopolitical climate, and by effective outcomes (the facts created).[17] As Hurst Hannum aptly points out, the commission "appear[s] to have based their judgments on geopolitical concerns and imaginary principles of international law, rather than on the unique situation in Yugoslavia."[18] He contends that "[t]he principle that borders should not be altered except by mutual agreement has been elevated to a hypocritical immutability that is contradicted by the very act of recognizing the secessionist states."[19]

Furthermore, the extension of the *uti possidetis* approach by the Badinter Commission in Opinion No. 3 to *internal* administrative boundaries of a fragmented or federalist state rests on extremely shaky grounds of policy and legal authority. The emergent legal authority in the decolonization setting was directed at the maintenance of *external* boundaries. In the opinion of the Badinter Commission, which invoked some of the language of the International Court of Justice in the dispute between Bukina Faso and Mali, *uti possidetis* "is a general principle, which is logically connected with the phenomenon of the obtaining of independence, wherever it occurs. Its obvious purpose is to prevent the independence and stability of new States being endangered by fratricidal struggles."[20] As Hannum confirms, the commission left out the end of the sentence of the original ICJ wording, which reads "provoked by the challenging of frontiers following the withdrawal of the administering power."[21] Furthermore, the court's dictum concerning *uti possidetis* is explicitly limited to situations arising out of decolonization. None of these considerations seems to apply, even indirectly, to the circumstances of the breakup of a federated state in which federal boundaries do not correspond, and even clash, with the ethnic or religious affiliations of the peoples living within them. The fundamental question, in fact, is not one of frontiers at all, rather it concerns the ways in which rearrangements of power and authority threatens the security of newly entrapped minorities who might have felt reconciled to the former federal arrangement, but who are unwilling to entrust their future to the new breakaway state. Validating such patterns of fragmentation is neither a matter of mechanically upholding or rejecting claims of self-determination nor is it a matter of acknowledging a de facto set of realities. It is, above all, a matter of democratic procedures and the secure protection of minority and group rights; it is a matter of acknowledging certain realities of power. Some beleaguered peoples are able to succeed in their efforts while others are doomed to failure.

A crucial point here is that the unconditionality of respect for territorial unity has been decisively breached in relation to the former Yugoslavia, and that the movements of separation launched by these developments were operationally, if not legally, invoking their right of self-determination. This entire process of constituting new states without protecting the constituent peoples or respecting their wishes was indirectly validated by granting widespread diplomatic recognition to these new states, as well as by their rapid admission to the United Nations, thereby legitimizing these particular challenges to territorial unity. In effect, what is accepted as valid by organized international society cannot be adequately understood by consulting abstract legal guidelines. The fact that the claims of independent statehood have generally corresponded with prior internal boundaries does not alter the breach of the fundamental effort of international law during the cold war era to reconcile the territorial unity of existing states with the exercise of the right of self-determination. Colonies were uniformly considered as unified entities even if their actual composition included antagonistic peoples whose regional identities were stronger than their attachment to the newly independent state.

The confusion generated by the Arbitration Commission of the European Community reappears, in a far more extended legal analysis, in a report prepared by five international lawyers in response to a series of questions set by the Committee of the Quebec National Assembly on May 8, 1992, to clarify the legal consequences of the possible secession of Quebec. The Pellet Report, as this document is commonly known, takes its name from Alain Pellet, a distinguished French jurist who drafted the initial set of responses.[22] It is, first of all, important to appreciate the limited scope of the Pellet Report. The authors are careful to restrict their responses strictly to the questions put to them, questions which are notable for what they fail to address, especially in relation to the extent and meaning of the participatory role of aboriginal peoples in the process of secession. The report also takes pains to point out its limited mandate. In the words of its authors, the questions "were asked exclusively from a legal perspective, and this study intends to situate itself solely within the field of law."[23] They also say of the report, "[i]n no way does it reflect any political preferences"; this holds true, then the report is quite unexceptional, but such a contention is unacceptable. The insistence throughout its analysis of the issues that the law is autonomous and clear is unconvincing and formalistic. It fails to take into account the alternative lines of interpretation being actively posited by diverse, often contradictory, political, and moral perspectives, and only by such failures can the report claim clarity and neutrality. The issues posed are so challenging, in part, because their disposition cannot be resolved solely by law, and therefore these issues inevitably confer on the government of Canada an opportunity and responsibility to address these claims in a manner that best contributes to the clarification of respective rights and duties, and to the well-being of the various peoples affected by any decisions that are taken.

Insofar as the rights of indigenous peoples are concerned, the Pellet Report concentrates on whether a right of self-determination inheres in their claims; if it does, the report maintains, then the crucial question is whether a claim of territorial independence is available to indigenous peoples and thereby validated. True, such a claim is one outer limit of an unconditional right of self-determination, but within the setting of the issues posed by the prospect of sovereignty, there are many additional intermediate questions, including the bearing of a majority claim of self-determination on the rights of minorities encompassed by the territory. There are several specific implications of Quebec separatism for the eleven indigenous peoples currently living in the province. The majority of these peoples have clearly expressed their wish to remain part of Canada. As such the question raised is whether such peoples can block separatist claims by insisting on their right to remain part of Canada and thereby prevent Quebec from becoming a separate entity. If accession to sovereignty by Quebec could be taken as already established, as is sometimes argued, the assertion by aboriginal peoples of a right to remain part of Canada would seem to have the odd legal appearance of challenging the territorial unity of the hypothesized new state of Quebec.[24] Such a mode of analysis seems highly artificial given the unresolved character of the underlying separatist claims, and given the right of indigenous peoples to participate regardless of what process is established to resolve the future status of Quebec and its relationship to Canada.

On the nature of self-determination, which the Pellet Report correctly calls "the heart of the controversy," the basic view is one of "variable geometry," to be applied in each instance in accordance with the wishes of the people involved. This, too, is accurate. What is more dubious, however, is the false clarity of the following assertion that the right of self-determination "is sufficient *only in colonial situations* to found the right of a people to acquire independence to the detriment of the State to which it is attached."[25] On the basis of both the more open-ended textual authorities, including the Declaration on Friendly Relations, and on the basis of diplomatic practice since 1989, the possibility of such claims of independence in noncolonial

situations is certainly not legally or politically precluded at this stage, and
the parameters of such a right are by no means fixed. The law on self-
determination is in flux, especially pertaining to indigenous peoples, and
is likely to remain so for the indefinite future, reflecting the ebb and flow
of both practice on the ground, doctrine as interpreted by various concerned
actors, and above all the realities of power and the vagaries of geopolitics.

The Pellet Report also conveys an artificial impression of definiteness in
law with respect to the treatment of the breakup of the former Yugoslavia.
As argued, the legal guidelines pertaining to self-determination convey an
impression of definiteness only if authoritative state practice is ignored.
Unlike the Badinter Commission's report, the Pellet Report, when discussing the *Case Concerning the Frontier Dispute (Bukina Faso v. Mali)*, man-
ages to acknowledge that the circumstances of Quebec are different than
those arising in the setting of decolonization. It contends, nevertheless,
that the Yugoslav experience is applicable on the basis of its "logic" pertaining to all situations "of accession to independence."[26] Such a generalization is unfortunate and is followed immediately by another misleading
inference: "[A]ll new States issuing from secession from a pre-existing State
have retained their pre-existing administrative boundaries, be they Singa-
pore, Yugoslav republics, or States produced by the collapse of the Soviet
Union; and in the latter two cases, the international community has very
firmly manifested its conviction that there is a rule in such situations that
needed to be respected."[27] In fact, the international community has exhibited considerable ambivalence with regard to Yugoslavia's preexisting internal boundaries, and with regard to its efforts to resolve the war in Bosnia.
The Vance/Owen and Owen/Stoltenberg diplomatic initiatives, as well as
those developed by "the contact group" (informal group designated to pursue settlement of war in Bosnia, consisting of the United States, Russia,
France, United Kingdom, and Germany) with broad UN backing, have
centered upon various plans for a radical redrawing of boundaries within
Bosnia, even in some scenarios envisioning entirely new confederations or
federations that link ethnic Serbian and Croatian minorities in Bosnia with
Croatia and Serbia. These negotiations refute the firmness of internal boundaries as the territorial basis for the division of a given state into two or more
sovereign states. Acceptable international boundaries depend on an assessment of the context, including the battlefield results of struggles among
the various "selves" that had been conflated to produce a "self."

Perhaps the most confusing dimension of the Pellet Report is its insistence that the emergence of a new state "is not a problem of law, but of fact."[28]
Of course, by definition, if a new state is postulated to exist, then the assertion is true, yet trivial. Such a formulation deflects attention from the most
crucial aspect of the actual situation: Given diverse and inconsistent claims
based on multiple separate appeals to the right of self-determination, under

what conditions can a new state come into existence validly, and with the requisite recognition by international bodies? Providing guidance on this question was outside the scope of inquiry of the Pellet Commission, and such a limitation greatly restricts the relevance of its findings and recommendations. Such a limitation of scope also renders dubious the central conclusion of the Pellet Report as applied to Quebec: namely, that under no circumstances can the province's territorial domain be altered in the course of accession to sovereignty, even though it was not previously an international entity.[29] This imposition of limits is misleading, as a process of accession is often a matter of negotiations, where competing and even antagonistic claims will need to be reconciled on the basis of legal guidelines, and their enlightened application. In other words, even a negotiated secession may not be acceptable if constituent peoples resist or effectively mount opposition to a change in status that shifts their formal allegiance without their consent.

A similar line of objection applies to the Pellet Report's treatment of the emergent right of self-determination enjoyed by indigenous peoples. It argues unpersuasively that the full right of self-determination, including secession, pertains only to colonial situations. The Report assumes, without providing supporting evidence, that aboriginal peoples are not appropriately entitled to claim such rights on the basis of their experience, which they generally interpret as "colonialist" in character, though in an extreme sense. The literature on the subject suggests a growing disposition to view indigenous and aboriginal peoples as victimized by extreme variants of colonization, even if not so denominated, and thus entitled, even at this late stage, to act upon such identity and to exercise whatever legal rights such a status implies. The crucial immediate issue, however, is often one of participatory rather than secessionist rights, which are acknowledged by the Pellet Report to pertain to all peoples (including those not entitled to claim independence because of their noncolonial status).[30] Yet because the Report takes accession as consummated it does not explore the ramifications of such participatory rights except in the most general terms: "For colonial peoples, this choice includes the possibility of independence; for others, it excludes independence, but signifies at once the right to one's own identity, the right to choose, and the right to participate."[31] It seems evident from context, and with reference to Thomas Franck's article on the emergent entitlement to democracy, that for the authors of the Pellet Report "participation" merely means democratic inclusion in the political community on a nondiscriminatory basis, and nothing else.[32]

What in fact needs to be clarified with respect to any attempted accession to sovereignty is the significance of the right of participation by objecting peoples. It is only by artificially postulating an already independent Quebec as an established fact that the Pellet Report can make the question of secession so central, and it thus considers any rights of the aboriginal peoples solely in relation to a consummated process.

The Pellet Report helpfully confirms that the rights of aboriginal peoples are emergent, gaining steadily in recognition under international law. The report also notes that the positing of a right of self-determination in the Draft Declaration on the Rights of Indigenous Peoples, now being considered by the Human Rights Commission, is likely to exert a significant influence, despite the fact that its degree of authoritativeness and impact is likely to remain uncertain for a considerable period of time. But the whole matter of the existence of such a right is determined to be "of little consequence" by the Pellet Report. The report contends that even in "the broadest conception of rights contemplated for aboriginal peoples, nowhere" is it "provide[d] that they should have a right of secession."[33] This puts the whole matter of self-determination for the indigenous peoples of Quebec in a quite distorting light. There is no claim being currently made or contemplated on the issue of secession by aboriginal nations. It is, at most, a matter of deciding whether there exists an outer limit restricting the right of self-determination should secession be claimed at some point. The central claim of the aboriginal peoples in present Quebec, however, is not secession, but their rights to avoid any change of circumstances that is perceived to be harmful to their existing arrangements and future prospects. The representatives of these peoples are also seeking to establish a prior right of consultation and participation, equivalent to that enjoyed by the official representatives of Quebec's provincial government. Aboriginal peoples do not want to be brought into the process of adjustment as an afterthought or to be placed in a situation where Quebec's separation is treated as a fait accompli. They also are seeking to avoid becoming a bargaining chip in future negotiations between federal Canada and provincial Quebec.

These issues of participation are important whenever existing states break into two or more parts. If objecting groups and minorities claim the right to exercise self-determination, then it is important to have a mechanism to evaluate the claim and draw appropriate legal conclusions. If the objecting groups content themselves with the status of being a "minority," then it seems most helpful to view complaints as a series of human rights challenges, possibly requiring special regimes of guaranty and protection. The failure to take such steps for the benefit of Serbian minorities in Croatia and Bosnia undoubtedly contributed to the downward spiral that erupted into vicious warfare in the 1990s. While the atrocities committed by the Bosnian Serbs are inexcusable, their sense of abuse and neglect in 1990 and 1991 was understandable and reasonable, especially considering Germany's encouragement of the Yugoslav breakup by way of extending diplomatic recognition to Slovenia, and especially Croatia, prior to any reasonable effort to reassure Serb minorities. There were also constitutional irregularities associated with the initial Bosnian claim of independence, which overlooked the requirement of legislative approval by a plurality that would have given the Serbs the power to veto any move to withdraw from the Yugoslav federation.

This analytic position reinforces peacekeeping approaches that rely on preventive diplomacy—acting before social, political, economic, and political tensions generate violence—which offers parties an alternative to war. As such, the right of self-determination in circumstances of multiple claims should be subject to a process of participation and assessment under respected auspices. This kind of approach will fail on some occasions, but it seems evident that if the global community is to learn from Bosnia and other similar crises, then the postcolonial extensions of the right of self-determination cannot be allowed to unfold on their own. It is instructive to note that where the breakup is mainly voluntary and the new entity does not contain significant objecting or threatened minorities, as was the case in Slovenia, such a cautious, preventive orientation is not appropriate. The presence of separate, indigenous peoples within the seceding entity also presents a special problem, especially if their representatives object to the contemplated change of status, as has been the case in Quebec. Two central questions are raised: Do such peoples enjoy their own right of self-determination, and does its exercise imply a full or partial right to take part in any negotiations that might produce an accession to sovereignty? This matter of an emergent right of self-determination for indigenous peoples will be explored in the next section, which introduces a special dimension into the conceptual discussion, since the peoples involved don't normally aspire to constitute themselves as a modern sovereign state.

INDIGENOUS PEOPLES AND THE RIGHT OF SELF-DETERMINATION

Another recent development of some consequence is the insistence by indigenous peoples, and their representatives, on claiming self-determination as a core right that befits their generally shared avowal of sovereignty and nationhood. The degree to which such a right of self-determination is currently part of international law remains uncertain and controversial. There is, to be sure, no binding formal instrument that establishes such a right, or, for that matter, that clarifies its scope, particularly in relation to international sovereign states within whose territory or territories such indigenous peoples and nations are situated.

At the same time, there has been a notable evolution of political consciousness with respect to such a claim, as well as a process of acknowledgment within the United Nations and on the part of existing states. It can be argued that the right of self-determination inheres in a people, and need not be established on its own; it can also be argued that the path of customary international law has been cleared to a sufficient degree to admit of the legal existence of a right of self-determination. Such matters are embedded in a gray area of legal controversy and are likely to remain so for the next decade or more.

What seems evident is that the wide array of potential self-determination claims by indigenous peoples around the world adds to the current confusion as to the status of the right and contributes to nervousness on the part of many diplomats about the persistence of this issue in this postcolonial era. The very notion of a "postcolonial era" can be called into question as well. France, for example, retains colonial possessions in the Pacific and Caribbean and shows no signs of giving them up, but rather seeks to avoid anticolonial opprobrium by characterizing its colonies as "integral" parts of France.

Also relevant is the contention by supporters of the claims of indigenous peoples that their exercise of the right of self-determination occurs within a "colonial" context, that such peoples have been severely "colonized" and are as entitled, if not more so, to self-determination as are those peoples that were formally categorized as "colonized." There is historical and ethical merit in such a perspective. However, even hinting at its full acceptance comes across as dangerous and politically unacceptable to the entrenched interests of the established world order. Accepting this perspective would open the way to gigantic territorial claims whose satisfaction would lead to devastating economic, political, and social effects for the dominant population, and such claims would presumably be resisted by violence if necessary.

What adds to the confusion in this setting is the intermixing of symbolic and substantive goals, and the deliberate blurring of this distinction by both sides. If the claims to the right of self-determination were clearly symbolic then it would seem less threatening to affirm the right. In reality, however, part of the symbolic value of the right of self-determination is that it contains within it at least the theoretical option of complete territorial sovereignty. The fact that such a claim cannot be successfully exercised and practically implemented within the setting of present world conditions does not altogether provide states with sufficient reassurance that they will not be faced with such challenges. If a right of self-determination is confirmed in its broadest implications, then at the very least the threat of secession can be used as a bargaining chip in negotiating circumstances, and there is no assurance that larger demands will not actually be insisted upon even if it would be irresponsible for an indigenous people to attempt to be fully independent. In other words, the impracticality of exercising a right of self-determination is no assurance that it will not be exercised.

No end of this problematic challenge is currently in sight. As with other aspects of the self-determination controversy, it is too late to withdraw its applicability in the situation of indigenous peoples. To attempt to do so would intensify conflict and would not be accepted by those who support a general improvement in the protection of indigenous peoples.

It is also worth noting the legal progress that indigenous peoples have made in recent decades. They are no longer seen merely as unprotected victims of the modernizing process, nor are their claims still limited to demanding protection by way of assimilationist norms of nondiscrimination. Indigenous peoples have now come to be recognized as groups whose autonomous way of life deserves protection. The question is whether this latter goal, which is now widely enough endorsed by states to qualify as a norm of customary international law, also implies a full right of self-determination. At this stage it is also plausible to view the duty of safeguarding indigenous autonomy to be a matter that is ripe for further negotiation and compromise. The law currently remains in a fluid condition, and awaits further clarification. The underlying problem is how to confer on indigenous peoples an appropriate entitlement without in the process creating an explosive situation with respect to contemporary realities.

It is now safe to say, in fact, that indigenous peoples' claims to the right of self-determination based on historical and sacred attachments to specific land currently risk a collision with parallel rights of self-determination by the people of the encompassing modern territorial state. These latter rights are themselves protected and entrenched, and the citizens who enjoy them feel little or no responsibility for the injustices that were allegedly done by their ancestors. In other words, the full exercise of the right of self-determination claimed by one group would infringe on the perceived rights of the other. What is needed is a process of mutual adjustment that somehow accommodates the essential claims of both sides. With good will and sensitivity such an outcome seems attainable in most instances, especially given the fact that most substantive indigenous claims now demand merely the safeguarding of rights and lands that they currently possess. Indigenous claims also include symbolic aspects about acknowledging the injustices of the past and making some gesture of rectification. The government of Canada has moved toward reconciliation by issuing a formal apology for 150 years of mistreatment of aboriginal peoples under its authority and by establishing a trust fund that would be available to such peoples in their efforts to sustain their way of life.

It is clear that the issues surrounding the debate over indigenous claims of self-determination are in many respects analogous to those informing the debate over ethnic minorities facing potential oppression or discrimination during the breakup of a previously unified or federated state. Both debates revolve around two fundamental questions: the first is whether the right of self-determination applies, and if so, does it allow for secession. The second involves the process: Are those minorities affected by the proposed breakup of a state entitled to participate in, and indeed give their consent for, such a change in political arrangements? In these respects, the situation of the Serbian minorities in Croatia and Bosnia structurally resembles that of the indigenous nations in Quebec that are insisting that there can be no valid change in constitutional structure without their participation and consent. The movement for secession in Quebec has not up to this point succeeded at the referendum stage, though it has gained strong support, and the issues raised are likely to remain unresolved for the indefinite future. Such uncertainty is bound to produce tensions and raise the anxiety level of those who oppose any change in constitutional status for Quebec.

A CONCLUDING NOTE

The evolution of the right of self-determination is one of the most dramatic normative developments in this century. During the height of the decolonization process, affirming rights of self-determination seemed fully in step with the march of history, having an overall positive effect on the human condition, freeing hundreds of millions from colonial bondage. A major result of this process was to extend sovereignty and statehood to all corners of the planet for the first time, and to transform the United Nations into a genuinely universal body representing virtually the whole of humanity.

Decolonization, however, in no way put an end to state-sponsored oppression, and statehood is still an unrealized goal of many victimized peoples worldwide. And yet promoting the right to statehood fundamentally conflicts with the general global geopolitical imperative of avoiding fragmentation. The breakup of the Soviet Union and Yugoslavia have dramatized these concerns, generating intense civil strife due to an array of efforts to reconstitute states in a manner that newly entraps other peoples, causing a collision of political wills and passions. Whereas the larger political entity may have tried to contain several overlapping nationalist identities, smaller fragments emerge as self-contained vehicles for a particular nationalism, and as such hostile to alternative nationalisms.

Despite these complications, however, to dismiss self-determination as an option is impossible at this stage. Its reality has sunk too deeply into the political and legal consciousness, and there remain in the world too many distinct peoples enduring alien and oppressive rule. The idea of self-determination recognizes that the legitimacy of *any* political arrangement depends on the will of the people subject to its authority.

There are no fully satisfactory solutions. In some settings, self-determination struggles can be avoided by a timely guarantee of group rights. In others, self-determination claims can be satisfied by moderate solutions that ensure self-rule and self-administration in the spirit of the Liechtenstein proposals. Still other contexts call for a phased process that moves from human rights to autonomy, and then, possibly, on to independence. The Liechtenstein proposals have the great merit of preserving the symbolic aura of self-determination while reducing its threatening substantive implications.

Limits appear the moment self-determination takes the form of a state-shattering movement in a setting where there is opposition both from the old unified state and from ethnic minorities in the new proposed state. In such circumstances, patient dialogue and diplomacy, the avoidance of violence on both sides, and the effective protection of human rights seems to constitute the most constructive approach, but clearly there are no panaceas.

In the background remains the core issue of maintaining overall geopolitical stability by limiting excessive fragmentation. The total number of sovereign states generally considered geopolitically manageable is two hundred, roughly the current level. An increase to 250 is widely regarded as the upper limit of manageability. To maintain this goal, state-shattering exercises of the right of self-determination must be kept at a minimum. And yet the promise of self-determination to all peoples makes it very difficult to find a principled basis in law for denying claimants who seem to represent a distinct people and have the will and capability to be a sovereign state.

The next chapter continues the inquiry into the delimitation of the right of self-determination, but with a focus on the matter of group rights, particularly those being insisted upon by representatives of indigenous peoples. The enlarging of the notion of human rights to protect fundamental aspects of collective identity is itself a contested undertaking. This enlargement goes against an earlier orthodoxy that conceived of human rights as belonging only to individuals.

Group Claims within the UN System 7

The Rights of Indigenous Peoples

ASSERTING GROUP CLAIMS

The issue of human rights has traditionally been focused on the rights of the individual. Protection of group identity, whether involving religion, culture, or gender, has generally been approached as a matter of individual freedom to engage in group activity without enduring discrimination or persecution. There is an increasing demand, however, to treat group rights as a truly collective concept.[1]

The relationship between the UN system and group claims is problematic, sharply contested, complex, and rapidly evolving. Patterns of practice and expectations cannot be deduced directly from either international law or the UN Charter, nor from an assessment of the attitudes and intentions of those who created the organization.

A central issue of conceptualization underlies this entire inquiry: How to relate the concept of the nation-state to the United Nations in the various contexts of group claims. There is, to begin with, a problem of terminology. The modern state, as a juristic matter, is the virtually exclusive source of authoritative nationality on a world level—granting or withholding the status of "national." Yet this statist appropriation of the symbols of nationality is also a way of suppressing, or at least subordinating, a psychopolitical sense of nationhood that is experienced by individuals and groups independently of, and often in opposition to, the "national" identity conferred by governmental act.

In many states, the existential reality is one of multinationality even if the legal reality is one of a unified nationality conferred by the sovereign center of state power. Some states are anomalous with regard to nationality. For instance, the United States has been generally successful in combining the psychopolitical and juristic sense of nationality in the face of ethnic diversity, but it has done so by way of shared beliefs, traditions, and experience, by giving substance and meaning to an overarching, nonethnic reality of citizenship. Those of Polish or Irish background, while generally feeling a strong identification with their country or origin, rarely question the primacy of their American "nationality" or claim a second national identity. Yet this sense of shared nationality is more a feature of the political identity that results from the rights, privileges, and aura of American citizenship than it is a wider ethnic identity that is coextensive with the state.[2]

An abused national minority that survives acute discrimination or persecution, or that has an active historical memory of a prior and coercively extinguished statehood, is almost certain to repudiate a political structure established by the coercing political power. The Baltic states' renewed resistance to continued Soviet annexation during the late 1980s illustrates this pattern. The persistence of strong feelings of distinct ethnic identity, coupled with this sense of historic injustice, is likely to produce a latent separatist movement for self-determination and restored statehood if the group has a sufficient density of population, enduring memories, and statist aspirations. If the surviving remnant lacks these features, its goals are usually expressed as demands for devolution or autonomy. From the United Nations perspective, however, the strong category of group claims is especially sensitive and problematic and is seen as threatening to the territorial integrity of important members. Overall, the United Nations has given a decisive priority to statist concerns about territorial unity. The statist approach is to consolidate control over disparate ethnic identities by insisting that minorities of whatever character owe a common allegiance to the state, and further, that solidarity among nationals is of a geographic scope coextensive with territorial boundaries.[3] Differently expressed, statist conceptions of nationality have successfully dominated psycholinguistic conceptions and earlier contrary experiences.

More concretely, from the perspective of international relations, a Kurd in Turkey is a Turkish national, and the sense of Kurdish nationality has no formal or legal transnational dimension that might otherwise establish links with Kurdish communities in Iraq, Iran, and Syria, or conceivably ground an appeal for relief to a wider international community. From this formalistic perspective there can be no Kurdish nation or nationality of international significance without a Kurdish state. Kurdish grievances, then, are generally reduced to the protection of individual rather than group or national human rights, including the right of an individual not to be persecuted because of his or her group identity.

In view of such legal and political realities, the intense drive to establish a nation secure in political, economic, social, and cultural domains inevitably spills over in part into a movement to obtain a state as a protective vehicle. The Zionist movement's struggle to establish Israel as a Jewish national home joined this sense of nation and state, as has the reactive struggle of the Palestinians to obtain their own state to uphold and protect claims of nationhood.[4]

The situation of indigenous peoples is different in some respects. Their objective in contemporary circumstances is generally the acknowledgment of their "nationhood" and a framework for assuring its maintenance. In essence, this amounts to a desired arrangement for autonomy that is given constitutional status within a state and that enjoys international backing, including some international legal process that provides remedies. Indigenous peoples generally realize that it is impossible or impractical to attain the international status of a sovereign state. What most political movements on behalf of indigenous peoples seek, then, is the competence to confer nationality on themselves, to generate enforceable limits on encroachment by the state and to protect domains of traditional life, including religion, sacred land, and customary fishing and hunting rights. To reach such goals it is generally not necessary for such a "nation" to insist on the status of a sovereign state. An indigenous people as an autonomous enclave within a territorial state may benefit from association with the larger political unit, provided the association is premised on unconditional respect for the fundamental traditions of the weaker unit.

There are, then, three categories of group claims that need to be distinguished:

1. Claims to equality of treatment and satisfaction of basic needs. Such claims assert the logic of human dignity and nondiscrimination.
2. Claims to restored, autonomous nationhood expressive of a primary political identity that is incompatible with assimilation into existing political entities. The limited character of such claims implicitly acknowledges that separate statehood is not feasible or desirable given the character of international society. Such claims to nationhood *within* existing state boundaries assert the logic of self-determination of peoples.
3. Claims to statehood reflecting a collective struggle to achieve control over distinct territorial units entitled to full membership rights in international society. Such claims invoke the logic of self-determination of peoples.

The United Nation's normative foundations are overwhelmingly statist. Notions of membership, sovereign equality, domestic jurisdiction, and the veto in the Security Council underscore the extent to which it is an organization of and for states. Furthermore, the territorial integrity of member states is affirmed as a prime basis of political order in the UN Charter. Nevertheless, there is a welcome degree of indeterminacy in the UN's constitutional framework, which is also evident in United Nations practice and evolution.

The overriding UN commitment to sustain peace provides a basis for involvement in ethnic conflict internal to states, despite the prohibition in Article 2(7) of intervention by the organization in matters essentially within domestic jurisdiction. The credo of self-determination is, under many circumstances of ethnic subordination, impossible to reconcile with statist notions of the "self." The recent activism of indigenous peoples, together with the presence of international human rights issues on various global agendas, has made deprivations of minorities, indigenous peoples, and subordinated groups, which are certainly not states, a matter of growing international concern in several UN institutional arenas.

This direction of UN evolution—slow and cautious, to be sure—toward support for group claims pertaining to rights, duties, and autonomy was not planned or predicted in 1945 at the UN's inception. The architects of the Charter, leading policymakers in World War II, were at the time understandably preoccupied with avoiding the recurrence of general warfare. All else, including issues of development and human rights, came later, as political trends created new configurations of power and influence. World leaders were disposed to build peace against the background of particular experiences such as the lesson of Munich, which was understood as teaching that aggression cannot be deterred by appeasement.

It is enlightening to compare the early history of the United Nations with the very different state of international relations during the formation and early operation of the League of Nations, particularly the competition between Leninist and Wilsonian ideas about self-determination and related strategies for the reorganization of political life on the planet. Both ideologies anticipated a reconstituted international political order based on normative commitments—Lenin calling for self-determination by oppressed classes, especially workers, and Wilson emphasizing the need, primarily in Europe, to take minority claims for autonomy into account.[5]

World War I was understood largely as a breakdown of the balance of power provoked by unstable political actors, and by tensions among restive ethnic minorities in several Balkan countries. In the postwar setting, preventing further conflict meant giving these larger and more volatile ethnic groups in Europe the prospect of self-determination and establishing a system under League auspices for the protection of minority rights.[6] This emphasis on upholding the rights of European minorities proved to be ineffectual in the face of the great economic and ideological forces that swept through world politics in the 1920s and 1930s. The crisis of confidence in the League's role developed not as a result of ethnic issues but in response to its ineffectual responses to Japan's aggression against Manchuria, Italy's against Ethiopia, and Germany's against a series of European countries.

By the end of World War II, the perception of danger had decisively shifted from a concern about the destabilizing influence of restive minorities. The new postwar focus was on the menace posed by totalitarian ideologies and militarist regimes, and more specifically, on the importance of democratizing the defeated Axis countries and protecting weakened states, especially France and Italy, against subversion arising out of links between large national communist parties and a world communist movement orchestrated from Moscow. The wartime consensus between the Soviet Union and the West broke down, in part, over whether this perception of totalitarian menace should form the basis of security in the postwar world.[7]

Against this historical and conceptual background, it is not surprising that problems of minorities were relegated in the immediate postwar years to the outer margins of political concern. With the onset of the cold war, two opposed blocs of countries took shape. Indeed, the political climate in both East and West favored strong states within their own spheres of influence, partly as assurance against ideological defection. As a consequence, the reality of minority grievances was hidden, or at least suppressed, beneath the mirage of strong, unified states, generally described, misleadingly, as "nation-states" to obscure their inherent heterogeneity and multinational character.

The persistence of these grievances was powerfully displayed by minority peoples in the Soviet Union during the late 1980s. Ethnic and nationalist agitation erupted in this period, but not because minority circumstances were deteriorating. It was rather that the Soviet moves toward democratization facilitated the expression of various long-smoldering forms of ethnic and nationalist discontent. As has been often noted, when oppressive structures are loosened, radical movements of resistance and challenge are likely to flourish, taking advantage of the new atmosphere of permissiveness. The problems of minorities have been much less significant in the Western bloc, but even there, the waning of cold war fervor encouraged the more vigorous pursuit of ethnic and minority claims in such seemingly stable and long-established states as the United Kingdom, France, and Spain—to say nothing of the explosive reigniting of ethnic tensions in the Balkan region. Such developments contributed to the breakup of Yugoslavia, leading directly to the worst European outbreaks of collective violence since World War II.[8]

To put it bluntly, the plight of indigenous and minority peoples was virtually invisible as an international issue when the United Nations was founded, and remained so for twenty-five years thereafter.[9] A number of factors explain this circumstance, especially as it relates to indigenous peoples:

1. the exclusion of issues related to the treatment of indigenous peoples from international political consciousness, an exclusion reinforced by the general

failure of indigenous peoples to participate or even gain adequate representation in most national political systems; their consequent demoralization,
passivity, and resignation; a lack of politically savvy indigenous leadership
that could advance a political cause on the stage of international diplomacy;
the frequent suppression of increasingly vocal and sophisticated indigenous
leadership;[10]

2. assimilationism and the homogenizing effect of modernism and consumerism;
a sense that indigenous cultures are outdated, if quaint, remnants of the past
that will naturally be swept away by the forward march of history;

3. the absence of global weight on the part of indigenous peoples and minorities, their lack of transnational constituencies, networks, and representatives
capable of mounting significant international protests or exerting leverage;

4. the shared statist interest of most UN members in keeping issues involving
indigenous peoples and minorities well hidden behind the shield of domestic jurisdiction;

5. the special concern of postcolonial states in Africa and Asia to safeguard their
territory against the genuine risks of dismemberment and civil warfare arising from tribally based autonomy and secession claims—or from any self-
determination movements outside the context of colonialism;

6. the special concern of the Soviet Union in avoiding the internationalization
of a variety of autonomy and secessionist claims from "captive nations"
located within both its bloc and its national territorial boundaries; and

7. the strong developmental and financial interest of dominant elites in appro-
priating land and resources owned or managed by indigenous peoples.

Despite this intensely unfavorable setting for the protection of group
claims within the UN system, the period since 1945 has been notable for
the increasingly assertive espousal of such claims and their growing acknowledgment, in a variety of institutional settings. Indeed, the achievements of
the United Nations, given its limited mandate, are all the more remarkable when compared with the lackluster record of the League of Nations.
The League mandate, though favorable to group claims, generated disillusionment, whereas the United Nations, proceeding without a legally binding mandate, has built a modest but improving record of achievement in
relation to many types of group claims, including facilitating the internationalization of the grievances of indigenous peoples in a form that enables
their direct presentation. This emergent concern about the well-being of
indigenous peoples is especially surprising given the enthusiasm for modernization in the postwar decades, and can only be explained by the relevance of some strong offsetting factors.

The remainder of this chapter seeks to identify and account for this unex-
pected, and probably undervalued, area of success by the United Nations;
it also seeks to consider some seemingly inherent limitations on the UN

role arising from the nature of the organization as a subordinate entity in a system of international relations that remains overwhelmingly statist. In sum, the United Nations has done more for group rights than could have been reasonably expected, but far less than necessary to reach the goals of (1) satisfying group claims using the established norms of international law and justice, partially as embodied in relevant human rights instruments, and (2) protecting indigenous peoples and other vulnerable minorities through the further development of human rights norms and legal regimes premised on ethnic autonomy and self-determination.

MOVES TOWARD ACKNOWLEDGMENT

Despite the low initial expectation for group claims within the UN system, varied factors have led to the gradual recognition of such claims by several UN organs. The relative importance of these factors has changed over time, depending on the issue in contention and the specific bureaucratic setting. The factors can be identified as follows:

The Growth of Human Rights

Overall, the UN system affirmed the promotion of human rights in a relatively perfunctory manner. As the full impact of the Nazi experience became inscribed upon international political consciousness, the international community realized that gross abuses of human rights were relevant to world peace and that limits upon the exercise of territorial sovereignty were organically linked to the maintenance of world peace. For the West, such an insight was both politicized and deepened by the perception of Stalinism as a renewed threat to peace and security, but it was also always conditioned by the realization that extensive sovereign rights continued to enjoy extensive support among elites.

The low status accorded group rights connected with ethnic or indigenous identity is evident in the text of the Universal Declaration of Human Rights as adopted in 1948. The document is overwhelmingly individualistic, although socialist and welfare-state influences are evident in its articles on rights to work, education, and welfare. Also, the document resonates with some distinctly American perspectives, especially the New Deal and Franklin Roosevelt's Four Freedoms. Group rights are indirectly acknowledged as vital for the achievement of an integrated society in which nondiscriminatory standards of treatment apply across the board to an entire population.

The two 1966 Covenants, however, provide the normative foundation for the basic claims of ethnic and indigenous peoples. Particularly significant is the endorsement in the shared Article 1 provision, which affirms that the right of self-determination belongs to "[a]ll peoples." However many times governments insisted that the rights of distinct peoples are subordinate to the territorial unity of sovereign states, Article 1 would continue to provide a conceptual wedge with which to put forth even the most drastic forms of group claims—namely, collective and separatist rights of autonomy and even secession.

An attempt to reconcile contradictory ideas of world order is found in the discussion of "the principle of equal rights and self-determination of peoples" that is embodied in the Declaration on Friendly Relations. On the one side, the ethos of self-determination for peoples is affirmed as a basic principle of international order under international life. The mandate to peoples can be satisfied in several ways: "The establishment of a sovereign and independent State, the free association or integration with an independent State or the emergence into any other political status freely determined by a people constitute modes of implementing the right of self-determination by that people."[11] In virtually the same breath, however, this apparent endorsement is qualified:

> Nothing in the foregoing paragraphs shall be construed as authorizing or encouraging any action which would dismember or impair, totally or in part, the territorial integrity or political unity of sovereign and independent States conducting themselves in compliance with the principle of equal rights and self-determination of peoples as described above and *thus possessed of a government representing the whole people belonging to the territory without distinction as to race, creed or colour.*[12]

Whether the notion of representing "the whole people" is taken formally or in a specific political sense is crucial to the significance of this qualification. In less ambiguous language, the Declaration of Principles in reinforcing limits to group claims of self-determination asserts that "[e]very state shall refrain from any action aimed at the partial or total disruption of the national unity and territorial integrity of any other State or country."[13] Yet such a limitation on the acts of other states is immaterial to those more prevalent threats to national unity and territorial integrity mounted by internal popular movements seeking to realize group claims for nationhood through a distinct political autonomy. Of course, nationhood can be achieved in a variety of governmental forms that do not involve dismemberment—for example, schemes for autonomy and self-government that can be accommodated within federal systems, or even as enclaves within unitary states. In any event, affirming peoples, not governments, as the agents of self-determination in noncolonial settings has opened a kind of Pandora's Box.[14]

The more modest contribution of the Covenants is the explicit acknowledgment of group claims as a specific and distinct dimension of human rights. There is an overall prohibition on discrimination based on group characteristics.[15] Another provision in the Covenant, this one on Civil and Political Rights, is specifically directed at the circumstances of minorities:

> Article 27. In those States in which ethnic, religious or linguistic minorities exist, persons belonging to such minorities shall not be denied the right, in community with the other members of their group, to enjoy their own culture, to profess and practice their own religion, or to use their own language.

Such an acknowledgment of minority rights, even though cast in terms of individual "persons," creates two possible modes of advocacy: either using nondiscrimination as a foundation for integration or assimilation into the political community as a whole, or asserting the right to safeguard a separate ethnic identity and character even if deviant from the outlook and interests of the majority. The aspirations of many indigenous peoples and minorities are to sustain their particular traditions and values; these in turn depend on equitable and respectful treatment as autonomous communities within the territorial and constitutional structures of a modern state. In effect, Article 27 also confers upon indigenous peoples—one kind of "ethnic minority"—the legally protected discretion to reject modernism in its various guises, although the precise modalities of such a rejection are not specified.[16]

One effect of this steady development of international legal standards in the human rights area has been to foster the general acceptance by governments of a formal obligation to treat people fairly and equally without regard to race, gender, and religion. The meaning of fairness has been increasingly elaborated in international treaty instruments, which are part of a considerable corpus of positive international law accumulated over the last four decades. The translation of legal standards into behavioral practices is by no means ensured or uniform, but the existence of authoritative standards does facilitate the presentation of claims on behalf of both groups and individuals who can put together a manifest case of "unfairness." Human rights in this general manner establishes a normative foundation for discussions and efforts within pertinent UN arenas on behalf of all categories of victims, including collective victims.

The Nuremberg Legacy

The prosecution of defeated Nazi leaders at Nuremberg created a general disposition to regard the treatment of minorities as a matter of international concern, indeed, as part of international law. More important, perhaps, is the fact that the Nuremberg proceedings indicted the international community for its tendency during the 1930s to look the other way during the period of Nazi persecutions, relying partly on the moral, political, and legal pretext of German internal sovereignty.

This perception led directly to the widespread acceptance of the Genocide Convention. The authoritative establishment of genocide as an international crime has enabled representatives of minorities and indigenous peoples to invoke international standards as part of their resistance against policies that are alleged to threaten the persistence of their group identity and ways of life.[17] As the debate surrounding the campaign against apartheid has disclosed, the boundary between peace and security issues and group claims has become blurred.

Other realities have contributed to this blurring process—the Amin regime in Uganda, the Khmer Rouge rule in Cambodia, the ethnic character of internal and transnational armed conflict in several African countries, and several horrifyingly deliberate efforts to eliminate indigenous peoples in Latin America.[18] As in other contexts, indigenous peoples, though arguably the most victimized and threatened category, have had the greatest difficulty finding governmental sponsors for their concerns within the UN system, and have often had to rely on underfinanced and understaffed nongovernmental organizations. The situation improved, at least at the level of awareness, with the creation and operations of the Working Group on Indigenous Populations, a UN subcommission that has met for several weeks almost every summer in Geneva, and that has produced reports and documents that have greatly clarified the overall indigenous outlook. Much attention and effort was focused for many years on drafting and gaining support for a Declaration on the Rights of Indigenous Peoples.[19]

The Demonstrative Effects of Revolutionary Nationalism

The post-1945 mobilizations of nationalist forces in Asia and Africa had an energizing effect on group identity, aspirations, and tactics. The colonial order, by its repressive and alien presence, had tended to suppress or constrain interethnic conflict. Removing the colonial presence created a situation of greater fluidity, which brought many ethnic rivalries to the surface.

Minorities—whether as ethnic group or tribal entity—became more assertive, seeking an active role in the construction of a postcolonial order, both to influence the state and to protect themselves against inequitable allocations of public resources. In other words, an unexpected side effect of the collapse of the colonial order was to stimulate other dimensions of intersocietal and intrasocietal conflict, as well as to draw into question the correspondence between statist boundaries and feelings of political identity.

Also, it soon became apparent that the ethos of self-determination as the foundation for legitimate nationalist movements could no longer be confined within a Third World anticolonial setting. The ambiguous character of nationalist identity and nationhood enabled groups subordinated to particular states, or groups whose historical and ethnolinguistic homeland encompassed a territory unrelated to the boundaries of a sovereign state, to make a variety of international claims of self-determination.

The importance of these developments for UN operations is evident. First of all, the fact that minority and indigenous groups appeal to UN bodies to press group claims builds international familiarity with and support for such claims, enhancing their overall acceptability. Second, the endorsement of self-determination by the UN is relied upon by militant factions of minorities and indigenous peoples to mobilize nationalist sentiments and expectations. The narrower UN construction of self-determination based on the acceptance of existing state boundaries and an emphasis on colonial relations, even if doctrinally authoritative, does not significantly constrain the political process within the organization or the various dialogues throughout the world that bear on minority and indigenous peoples' rights.[20]

The success of nationalist movements in anticolonial settings also had broader effects that made it evident that the relation of forces in liberation struggles could not be assessed on the basis of ratios of military power alone. Political will, a persevering leadership, and legitimacy on an international level came to be seen as vital resources in such struggles, and moreover, as available to minorities and indigenous peoples affirming their own nationhood and seeking a political framework capable of sustaining autonomy. The United Nations has played a critical role on a symbolic level, lending legitimacy to group claims with nationalist components.

International Terrorism

The rise of international terrorism in the 1970s was associated in many instances with the desperate political violence of abused and repressed ethnic minorities and "captive nations." Had the United Nations acknowledged this influence, it would have effectively validated terrorism as an instrument of rectification. It is difficult to avoid the impression, for example, that the historic plight of the Armenians in Turkey became far more of an international concern after widespread terrorist attacks on Turkish diplomats by Armenian groups.[21] More generally, the growth of interest in group claims within the United Nations coincided with the threats posed to peace and security in international society by disenfranchised and severely oppressed groups and peoples. If such political terrorism were to disappear it seems quite likely that many of these issues of group claims would slip from public awareness and once more be left exclusively to the discretion of territorial governments.

Geopolitical Factors

The extension of geopolitical rivalries to contexts involving group claims is a common feature of world politics, especially when ideological alignments are at stake. Reliance on geopolitical forces is often precarious for persecuted groups, but it is also often the only basis for mounting an effective challenge to existing arrangements. Anticolonial struggles in Angola and Mozambique became entwined with the play of geopolitical forces in the region. The effect was both to strengthen the drive toward self-determination by rival movements competing for influence and to magnify and perpetuate patterns of ethnic conflict. As a result, group claims have been given more salience than previously in those United Nations settings where peace and security concerns—high politics—are addressed. For better or worse, geopolitical rivalry ensures the internationalization of many of the claims by those minorities and indigenous peoples whose plight carries serious geopolitical implications.[22] In contrast, the absence of geopolitical tension in a given situation tends to keep group claims more or less invisible at an international level. Governments still have considerable latitude to rely on repression in the absence of a politically interested outside strategic power or an external sponsor that can protest effectively on behalf of the victims.

The moderation of the geopolitical tensions associated with the cold war seems to have had contradictory effects on the global policy agenda. Soviet policies of democratization in the 1980s opened a space in which suppressed ethnic claims were vigorously asserted, claims that burst forth more strongly with the Soviet collapse. It was easy in the early post–cold war days to see the outbreak of ethnic conflict in the Soviet republics and bloc countries as a confirmation of earlier claims that the Soviet Union had been a uniformly cruel, repressive state. The Soviet state was generally restrained from acting coercively in this setting, especially as its priority during the Gorbachev years was to improve its international reputation.

The decline of a strong central state contributes to micronationalist frustrations. Weak states are vulnerable to the rise of various movements seeking autonomy, and sometimes independence. The former strong state, fearful of fragmentation, is tempted to react coercively, as Russia did in response to Chechnya. In the absence of a deep geopolitical rivalry that could give global meaning to all events, the geopolitical powers in the post–cold war era generally allowed weak states to disintegrate, believing that such events would have little bearing on regional or global status quo.

The Ecological Ethos

The surge of anxiety about environmental decay has produced a growing appreciation of nature and conservation, and of the inherent connections between lifestyle, world view, and ecological viability. In this spirit, a new set of ecological guidelines has encouraged a greater appreciation of the attitudes and behavior of indigenous peoples. Instead of being pitied as "backward" or "primitive," such peoples are now seen as having been more successful than modern societies in enabling sustainable development over long time periods. Earlier assumptions that modernization was the only desirable path seem clearly invalid, and the opportunity to learn from premodern peoples seems sensible and relevant. At the same time it is important to realize that premodern peoples also made severe ecological mistakes that frequently doomed their particular society to extinction.

In the wake of this reevaluation the United Nations changed its approach to indigenous peoples from one of removing obstacles to cultural assimilation to one favorable toward traditional patterns of existence, including retention of sacred land.[23] In the mid-1980s the plight of indigenous peoples became an important global concern, one that stood at the intersection of environmental policy and human rights. At the same time it came to be appreciated that indigenous peoples could not be adequately represented through the intergovernmental channels of the state system. Indigenous peoples' issues have since gained greater access to UN human rights forums (especially the Commission on Human Rights and its subcommission on the Prevention of Discrimination and Protection of Minorities). This in turn has helped bring about the formation of the Sub-Commission's Working Group on Indigenous Populations, which has convened annually in Geneva for the past twenty years. The evolution of tactics on the part of indigenous organizations themselves, notably their increasing recourse to international bodies, represents a more activist response to a long, demoralizing experience of expense, frustration, manipulation, oppression, and exploitation on the domestic level. Whether this internationalization of their struggle for justice will achieve material benefits is difficult to assess. It does seem to be the case that increased international salience for the grievances of indigenous peoples leads to greater sensitivity to such claims within intranational settings.

The NGO Dimension

The heightened recognition of group claims was facilitated by the rapid growth and activities of nongovernmental organizations devoted to human rights, the environment, women's issues, and indigenous peoples. These organizations put pressure on the United Nations and underscored the plight of minorities and indigenous peoples in a variety of settings. The transnational scope of many of these NGOs helped to mobilize support for group claims and developed materials and expert testimony on the problems posed. The enhanced status of group claims on a global level encouraged NGOs to rely on international law arguments as a way of reinforcing the efforts of minorities and indigenous peoples to gain protection or autonomy within a particular sovereign state. Greater UN attention to self-determination norms fed back into domestic political processes as minorities, indigenous peoples, and nongovernmental organizations employed these norms to support claims based on rights and equitable considerations in a variety of domestic contexts. Nongovernmental organizations served as important channels of communication between the United Nations and the claimant constituencies.

Rebuilding the UN Role

At its inception the United Nations was conceived mainly as a vehicle for collective security in the postwar world. The overriding concern was peace based upon a conception of bringing the weight of the organized world community to bear on the initiator of aggression. Through 1956 it is arguable that the United Nations lived up to much of its promise, protecting South Korea in 1950, and in response to the Suez Campaign of 1956—both apparent instances of an "armed attack" across an acknowledged international boundary. Whether Article 2(4)'s prohibition of the use of force "died" after 1956 is a matter of scholarly controversy. But surely the capability and willingness of the United Nations to side effectively with victims of armed attack became seriously weakened, and despite the Gulf War has not recovered as of the end of the twentieth century. The geopolitics of the cold war superseded the UN Charter, and the political challenge from the Third World eroded the perception that the main UN organs were respectful of constitutional constraints.[24]

The declining effectiveness of the United Nations in the domain of peace and security was somewhat offset by the increasing effectiveness of the organization in two areas of relevant concern: standard-setting (especially with respect to human rights and self-determination) and consciousness-raising (especially in relation to emergent problems of global concern).

In both respects, the espousal of group claims benefited. One can conjecture that as the United Nations found itself blocked by East-West and North-South tensions, it shifted to undertakings that seemed to transcend the deep cleavages in international life. The relative failure in the peace-and-security domain probably gave greater prominence to these undertakings, and helped to put issues involving minority rights and the protection of indigenous people back on the global agenda. The process developed a cumulative momentum in the Human Rights Commission and the sub-commission's Working Group on Indigenous Populations. Even if the predominant UN intentions were to engage these issues minimally and selectively, NGOs were able to push beyond such modest limits, usually with the help of mobilized constituencies that addressed their claims to the United Nations. Often the UN response was inconclusive, helping to create a basis for further involvement.

EVALUATING THE UNITED NATIONS ROLE

The contributions of the United Nations to the protection of minorities and indigenous peoples are difficult to evaluate in terms of policy and behavioral effects. The United Nations has not employed coercive means on behalf of group claims; instead, its role has been indirect and atmospheric, altering the climate within which these issues are perceived and resolved. Especially in relation to the situation of indigenous peoples, the mere achievement of visibility has seemed a tangible gain. Whether it is a sufficient gain to neutralize destructive pressures is another matter, and one that can only be addressed on a case-by-case basis, and over a considerable stretch of time.

Consciousness-Raising

UN auspices have been exceedingly useful in facilitating a greater global awareness of group claims. This awareness includes the realization that group claims now enjoy a formally acknowledged status, one not as widely endorsed as that enjoyed by individual claims, but still well within the domain of positive international law. Group claimants thus enjoy a stronger position in policy debates, and in ongoing norm-creation processes. The support for humanitarian intervention as a response to ethnic cleansing dramatizes the turn toward effective international action on behalf of brazenly threatened group rights.

The United Nation's role in fostering general awareness encourages the gathering and dissemination of information, especially where sanctions and implementation of decisions are not feasible. Discussion within UN settings affects world opinion about a particular government's behavior, and has apparently led governments on several occasions to institute expedient and partial reforms.

The United Nations has provided the resources to gather information and issue reports that exert considerable influence on global perceptions.[25] This dynamic can strengthen the presentation of claims in both international and domestic settings. The organization has also stimulated widespread global interest and concern in other areas, especially on matters of indigenous peoples. Its role can be seen as educative in the fundamental sense of changing societal attitudes and perceptions.

Standard-Setting

One of the most important contributions made by the United Nations has been its symbolic support of claims put forward by aggrieved individuals and groups. The struggle to appropriate symbols of legitimacy is of particular significance for those claimants that lack the material capabilities to mount direct challenges. In the setting of group claims, the UN system has been creative and productive at the conceptual level, legitimizing certain expectations and clarifying the character of others.

Despite efforts by UN officialdom to restrict Article 27 to the protection of negative rights (that is, protections against abuse) and nondiscrimination, concerned communities have increasingly moved toward the assertion of affirmative group claims to realize various degrees of autonomy. So far, UN organs have not ventured into this contested area very much, presumably because most representatives to its organs are beholden to statist notions of governmental supremacy. There are great opportunities for the United Nations to develop a range of policy instruments for the realization of affirmative group rights, and of schemes for devolution, autonomy, self-government, federalism, and self-administration.[26] Such activity is unlikely unless stimulated by public opinion and a determined effort on behalf of minorities and indigenous peoples and orchestrated by a coalition of human rights NGOs.

The circumstances of indigenous peoples are more difficult and uncertain than ever.[27] Challenging the assimilationist rationale embodied in the International Labor Organization Convention No. 107, now revised by the newly adopted Convention No. 169, has had two effects: (1) the gradual acceptance that the plight of indigenous peoples is an appropriate item on the agenda of human rights and self-determination; and (2) the shift in indigenous rights discourse from the promotion of assimilation (in the face of discrimination) to the promotion of sustainable autonomy (in the face of assimilation). The normative solution of a generation ago has become the normative challenge of the current generation.

Both of these developments are essential preconditions for effective action, but they offer no assurance that indigenous peoples can avoid severe displacement, even extinction, given the magnitude of adverse pressures. Each particular situation has its own dynamics, and its own balance of opposed forces. What seems evident at this stage is that UN activities improve the prospects that government policies of assimilation and relocation will be challenged and discredited by groups willing to invoke UN-generated international standards. Domestic resistance to governmental disregard of the development and well-being of indigenous peoples is reinforced by international validation and enhanced media interest.

In a more explicit vein, the subcommission's Working Group on Indigenous Populations, after years of discussion and many drafts, finally agreed upon a Declaration on the Rights of Indigenous Peoples in 1994.[28] The general character of the declaration shows the degree to which the mobilization of indigenous peoples within the United Nations has reshaped standards and the overall normative climate, in which it is now widely agreed that indigenous groups qualify as a "people" within the legal meaning of the right of self-determination. Whether these modifications will be accepted by the UN system as a whole remains uncertain. Shortcomings aside, this past decade of UN activity has decisively influenced, at least for the time being, the salience and normative orientation of indigenous peoples' claims.

Similarly, minority rights are receiving more attention in UN human rights arenas. To some extent this attention is the result of widespread and highly publicized ethnic conflict. The UN process has often been effective as a channel for expressing censure of discriminatory policies and practices directed against minorities. Censure generates and reinforces pressures associated with world public opinion, and tends to give greater political weight to minority grievances. The relative effectiveness of such pressures varies, of course, from setting to setting, depending on an array of contextual factors.

Networks and Feedback Mechanisms

One of the most impressive achievements of the United Nations is to provide arenas in which a variety of claimants can establish productive links and find common ground. A learning process occurs as groups seek to build on successes and avoid failures. The presentation of arguments over time builds a pool of knowledge that leads to greater sophistication. The natural course of events produces reports, comprehensive declarations, a cadre of specialists, and cooperative relations among claimants.

The transnational network generated in relation to indigenous peoples over the last decade has been greatly facilitated by the United Nations and by the formation and activities of the Working Group on Indigenous Populations, which has been in existence since 1981. The list of participating organizations in the Working Group and other human rights arenas is itself an impressive enumeration of the range of active NGOs. At the annual sessions of the Working Group, information about deteriorating conditions and ongoing struggles is shared, social and organizational relations are established, and demands for specific kinds of UN support are put forward. A sense of global presence is achieved, helping the leadership of these vulnerable groups to feel that their efforts are part of a wider transnational undertaking with its own unity rather merely a series of isolated and lonely stands against the overwhelming power of a modern state.

What political process emerges from this global presence is difficult to discern, as it is in the early stages of gestation; even more difficult to ascertain is the substantiation of tangible results. It seems reasonable to identify at least two provisional impacts: (1) States seem somewhat more deterred than previously from committing atrocities against minorities and indigenous peoples. That is, atrocities may and do still occur, but the motivation to avoid them seems greater due to the prospect of censure within the UN framework.[29] (2) Other actors associated with protective roles are strengthened in their resolve by this prospect of UN concern. The UN role is part of a wider buildup of capabilities and awareness to protect vulnerable groups against encroachment. The expansion of relevant NGO activity is of particular importance.[30]

It is evident that territorial states remain by far the most powerful actors within UN settings, placing financial, constitutional, and most of all, geopolitical limits on the sort of responses that are feasible. States have protected each other's territorial supremacy in these matters of minority rights, but have discovered a variety of normative and geopolitical incentives to highlight the specific conditions of deprivation involving group rights that exist in certain states. This "opening" on behalf of group claims suggests the extent to which geopolitical rivalry, genuine moral concern, public pressure, war, international public order, and international reputation qualify a logic of pure deference by states to each other's internal sovereignty.[31] The compromise is struck along the boundary between coercive steps that achieve behavioral change and initiatives of persuasive or symbolic purposes that raise consciousness and build support. This boundary is not consistently drawn.

One important generalization can be applied to the evolving character of the United Nations. Over the years the organization has moved away from its initial war-prevention focus toward a broader undertaking, one with varying emphases that reflect a shifting political climate.[32] One notable area of evolution has been the extension of protective concern to several categories of vulnerable people: refugees, disaster victims, the very poor, and other individuals and groups deprived of basic human rights, including the primary concern of most indigenous groups to enjoy a right to maintain their traditional way of life distinct from the dominant culture of the state. This sense that protecting the most vulnerable lies at the core of justice has helped the United Nations manifest a sympathetic interest in the plight of indigenous peoples.

Can the United Nations go further in the future? Will a strong statist backlash soon ensue? Should the organization confine its activities to symbolic, informational, and educational functions? To what extent is the United Nations already rubbing up against the constraints of the state system, which controls the purse-strings? The struggle of the Working Group on Indigenous Populations just to stay alive and to sustain a fairly independent line of activity is emblematic of the push and pull of political forces on these matters of group claims. These factors are further complicated by the various agendas and priorities of global market forces.

The surprising failure of the United Nations to take affirmative, as opposed to preventative, action with regard to group claims poses a particular challenge for the future, especially given the enormous human tragedies unfolding around the world as a consequence of clashes between an aggrieved minority and a suppressive state. It would seem that the United Nations can play a more assertive role in relation to potentially bloody minority problems since its undertakings are no longer driven by cold war attitudes. Protecting minorities is more than an extension of human rights, it has also become a matter of upholding international peace and security. As strategic conflict has receded, intrastate violence has assumed greater global importance.

Of course, to promote stability and justice under these circumstances rests in the end on building greater support for "natural political communities" as the basis of stable and just states. Given the rising militancy of ethnic and religious minorities in many settings, the alternatives for the future seem to be either the adoption of a creative and humane approach to building frameworks for autonomy or the continued recourse to violent repression. The latter, besides being violative of human rights, is also likely to undermine war-prevention goals, since minorities are often transnationally linked in ways that frustrate attempts to contain their problems within the territorial limits of a single state—as is the case, for example, with the Kurds, Tamils, and Kashmiris. These issues of minority protection and rights are likely to be a major test of the capacity of the United Nations to exert a positive influence on international life in the first decade of the twenty-first century.

The next chapter will examine this idea of collective identity from a different angle, that of non-Western civilizational and religious perspectives in general, and that of the Islamic world in particular. It will also consider the claim that the entire structure of world order, and its evolutionary dynamics in recent centuries, have been biased against such non-Western perspectives. Such an investigation, as we shall see, turns the hypothesis of "a clash of civilization" on its head.

The Geopolitics of Exclusion

8

The Case of Islam

CIVILIZATIONAL PARTICIPATION AS A HUMAN RIGHT

In *Twilight of the Gods* Nietzsche insists that what makes Socrates interesting to the modern mind is not his thought or method, but the extraordinary societal significance for Athens of having taken so seriously such silly and banal ideas. Huntington's clash thesis can be regarded in a similar spirit. What is interesting about the piece is not the argument, as such, which seems both simplistic and implausible, but its extraordinary resonance around the world. No other short essay, even the famous "X" article of George Kennan, has elicited such an intense response. It remains important to ask, "What is this resonance telling us?"

I believe that this resonance is closely related to the interplay of particulars and universals with respect to the normative architecture of the world late in the twentieth century. The emergent importance at this historical moment of *civilizational* identity as a potent political, moral, and psychological force is an aspect of a more multifaceted challenge to the hegemonic, almost monopolistic, dominance of *statist* identity. In fairness to Huntington, his starting point is similarly conceptual, asserting that for the long cycles of human experience, the significant unit of collective identity was something resembling what we now call a civilization rather than that which we label as a state, the latter enjoying prominence, and then preeminence, only in recent centuries. Huntington, along with many others, sees the state as being in a waning phase, but unlike most commentators, he believes the defining emergent reality is not "the global village," "the borderless world," or more dynamically, "globalization," but rather inter-civilizational reality.[1] For Huntington, this reemergence of civilizational identity implies, above all, a reconfiguration of geopolitical patterns of conflict, which in its essence will result in a new world order framework. A less radical, perhaps more reasonable vision, while similarly questioning the intellectual viability of statist conceptions of world order, sees such a global reconfiguration mainly as a result of the significance of global market forces and the rise of nonstate political actors. Such a vision holds that the various dimensions of globalization, especially its economic and cultural dimensions, are of defining importance with regard to superseding a world order system based upon the interaction of sovereign states. This vision does not preclude Huntington's assertion that intercivilizational relations are of ever greater significance for world order thinking, and particularly so with reference to human rights, political ideology, and the future of nationalism. Yet this significance is not necessarily tied to the issue of cultural relativism or to related challenges to universalist claims put forward on behalf of international human rights standards and procedures.

What is central to this inquiry is an exposed deficiency of the human rights enterprise, namely the essentializing of non-Western civilizations as monolithic realities, particularly Islam, and their treatment in a discriminatory fashion with respect to participatory rights. At issue is not the broad array of established human rights, as such, but the posited human right to participate, directly or indirectly, in the authority structures, processes, and practices that together constitute world order. Each element of this perspective requires some explanation and is controversial. A series of questions establishes the domain of inquiry: How has Islam been the victim of discrimination on a global scale? In what respects does such discrimination raise issues that are properly treated as falling within the scope of human rights? And even if it is granted that human rights can be encroached upon at a civilizational level, how can the character of such rights be validated and implemented? Can international law be extended to serve as an effective vehicle for achieving equitable intercivilizational participation in world order structures and processes without eroding its achievements in regulating state-society relations by way of protecting individual human rights? If this category of rights pertains to all that is "human," why should civilizational differentiations be taken into account?

Perhaps an appropriate point of departure in addressing these questions is by reference to what might be called "the geopolitics of exclusion," both with respect to the dynamics of global governance and to those substantive and symbolic issues that seem to be of greatest concern to the Islamic world. By using such terminology, one does not necessarily imply a conspiracy among Western leaders to achieve such exclusionary goals, nor does one claim that a historical examination uncovers a consistent, deliberate pattern of discrimination. Indeed, the implementation of exclusion occurs mostly as a result of what might be labeled "false universalism," a process of depicting the particular and partial as if it were synonymous with the general, not only with respect to substantive outcomes, but more crucially in relation to the processes by which these results are reached. At the risk of entering upon the treacherous terrain of cultural constructivism, one could trace this false universalism mainly to the Enlightenment, with its reliance on decontextualized reason, as embodied in the language, ideas, diplomatic style, experience, and rules of representation that originated in Western Europe and gradually evolved into a global framework of sovereign, secular, territorial states over a period of centuries—a process that is conveniently, yet arbitrarily, linked to the Peace of Westphalia in 1648. This evolution is convincingly depicted by Stephen Toulmin in his book, *Cosmopolis*, which shares the view that the era of statist dominance is gradually coming to an end. Toulmin, however, sees the sequel as being global humanism, rather than an intercivilizational ethos or some more complex tapestry of overlapping and intersecting identities. This latter conception of world order has often been analogized to the multiple, interpenetrating levels of authority associated with medieval Europe.[2]

In effect, the universalism that has been called "false" is a mask worn to obscure Western civilizational hegemony. This mask has been worn so long that it is indistinguishable from the face itself for wearer and beholder alike. As would be expected, such a hegemony is far greater than the sum of its political, economic, and even cultural parts, as it is civilizational—that is, it includes distinctive ideas, memories, beliefs, practices, misconceptions, myths, and symbols that go to the very core of human identity. In contrast, a true universality would acknowledge significant difference, as well as sameness, in constituting a world order based on procedures and norms explicitly designed to ensure equitable participation by each major world civilization.[3] Intercivilizational equality, as a constitutive principle of world order, seems to add a category, as well as a dimension of complexity, to what David Held, Daniele Archibugi, and others have been so usefully describing and advocating under the rubrics of "cosmopolitan democracy" and "cosmopolitan governance."[4]

The point of the present inquiry is not at all to enter into a discussion of the substance of difference, matters of relative merit, or the outer limits of legitimate difference, but only to support the view that the neglect of civilizational participation for Islam has produced a series of partially deformed institutions, practices, and perceptions. It should also be understood that there is an enormous range of intracivilizational differences in Islam that also need to be democratically and nonviolently negotiated as part of a human rights process. The emphasis here is far more modest, and in a sense preliminary: simply that *at this historical juncture* civilizational identity is sufficiently genuine for a sufficient portion of the more than one billion persons on the planet who consider themselves Muslim to be treated as an *essential* category in evaluating the legitimacy of world order structures and processes.[5] Reinforcing this contention is the increasingly articulate expression of grievances and demands on the part of those who affirm their Islamic identity, and those who increasingly adopt a critical stance of normative and emotional distance from the imposed Western structures and processes of world order, while themselves affirming the quest for worldwide peace and justice.[6]

The specific objective of this chapter is to link this analysis more directly to a concern with human rights. The contours of this concern can be briefly outlined: we are in the midst of a period in international history in which the normative architecture of international society has been increasingly expressed by reference to a human rights discourse that combines, somewhat confusingly, ethical, political, and legal perspectives; these perspectives are intertwined in various ways, but more in the form of claims, grievances, and practices than as binding rules and standards. To a large extent, this human rights discourse is unavoidably perceived, with varying degrees of justification and opportunism, as tainted by false universalism and as an expression of Western hegemony, one feature of which has been, and continues to be, the suppression of civilizational identity and difference—particularly Islam, which has historically been perceived as a threat by the West.[7]

The prevalence of the human rights discourse is anchored by the embodiment of the human rights tradition in contemporary international law, primarily by means of a series of declarations and agreements affirmed by states—most notably, the Universal Declaration of Human Rights, the two Covenants of 1966, and a series of regional formulations and conventions addressing such specific concerns as racial discrimination, women, and children. On an *intra*civilizational basis this tradition has been subjected to various kinds of assault, especially by those who affirm Marxist and socialist priorities and who were offended by an overly individualistic conception of rights that included extensive protection of private property rights; the little appreciated—and rarely implemented—reality is that the human rights tradition as entrenched in international law carries forward a compromise between market-oriented individualism and welfare-oriented social democracy.[8]

Additionally, from the beginning of this century there have been imaginative and quite successful efforts, particularly by Latin American jurists, to challenge a series of exploitative and unequal relationships protected by international law in relation to foreign investment, extraterritorial criminal jurisdiction, and interventionary doctrines.[9] Such juridical critiques and innovations were framed as objections to the then prevailing character of interstate, not intercivilizational, relations, especially in the context of interventionary diplomacy and colonialist statecraft. In the 1960s and 1970s this intracivilizational critique from various Third World perspectives was generalized to stress the overall unfairness of the way rights and duties were distributed on a North-South basis, and was politicized within the United Nations, especially the General Assembly, in the form of calls for a "New International Economic Order" that were articulated in a series of declaratory, quasi-legal instruments.[10]

The categories of North and South were very generalized designations, as were the terms *Third World* or *Non-Aligned Movement*, which were reformist references to historical, geographical, and developmental affinities and coalitions, and which did not imply cultural or civilizational solidarity or experience. These normative initiatives designed to promote mainly global economic reform were effectively disregarded as a result of a powerful market-oriented backlash associated with the neoliberal orientation championed in the 1980s by Margaret Thatcher and Ronald Reagan, and with the widening fissures in the Third World that resulted from modernizing strategies that yielded high growth rates and surging export markets for a number of Pacific Rim countries.

What has survived in the 1990s, at least rhetorically, from the normative pressures for a more equitable international economic order was a new notion called "the right to development."[11] Whether this right currently has any operational content is doubtful, and yet important legal scholars have lent support to its validity. Although difficult to demonstrate, it would seem that the status of the right of development has shaped the way the international agenda on such other issues as environment, population, and human rights generally is addressed, at important consciousness-raising UN conferences.[12] However, such efforts to register as a "right" the perceived grievances of disadvantaged nations in relation to existing world order are linked to an inquiry into how to overcome a circumstance of intercivilizational inequity when the claimant is neither individual, minority group, nor state entity, but rather, a civilization itself. These categories, it should be pointed out, are overlapping rather than mutually exclusive identities.

The first truly intercivilizational critique of the prevailing human rights discourse and its world order implications emerged, somewhat surprisingly, from the concerted struggle of indigenous peoples in the 1980s and 1990s.[13] This struggle took shape against a background (and foreground) of exclusion, discrimination, and persecution, even extermination, assimilation, and marginalization—all factors expressive of confusing admixtures of arrogance, racism, and ignorance. These extraordinary efforts of indigenous peoples to protect the remnants of their shared civilizational identity, an identity that was coherent and distinct only in relation to the otherness of modernity, achieved two results of direct relevance to the position taken in this chapter: first of all, it exposed the radical inadequacy of a civilizationally "blind" approach to human rights, by which is meant the utter failure of the modernist instruments of human rights to address in any satisfactory way the claims, values, grievances, and outlooks of indigenous and traditional peoples; and second, transnational activism by indigenous peoples in the last two decades has given rise to an alternative conception of rights that has been put forward after a long process by previously excluded civilizational representatives.

In this regard, a revealing contrast comes to light: this recent authentic expression of indigenous peoples' conception of their rights contrasted with that of earlier mainstream human rights instruments claiming universalism. Also revealing is a comparison between these efforts by indigenous peoples on their own behalf and the paternalistic efforts of the International Labor Organization to set forth a legal framework for the rights of indigenous peoples. Such comparisons confirm the contention that participatory rights are integral to a legitimate political order, as well as to a reliable clarification of grievance, demand, and aspiration.[14] This alternative conception has been developed by indigenous peoples in an elaborate process of normative reconstruction that has involved sustained and often difficult dialogue among the multitude of representatives of indigenous traditional peoples over a period of more than fourteen years, during which time these representatives have come together at the Informal Working Group on the Rights of Indigenous Population, set up under the Human Rights Commission's Sub-Commission on the Prevention of Discrimination and the Protection of Minorities. The Sub-Commission recently issued a Draft Declaration on the Rights of Indigenous Peoples, which is now being considered within the wider UN system. It is doubtful whether this Declaration of the Rights of Indigenous Peoples will be validated by state-centric procedures. In effect, government representatives remain the gatekeepers within the UN system, and it's these heads of state who are upholding the still ascendant false universalism.[15] The resistance being mounted in reaction to this broader, participatory vision of human rights is mainly centered on certain perceived tensions that could result if a right of self-determination were to be legally guaranteed for indigenous peoples. The extent to which this struggle of indigenous peoples succeeds or fails is conceptually and substantively unrelated to this inquiry into Islamic exclusion, except as a concrete example of the surfacing of a different type of intercivilizational challenge within the same approximate historical time interval.[16] Of course, the indigenous peoples' struggle also reinforces the point that unless authentic participation in the rights-creation process occurs, the results are not likely to be genuinely representative and the whole process will be regarded as illegitimate and alien by those who did not participate.

UNDERSTANDING THE GEOPOLITICS OF EXCLUSION

At this point, it seems important to set forth the basic elements of the argument for "normative adjustment" in response to the intercivilizational challenge being mounted from an Islamic perspective. Normative adjustment is understood in two senses: first, it is a reshaping of the human rights discourse to make belated provision for intercivilizational participation on the basis of equality; second, it is a move to legitimize world order by improving the procedures for intercivilizational participation and by establishing better means for equitable civilizational representation in the main authority structures of the world.

Although the wider conceptual and normative concern is one of intercivilizational participation in general, this chapter focuses on the specifics surrounding Islamic exclusion and its implications. Arguably, a parallel inquiry could be made from a Confucian or Hindu or African perspective, as well as from a variety of indigenous peoples' perspectives. In any event, if the primary question is either the existence of a civilizational right to participate or the role of equitable civilizational participation in a legitimate world order, then the wider inquiry is tied to this narrower one that dwells upon Islam. The narrower focus has the advantage of responding to the subjective side of civilizational exclusion in the crucial sense that Islam perceives itself as having been long victimized within the framework of world order, and in turn, is frequently perceived in the West as posing a multidimensional challenge. It is important in light of this adversary intercivilizational interaction to assess whether there appear to be objective grounds for the subjective claims of grievance. It is in this spirit that the following steps in the argument will be taken:

- identifying the psychopolitical sense of grievance and difference that is characteristic of Islam's civilizational self-image in relation to the West and to world order in general;
- a presentation of empirical, yet anecdotal, evidence in support of the view that Islam has been excluded from world order arenas and subjected to discriminatory regimes of control and prohibition;
- an insistence that the combination of perceived grievance and objective grounds provides the basis for "normative adjustment" and the enhancement of the legitimacy of contemporary structures and processes of world order;
- the conclusion that the case for normative adjustment could be sealed by extending human rights to incorporate civilizational participation, initially for the Islamic world, and eventually for any civilizational unit of major stature in the present system of world order.

It is important, at this point, to restate the parameters of this analysis: that the geopolitical exclusion of Islam is real, that it has negative world order consequences, that its rectification would be of benefit to Islam, and that expanding human rights coverage to include civilizational rights of participation provides one, but only one, mode of rectification.

This emphasis upon the deficiencies of the human rights tradition as perceived and appraised from a civilizational perspective is not without potential risks. It might provide indirect, and unintended, support for oppressive and extremist tendencies, religious or political, that wish to avoid external standards of accountability as embodied in human rights treaties and international law. Also, the efforts of domestic opposition movements, intent on promoting democracy and human rights, may be discredited to the extent that the false universalism argument gains ground. In one respect, the flaws of false universalism may be less immediately linked to the well-being of society than are the effects of arbitrary and exclusionary rule and the encouragement given to extremist religious traditions.

How can this dilemma be resolved? One can start by relying on the normative expressions of rights largely evolved in the West but interpreting them through a process of intercivilizational dialogue and legitimation. It is also possible to mediate some of the rights through civilizational filters in such a manner as to situate their authority within the framework of Islamic or other non-Western civilizations; and it is possible to clarify genuinely universal claims that continue to be denied by a reliance on civilizational authority.[17] Prohibitions on cruelty and torture, for example, have widespread multicivilizational roots that can reinforce the conventional claims of international law even as it is being argued that these conventional claims are tainted by the inequitable geopolitical circumstances surrounding their evolution.

These are not abstract concerns. There are a series of ongoing struggles in non-Western countries in which the central national concern is either religious and secular tolerance or democracy and human rights as the basis of opposition to an established order. The analysis that follows, which gives support to a civilizational line of critique, is not meant to lend aid and comfort to oppressive and intolerant social forces in any setting. The intent is, rather, to show that the redress of intercivilizational injustices will over time reinforce the struggles to achieve intracivilizational justice. Such a conviction also reflects the view that the framing of inquiry by exclusive reference to individuals and to sovereign states, as is done in the current human rights context, is not sufficiently sensitive to the new realities of economic globalization and to the shifting character of political identity, which is increasingly focused on ethnic, religious, and cultural factors.

CONTEMPORARY WORLD ORDER VERSUS AN ISLAMIC PERSPECTIVE

There is little doubt that there is a generalized Islamic sense of grievance that overrides the very deep intracivilizational cleavages (on the level of state, class, religious tradition, and geographic region) that currently exist in the Islamic world. Possibly less self-evident is an appreciation that this sense of grievance is coupled with an Islamic civilizational self-image that is capable of providing an alternative normative grounding for world order. The psychological and political confirmation of these assessments can be gleaned from many sources and is sufficiently established that it doesn't need elaborate documentation.[18] The nature of these collective Islamic grievances is perhaps best expressed by Ahmet Davutoglu in a passage from *Civilizational Transformation and the Muslim World*:

> There has been a tendency in recent years in western political and intellectual centers to misrepresent Muslim societies as incongruous elements in the international order. The issue of Salman Rushdie and the discussions of the Islamic dress code in France and Britain have provoked historical prejudices against Islam. The mass media has been extensively used to strengthen this imagination. Lastly, in the Gulf crisis, although the other front was also supported by many Muslim-populated states, Saddam has been misrepresented as the symbol of the increasing threat of Islamic fundamentalism.[19]

The point here is not to evaluate these perceptions of misrepresentation, but to consider such an understanding as typical of perceptions in the Islamic world. In a similarly useful passage, Davutoglu extends this sense of grievance to the functioning of world order:

> [T]he Muslim masses are feeling insecure in relation to the functioning of the international system because of the double standards in international affairs. The expansionist policy of Israel has been tolerated by the international system. The *Intifada* has been called a terrorist activity while the mass rebellions of East Europe [*sic*] have been declared as the victory of freedom. There was no serious response against the Soviet military intervention in Azerbaijan in January 1990 when hundreds of Azeris were killed while all Western powers reacted against Soviet intervention in the Baltic republics. The international organizations which are very sensitive to the rights of small minorities in Muslim countries, did not respond against the sufferings of the Muslim minorities in India, the former Yugoslavia, Bulgaria, Kashmir, Burma, etc. The atomic powers in some Muslim countries like Pakistan and Kazakhstan have been declared a danger when such weapons have been accepted as the internal affairs of other states such as Israel and India. Muslims who make up about 25 percent of the world's population, have no permanent member in the Security Council and all appeals from the Muslim World are being vetoed by one of the permanent members. The Muslim masses have lost their confidence in the international system as neutral problem-solver after the experiences of the last decade.[20]

Again, it should be emphasized that it is not the accuracy, or even the reasonableness, of such assertions that is being argued (although the overall indictment seems accurate and reasonable), it is the extent to which they crystallize the collective Islamic perspective.

The deeper argument, of course, moves beyond rhetorical criticism to the claim that Western civilization as the dominant force in international life is having a destructive impact and that Islam, properly understood, presents a constructive alternative. Davutoglu also presents this case clearly, arguing that Western-style economic globalization is in the process of destroying the other "authentic cultures and civilizations" that together constitute world order.[21] In effect, Davutoglu argues that the Islamic recovery from a long period of suppression, culminating in the colonial era, offers the world a strong and coherent alternative to what he calls "the modernist paradigm."[22] In essence, then, the foundational premise of the argument here is an evolving Islamic self-image—first, as the aggrieved claimant of civilizational rights, and second, as a potential contributor to the emancipatory project of an ethically (and civilizationally) enhanced world order. In effect, in their more assertive expression, Islam and its proponents are committed to the rescue of the West (and others) from the calamity of modernism.[23]

ASSESSING ISLAM'S GRIEVANCES

Accepting the insistence of influential anthropologists that all knowledge is "situated knowledge," that is, reflecting the experience and outlook of the observer, and eschewing any pretension of an Olympian position above the fray, it still seems possible and useful to evaluate the reasonableness of Islam's sense of grievance and significant difference as it affects the character of human rights claims at a global level. Indeed, such an assessment underlies both the critique of false universalism and the argument favoring the incorporation of rights of civilizational participation into the discourse and protective framework of international law.

There is little doubt that much of the recent discussion of Islam and the West, whether in the form of journalistic portrayals or academic writings, is afflicted with orientalist stereotypes that validate hostile behavioral and policy responses. Since the globalizing hegemony of the West tilts this debate, especially by its dominance of mass media, there is a strong disposition to perceive Islam as disposed toward violence and extremism, driven to terrorist action by hostility toward the West and Western values. This perception was consolidated by the media glare directed at Ayatollah Khomeini's Islamic revolution in Iran during its most militant early phases, climaxing with the hostage ordeal in the American Embassy in Tehran, which dragged on for many months until it was resolved in January 1981. This prevailing perceptual framework helps explain the extent to which the literature on Islam's relationship to the West is preoccupied with the question of whether Islam does or does not pose a threat. Even the writings most sensitive to the Islamic reality (Esposito, Fuller & Lesser) seek mainly to reassure the West that Islam is not as militant as is often presented, that even political Islam is heterogeneous and is not necessarily aggressively disposed toward Western interests, and that it is important for its own strategic interests that the West not convert the Islamic threat into a self-fulfilling prophecy. What these moderating Western perspectives tend not to do, except by way of acknowledging the historical extent of prior Western encroachment and abuse, is to examine the plausibility and structured character of Islamic grievances and the desirability of a world order reconstructed to accommodate intercivilizational identities and aspirations.

The validity of the main grievances enumerated by Davutoglu and others can be briefly assessed as follows:

Participation in the United Nations System

The Muslim world comprises more than one billion adherents spread across more than forty-five countries, yet no permanent member of the Security Council is part of the Islamic world, and in most proposals for UN reform, calls for the expansion of the Security Council usually do not propose rectification. This, to be sure, partly reflects the statist and Eurocentric origins of the United Nations at the end of World War II. It may also reflect the failure of Islamic countries to press harder for representation of this character in the most symbolically important organ of the United Nations. But the impression of exclusion is reinforced by the realization that none of the secretary generals of the organization to date have been of Muslim faith, and very few of the important specialized agencies have been headed by a Muslim. Again this can be explained, in part, by the contention that officials are selected on the basis of secular criteria of merit and political support, not because of ethnic or religious identity. Yet when combined with other factors, there would be reasonable grounds for believing that Islamic participation could make a difference with respect to the role of the United Nations on such issues as Palestinian self-determination and the status of Jerusalem, the approach to international terrorism, and the maintenance of the nuclear nonproliferation regime.

The Bosnian diplomatic and peace process can also be viewed as one that denies the Islamic world a sense of equitable participation: each of the factions except for the main victims of atrocity and aggression, the Bosnian Muslims, were represented in high-profile diplomacy by an external actor with corresponding civilizational ties;[24] Turkey, a steadfast member of the Western alliance, and the only European state with an Islamic identity, although highly secularized at the level of the ruling elites, was not included in the "contact group" of countries with a special role in the peace process, while Russia, with less of an organic or geographic link to the conflict, was included. In isolation, this pattern in Bosnia might not warrant comment, but as part of the larger picture, it does seem to add some confirming evidence of a geopolitics of exclusion.

Double Standards

Here again it is difficult to circumvent the subjectivity of interpretive standards. Nevertheless, the orientation of the media and of United States foreign policy has seemed to produce consistent support for actors pursuing goals inimical to Islamic interests, as well as opposition or indifference to issues of major symbolic and substantive concern to Islamic interests.[25] To varying degrees the Arab-Israeli conflict has been the dominant paradigm for many years, fostering an impression that Israeli violence against Palestinian refugees and neighboring states constitutes generally acceptable acts of war and expressions of security policy, while Palestinian violence is treated as "terrorism" of a character that undermines whatever political and moral claims may exist to support the Palestinian struggle. Similar impressions of double standards have arisen in Bosnia, Chechnya, and Kashmir, making it seem probable that if the identities of victim and perpetrator had been reversed, the international response would have been altered. Such a pattern exists, and although each instance can be partially explained by other factors such as deference to the coercive power of a territorially sovereign state, or the infeasibility of challenging major states acting within their own geographical zone of dominance, the cumulative trend in relation to crisis situations, as well as the selective reliance on international law to condemn and condone, gives the accusation of double standards a rather strong air of validity.

A Discriminatory Nonproliferation Regime for Nuclear Arms

Aside from China, the declared nuclear weapons states are Western in orientation, and claim a continuing right and intention to retain possession of this weaponry of mass destruction, and even to proceed with further development. At the same time, states with genuine security concerns are being denied, to the extent possible, access to such weaponry. But even this dual structure is not being implemented in a uniform way. Communist states (North Korea) and Islamic countries (Iraq, Iran, Libya, and Pakistan) are the object of strong nonproliferation efforts, while the acquisition and continuing development of nuclear weapons in Israel are completely ignored, and according to some sources, deliberately facilitated.[26] The media reinforces this impression by writing about Pakistan's acquisition of nuclear weapons in terms of the threat of an "Islamic bomb," even though Pakistan's motivation is clearly directed at offsetting India's military and nuclear threat.

No serious journalist would dare write about a "Jewish bomb" or a "Confucian bomb" or a "Hindu bomb." The resulting impression is clear: civilizational identity does count, but only negatively, and only if it is Islamic. Such a double standard, as reasonably perceived from an Islamic perspective, is taken as irrefutable proof of an anti-Islamic structure of world order. Again there are extenuating circumstances, ranging from Israel's isolated and endangered situation (a situation, for that matter, that would apply to North Korea and to several other states seeking to possess a nuclear option?) to the Western impression that there is an Islamic threat that could materialize in a dangerous way if backed by nuclear arms. Nevertheless, the implementation of the global nonproliferation regime appears to have an anti-Islamic component.[27] This pattern of perception persists despite India's decision to test nuclear weapons in May 1998, which inevitably led to Pakistani tests shortly thereafter.

Punitive Peace

It is worth contrasting the way in which Serbia and Iraq have been treated in the early 1990s after cessation of hostilities, lifting sanctions, and rapid restoration of normalcy in the instance of Serbia as compared to intrusive intervention and the maintenance of sanctions that are wellknown to have caused prolonged great suffering and loss of life to the poorest sectors of Iraqi society without contributing to the downfall of Saddam Hussein's regime.[28] Janna Nolan points out that the West's sustained effort to inspect and disable Iraq's military infrastructure, especially its weapons of mass destruction, has "some parallels to the Allied program to disarm Germany after World War I."[29] The failure of the Versailles punitive approach led to the abandonment of an imposition of humiliating and punitive conditions in the wake of military victory partly because it was seen as contributing to the rise of fascism, but now such an approach has been resurrected, mainly by unilateral action, against Iraq, and even extended in certain respects to Iran. There seems good grounds, then, for regarding such policy approaches to countries in the Islamic world as aspects of a broader pattern of initiatives that follow from the geopolitics of exclusion. Even the language of containment, central to the West's posture vis-à-vis the Soviet Union, has been adapted and invoked in relation to Iran and Iraq. This latter policy is explained by Washington policymakers under the rubric of "double containment."

Policymaking and Participation in the World Economy

As with the permanent membership of the Security Council, the Group of Seven, the directorate of the world economy, includes no Islamic state. Would not Indonesia, Malaysia, or Saudi Arabia have as good a claim for membership as Canada or Italy? In an era of globalization, with the Asia-Pacific region in the ascendancy, it would seem reasonable to expect greater representation in economic power structures for Islamic countries. The same pattern of exclusion also pertains to the Bretton Woods institutions, which are consistently administered by officials drawn from the West. A further source of suspicion is the drastic international response to the disclosures of fraud on the part of the Bank of Credit and Commerce International (BCCI), whose immediate, forced dissolution represented the demise of the only international bank with primary Islamic funding and direction.[30]

Responses to Terrorist Incidents

There does seem to be hostility toward Islam on the part of global media and in Western governmental responses to major incidents of terrorism. Such a pattern can be discerned in the differences with which the U.S. government responded to the World Trade Center bombing in New York City on February 26, 1993, and the bombing of the Alfred P. Murrah Federal Building in Oklahoma City on April 19, 1995. Perhaps most revealing was the reflex of suspicion directed toward political Islam, despite the timing of the Oklahoma explosion, which coincided with the anniversary of the Waco, Texas, raid on the Branch Davidian cult—an event that was known to have greatly agitated rightist militias and led several of them to contemplate retaliation. Once it was determined that the perpetrators were white American extremists, however, the U.S. government's reaction to the Oklahoma bombing was to investigate whether excessive force had been used in the Waco raid, to dismiss several of the officials who seemed responsible for staging the raid, to pay compensation for excessive federal force used in another attack on a survivalist family in Montana, and to strengthen international laws on terrorism. In contrast, the prosecutorial strategy in the World Trade Center bombing relied on a tenuous conspiracy theory that would cast the widest possible net to ensnare even those indirectly involved in the Trade Center bombing, especially the Islamic religious figure, Sheik Omar Abdel Rahman, was indicted and prosecuted. In the Oklahoma City bombing, however, the indications are that the U.S. government limited indictments to those individuals accused of being perpetrators or accomplices. The prosecutor in that case also agreed to move the trial from Oklahoma in deference to the defendants, while a similar motion for a change of venue was denied the Islamic defendants in New York, where the atmosphere was probably even more volatile.

Stigmatization of States as "Outlaw" or "Rogue"

The stigmatization of several sovereign states as "outlaw" or "rogue," especially by the United States Government, has again seemed to frame the Islamic world as the main irritant to world order, putting it in the company of such aging Communist regimes as Cuba and North Korea. Libya, Iran, and Iraq have been consistently treated as outlaws, with varying degrees of justification, but always with the underlying message that an Islamic orientation, if militant, will be dealt with as aggressively as possible, while troublesome non-Islamic states, such as Burma in recent years and South Africa during most of the apartheid period, are dealt with by way of "constructive engagement."[31]

The Right to Democratic Governance

After the cold war, the West proclaimed its commitment to the spread of democratic governance, which meant especially the encouragement of constitutionalism in the form of multiparty elections. Yet its concern with the spread of political Islam apparently led it to overlook the 1992 coup in Algeria that deprived Islamicists of an anticipated electoral victory.[32]

The Unevenness of Compassion

Media treatment of suffering in the Muslim world tends to be abstract, general, and scant, if given at all, and is dwarfed by repeated inquiry into the tactics and mentality of Islamic extremism. Little attention is given to understanding the moral and political pressures that might explain the desperation that induces such highly publicized extremist behavior. The support given by Palestinian refugees and some anti-Western governments (e.g., Libya and Iran) to horrifying acts of terrorism is appropriately noted, but not the Israeli calls for ethnically based vengeance (random attacks on Palestinians, collective punishment, chants of "death to the Arabs!"). These are admittedly delicate, complicated matters of assessment, yet the imbalance seems clear. Just as the small statistical advantage enjoyed by the house in gambling casinos ultimately yields immense profits, so a seemingly trivial imbalance in the appreciation and publicizing of justice claims can ultimately translate into a decisive, even overwhelming power to sway public opinion in favor of Western biases.[33]

My contention is that Islamic perspectives have not been equitably represented in key authority structures and processes of world order, which helps to account for the impression and actuality of an anti-Islamic bias in addressing controversial issues on the global agenda. It seems clear that if civilizational rights of participation existed, such an impression and its reality would be diminished, and likely, the policies produced would be more balanced and would be perceived as such from Islamic perspectives, if assessed on an intercivilizational basis. Such an analysis is minimalist in the sense that it does not give weight to the antimodernist, antisecularist, antiglobalization dimensions of the Islamic critique of world order; nor does it address the contention that the Islamic model, which balances community values more evenly against individualist claims, would contribute to a more stable foundation for social relations around the world and increase prospects for intercivilizational understanding.

THE DIFFICULT CHALLENGE OF NORMATIVE ADJUSTMENT

Normative adjustment implies a mutually reinforcing combination of moral, political, and legal developments, combined with supportive historical circumstances. In concrete terms that relate to present world order, such an adjustment refers to alterations in patterns of practice and modes of participation in authority structures and processes. It means addressing reasonable grievances. More specifically, in the setting of this analysis, it means correcting the grievances outlined in the prior section. With reference to Islam it means conferring and safeguarding rights of participation based upon civilizational identity. As such, this particular normative adjustment cannot be effectively achieved within the traditional framework of statism, even an enlightened statism that confers rights more equally on individuals, minorities, groups, and peoples.[34] To date, it has been indigenous peoples who have met with the most success in transcending the Westphalian statist model and in achieving recognition, both symbolic and substantive, as a distinct civilization.[35]

Even given these successes, however, the prospects for successful normative adjustment with respect to overcoming what has been called the geopolitics of exclusion are cloudy at best. For one thing, there is as yet no clear consensus that such exclusion is occurring, and those aggrieved have so far not chosen to present their grievances in these terms. For another, there are strong policy grounds on the part of those social forces that benefit from false universalism to resist claims premised on civilizational identity and difference. Such resistance tends to be particularly strong when recognition of such identity would seem to benefit Islam. Finally, Islam is far from united in its self-definition with respect to normative adjustment, with some portions of the Muslim world accepting the premises of globalization, secularization, and a statist world order.

The history of normative adjustments is varied and highlights above all the intertwined role of morality, politics, and law. Particularly salient milestones include the prohibition of the international slave trade, the recognition of the right to self-determination, the process of decolonization, the antiapartheid campaign, the recognition of genocide as a distinct crime, and the realization of civil and political rights. Each instance forms a complex narrative that generates a wide range of appraisals, but each discloses a degree of normative adjustment that resulted in some change in authoritative language and practices. It is illuminating to consider projects of normative adjustment that resulted in substantial failure: the attempt to define aggression, the attempt to establish a collective security system, the attempt to bring to the fore economic and social rights.

The normative adjustment that is appropriate for Islam depends on the character of the grievances and the remedies being sought. Clearly, effective normative adjustment on behalf of Islam must begin with a more equitable participation in authority structures (the United Nations, the administration of the world economy) and an acknowledgment of civilizational identity. Of course, even if such a position were to be generally accepted, difficult problems remain in defining the specifics of representation and the contours of civilization units. Despite these obstacles, certain favorable conditions exist with respect to the prospect for normative adjustment: the reality of an Islamic resurgence and sense of grievance; the established reasonableness of the core grievances; the political interest of non-Islamic leaders to avoid a hostile intercivilizational encounter and the successful precedent set by indigenous peoples.

WHY HUMAN RIGHTS? WHY CIVILIZATIONAL RIGHTS?

The last half of the twentieth century has been characterized by an increasingly prominent process of legitimation of grievances and the subsequent recognition of rights. This has occurred generally in relations between individuals and their governments, and then with respect to more specific categories of claims relating to group discrimination, children, women, environment, and even food, peace, life, and development. In the current context, however, recognition of these human rights all too seldom translates into behavioral implementation and enforcement. Invoking human rights to alter conditions of perceived and actual injustice in the world involves all of the ambiguities and frustrations of "soft law."[36]

The main argument for suggesting a civilizational level of protection for human rights at this stage of history is largely based on the empirical circumstances that have been described, and which have given rise to serious claims of grievance and pose dangers of conflict. The articulation of a right of civilizational participation on behalf of Islam would itself be an enlightening educational process. An additional benefit would be to challenge the false universalism of globalization and suggest an alternative in the form of an intercivilizational world order that combines the ecological and biological conditions of unity with the civilizational realities of difference and self-definition.

The advent of such an intercivilizational world order would not come without costs. It could weaken democratic forces in existing Islamic states seeking to uphold a secular conception of relations between religion and the state, and to protect the freedoms and autonomy of individuals. In this regard, even if the human rights framework deserves criticism on a civilizational level, it is still valuable, even indispensable, to the struggles being carried out at the level of the sovereign state in such countries as Turkey and Egypt. This tension is essentially a creative one, that weighs the need to assert the relevance of current human rights norms against the need to repair the human rights framework to overcome gross Western biases. To accord Islam such a civilizational status would be of great symbolic and substantive benefit in the current world atmosphere, and it could provide the basis for establishing the first true universalism in human history.

While such concerns about civilizational rights remain largely conceptual in nature, the challenges posed by extreme abuses of human rights, especially genocide, are brutally concrete. In the face of such wide-scale atrocities, there is an evolving transcivilizational commitment to override the pretensions of sovereignty in the face of genocide. In these circumstances, the deficiencies of world order are brought to light by the failure of the organized international society to act either preventively or reactively to episodes of genocide. The tragic experiences of Bosnia and Rwanda in the early 1990s, as will be seen in the next chapter, vividly exposed this gap between promise and performance.

The Unmet Challenges of Genocide in Bosnia and Rwanda 9

DEPICTING THE CHALLENGE

Unquestionably, the epicenter of Robert Jay Lifton's influential and highly significant scholarly oeuvre is a preoccupation with genocide, and particularly with what he identifies as "the genocidal mentality." Whether it is the Holocaust, Hiroshima, the nuclear threat, the Vietnam War, or even the Armenian ordeal in Turkey, Lifton's psychohistorical inquiries have exposed the main dimensions of the genocidal phenomenon, explaining how both its architects and perpetrators go about their bloody business and how a complicit population removes itself from real knowledge, and hence from any realization of their own interventionary responsibility. Lifton's most provocative and threatening, yet also most valuable, finding is the dual reality that those who commit genocide are not far removed from the rest of us and that all of us, by societal circumstance or by drawing down a numbing curtain over our feelings, are actual or potential culprits. In essence, Lifton's work imparts the disquieting news that there is a fearsome normalcy about genocide that makes efforts to portray its occurrence as abnormal deviance profoundly misleading, and worse, that encourages complacency.

Lifton's position is that a scholarly inquiry into the roots of genocide in human personality and social structure is indispensable for purposes of explanation, prevention, and opposition, and that a moralistic denunciation on its own is an empty gesture that obscures the pervasive and continuing potential for genocide to erupt almost anywhere on the societal landscape of humanity. Lifton's studies of genocide are not at all intended to reconcile us to its occurrence, but quite the opposite. Lifton's abiding concern is to explicate evil in its most extreme forms, with the intention of identifying the menace and protecting against the shared human susceptibility to engage in genocidal behavior under certain conditions. Lifton believes strongly in the human responsibility to avoid direct or indirect participation in genocide, and seeks to clarify this human responsibility whenever genocide presents itself in our world. To grasp Lifton's overall political message, then, is to acknowledge the pervasiveness of a genocidal threat, and simultaneously to insist on the ethical imperative of active resistance by all nonviolent means. It is important to realize that our engagement with genocide can often involve the unwillingness to confront its reality through the psychodynamics of denial, which Lifton associates with "numbing," a condition of passivity that is both deliberately induced to manage the citizenry and easily embraced by citizens to avoid the discomfort of deciding what to do about a genocidal challenge.

Given this background, then, it is hardly surprising that Lifton should have been so profoundly challenged during the past several years by the collapse of the Yugoslav state and the ensuing ordeal of Bosnia. In his introduction to Zlatko Dizdarevic's *Sarajevo: A War Journal*, Lifton illuminates this challenge: Genocide, by definition, is an ethical scandal. But the added scandal of Bosnia is "the whole world's viewing genocide and doing no more than pretending to combat it. . . . We have betrayed both the Bosnians and our own more decent and responsible selves. More than that, in tolerating— and periodically facilitating—visible genocide, we have to a degree entered into a genocidal mentality."[1] Indeed, Lifton contends that unlike Germany in the 1930s, when the Nazis went to great lengths to hide their genocidal designs and behavior, in Bosnia there has been "full knowledge of the genocide," as "nothing was hidden from us," thereby putting all of us in "a new category in our relation to genocide, that of informed bystanders." Although Lifton's preoccupation with the genocidal aspect of the Bosnian conflict is articulated in universalistic language, there is, at least implicitly, an intensifying rationale for response, given the conflict's civilizational locus in Europe, reminding us all of the pledge "never again," a pledge made in various forms by representative civic voices in the liberal democracies, possibly as a partial atonement for the abject passivity of the West during the rise of Hitler and Naziism. Without taking account of the European locale of Bosnia, it is difficult to explain the relative absence of concern about such more unambiguous instances of recurrent recourse to genocide in Rwanda, as well as in relation to such earlier genocidal episodes in Cambodia, Burundi, and East Timor.[2]

Despite this seemingly depraved complicity, Lifton observes that "[h]ere and there, Americans have been able to transmute their psychological confusion into a constructive stand for multilateral intervention in Bosnia." And somewhat more explicitly, Lifton feels that it is "never too late to change course," by "remobilizing our world organization, and ourselves in serving it, and empowering it to make use of its own charter to intervene to stop the killing and establish conditions for democratic behavior and sustained peace."[3] Lifton essentially calls for intervention, under the auspices of the United Nations, of sufficient magnitude to stop the genocide. The political imperative occasioned by genocide, then, is to draw a clear line between official policies that merely pretend to respond to genocide and those that promote "constructive intervention," a coercive course of action that is intended to have a reasonable prospect of ending the genocide.

It seems appropriate to relate more personally at this point to Lifton's approach on these matters. I have over the years been deeply and variously instructed by Robert Lifton's theoretical and empirical work on genocide, including his strong appeal for responsive action based on conscience, historical memory, and species solidarity. But while fully subscribing to this framework of analysis I have had difficulty sharing the specific application of the approach to the actualities of the Bosnian tragedy. It is now my intention to explore here some of my reasons for taking a different path; my aim is not to reargue the case against "intervention," but to depict what must be done if genocide of the Bosnian sort is, indeed, to be effectively opposed.[4]

This divergence from a close and trusted friend is inevitably disturbing, especially given a long previous experience of convergence. During the latter stages of the Vietnam War Robert Lifton and I were comrades in the civic struggle to end America's involvement in the quickest possible manner, with the least additional violence, death, and destruction. We were particularly appalled by the war's cumulative tendency to generate atrocities against Vietnamese civilians, and regarded that tendency as a direct consequence of ideas and doctrines that underpinned the American military effort in Vietnam.[5] In that setting we were united in our opposition to the American intervention in Vietnam, and called for its end with acts of civil resistance and expressions of solidarity with those who would not participate in the killing. In this regard, anti-interventionism united progressive opinion and activism throughout the cold war era. What has been striking ever since the Gulf War is the extent to which interventionism has divided the moderate left. Add to this the fact that the Soviet collapse, combined with the spread of a market-oriented ethos of political and economic development, has caused widespread confusion and disarray in progressive ranks, and this condition may help explain why the intervention debate within progressive circles has been so acrimonious and disappointingly inconclusive.

What is the root cause of this division? Is it a failure to agree on the facts? Differing moral assessments? Divergent political approaches? The disagreement, in essence, relates mainly to the different ways that moral imperatives and prescribed political action are combined in practice by complementary yet distinct styles of thought in the search for a proposed course of action. It is a difference between what can be called morally conditioned political advocacy and politically conditioned moral advocacy. In the former instance the mandate to act is derived directly from the severity of the suffering being inflicted, while in the latter the mandate to act is shaped primarily by geopolitical constraints and the political will of potential intervenors—particularly the U.S. government, the United Nations, the main governments of Europe, and the various European regional actors (NATO, OSCE, WEU). In the case of Bosnia, the essential question was: Were these actors ever reasonably capable of mounting a morally conditioned constructive intervention against genocide?

The fact is that these governmental and intergovernmental actors are abstractions, not persons, and that the officials who shape the policy-forming climate are diverse and to varying degrees receptive to citizen pressures based on moral appeals, and further that in a democratic society, citizens should normally exhaust available channels of persuasion before writing off the government as unalterably opposed to the policy initiatives being urged, in this instance intervention to stop genocide. It is also clear that civic encouragement for initiatives to prevent genocide, such as the securing of safe havens in Bosnia, was an entirely justifiable, politically plausible, humane, timely, and constructive line of policy advocacy. Yet such a course of action was still not sufficient to challenge and stop the genocide in Bosnia. In reality, an interventionary option was never seriously proposed in relation to the struggle going on in Bosnia. Regardless of subsequent events, it remains important for many reasons to understand why this was so. Such an understanding is indispensable if we are to commit ourselves to work for the ideological and institutional reforms that might yet make the twenty-first century unsafe for future practitioners of genocide.

WHY INTERVENTION TO PREVENT GENOCIDE WAS NEVER A GENUINE OPTION FOR BOSNIA

There is always an element of uncertainty in asserting what would have happened if this or that had been done in the past: What would the Bosnian Serbs have done if the gun emplacements surrounding Sarajevo had been bombed by NATO in 1993? or if the safe haven at Gorazde had been protected in March 1994? or if the arms embargo had been lifted or never imposed? There is reason to believe that "shallow" intervention of this character would not have significantly altered Serb goals or behavior, nor would Serb resistance to such measures have led the United Nations, NATO, or major states to commit themselves to a deeper intervention of sufficient scale. More likely, the reverse dynamic—withdrawal of any external presence and quite possibly an expanded war/genocide zone—would have ensued.[6]

Such a pessimistic assessment seems to find ample corroboration in similarly restrained responses in places like Somalia, Rwanda, and a number of other humanitarian disaster areas. This pattern discloses some willingness to act in a mitigating role, but not to take on the far more formidable task of political reconstruction in the face of entrenched, indigenous resistance. It is possible to contend that the 1994 U.S./UN intervention in Haiti undercuts this line of interpretation; it also raises the question as to whether Serb capitulation would have resulted from a tougher international stand on Bosnia early on in the conflict. For a variety of reasons, the Haiti intervention did not provoke resistance, and therefore the depth of the commitment was never tested. That said, there is virtually no reason to believe—given the ultranationalist passions unleashed in Bosnia, as well as its history and regional power rivalries—that such an intervention in Bosnia would have met with similar passivity.[7]

This matter of political preconditions in relation to intervention in Bosnia needs to be examined in light of past occasions in which the persistence of genocide was successfully challenged: the liberation of Nazi death camps; the Vietnamese liberation of Cambodia from the Khmer Rouge in 1979; India's invasion of East Pakistan in 1971 resulting in the formation of Bangladesh. In each instance the effort was massive, engaging the maximum energies of the intervening side, and in each case, emancipating the victim population was definitely incidental to the main interventionary goals and the pursuit of strategic security interests. In other words, sufficient intervention, given the structure of world order and the mind-set of political leaders is *always* interest-based, never values-driven. In these terms, the tragedy of Bosnia was that its survival as a humanistic, multiethnic political entity was perceived as principally a matter of values, and only peripherally as a strategic goal.[8]

There are several conclusions that emerge from this analysis of the challenge of genocide in Bosnia:

1. External actors (both governmental and intergovernmental) did not perceive their interests to be seriously engaged in former Yugoslavia, and thus were never prepared to commit to anything but shallow intervention.

2. The main realist rationale for even shallow intervention in Bosnia, aside from public outcries that "something be done," was the early termination and, above all, the containment of the conflict, including the outflow of refugees, and not the prevention of genocide, or even the prevention of aggression.

3. The humanitarian element in the unfolding diplomacy of shallow intervention was mainly a response to "the CNN factor," its intent being merely to minimize civilian suffering but not to undo the effects of ethnic cleansing, nor did this policy embody the view that genocidal policies must not be allowed to succeed or that the survival of secularism in the former Yugoslavia was a strategic interest for Europe and the United States.

4. Shallow intervention never appeared to have had any serious, credible prospect of altering Serbian goals or conduct in Bosnia, although Serb adjustments in timetable and tactics might have resulted from additional initiatives designed to challenge their project.

5. Deeper intervention to prevent genocide and aggression would have required a major commitment of resources and occupying forces for a period of uncertain duration, which never became a possibility because of the absence of perceived strategic interests.

6. Challenging genocide by interventionary diplomacy is unlikely to occur unless such a challenge is entwined in larger strategic interests; such a condition seems unlikely to change until political leaders are ideologically reoriented to regard moral, legal, and humanitarian concerns as integral to the pursuit of national interests in a globalized world order.

This assessment, given uncertainties of facts and the unresolvable character of "what would have happened if," is necessarily contingent and conjectural. Only a minimal conclusion is possible. It does seem safe to conclude, however, that an appropriate intervention in Bosnia, in the words of David Rieff, "would have been neither cheap nor easy," and that to claim otherwise is to engage in "loose talk" inconsistent with the past history of interventionary diplomacy.[9]

MEETING THE CHALLENGE OF GENOCIDE IN BOSNIA AND ELSEWHERE

If a sufficient intervention is not possible, what can be done to reduce suffering and to work toward the effective elimination of genocide from human experience? More specifically, what can be done within current political space to go beyond the prevailing politics of gesture? And what can be done ideologically and structurally to protect humanity against genocide in the future? Given the current climate of politically conditioned moral advocacy, emphasis should be placed on overcoming the political obstacles that block the implementation of widely shared moral imperatives.[10] Also, each specific genocidal context presents its own problems and opportunities relevant for the formation of policy, making broad generalizations inappropriate. Yet from a context-specific analysis of the situation in Bosnia emerge a number of broader implications.

Democratic Empowerment
The politics of gesture in relation to Bosnia emphasized a mixture of humanitarian assistance for civilian victims with a heavy Western diplomatic effort that was prepared to ratify most of the results of ethnic cleansing and to treat Serbian political and military leaders as the legitimate representatives

of their people, despite their role in committing severe violations of the laws of war and of the Genocide Convention. Such an approach is morally incoherent, yet it is reflective of the geopolitical priorities at stake, which are to produce a settlement that will end the violence, thereby avoiding any spillover into other parts of the Balkans, as well as to reduce pressures associated with large numbers of refugees. But it is not responsive to the essential challenge of genocide, either by way of prevention or accountability.

In this regard, transnational links with local democratic, antigenocidal social forces throughout the former Yugoslavia, whether Serb, Muslim, or Croatian, could be of great importance in reshaping the dynamics of self-determination. Since intervention from without is unavailable or severely problematic, if intervention from within and from below could help reverse the reductive effect of treating criminal rulers as legitimate leaders. Helsinki Citizens and the Campaign for Peace and Democracy have been creatively experimenting with this type of transnational civic diplomacy, drawing on the experience of the 1980s, when West European and North American peace forces joined with dissidents in Eastern Europe and the Soviet Union in successful indigenous efforts to promote human rights and democracy, weaken governing elites, erode their legitimacy, and even undermine their will to rule. The struggle against genocide needs to become part of the agenda of what is being called "cosmopolitan democracy," which supplements the role of states with transnational association of citizens joined by normative commitments rather than by self-serving intergovernmental alliances.[11]

Criminal Accountability

It is also crucial to mobilize public opinion behind efforts to implement existing norms and procedures prohibiting genocide. The Security Council, in Resolution 808 (February 22, 1993), responding to pressures to act, authorized the establishment of a war crimes tribunal to address crimes associated with the wars in former Yugoslavia; it was later expanded to encompass the killing fields of Rwanda. It can be argued that such an initiative is ill-conceived, given the absence of other elements of an interventionary diplomacy, and tends to interfere with efforts to moderate the conflict through a negotiated settlement.[12] Yet in its capacity to limit the authority of states and political movements to engage in genocidal violence, the pedagogical and punitive potential of the war crimes approach is considerable, and has already rekindled long dormant moves to establish a permanent international criminal court under UN auspices. Such an institutional innovation will not occur in a useful form unless it is promoted vigorously by transnational democratic forces as an essential ingredient of an emergent global civil society. In effect, although such a tribunal was established in an atmosphere of overall ambivalence, it can at this stage be used at the very least to document the horrors of genocide and to provide a measure of solace to survivors. It also strengthens an international consensus to take steps to create an independent enforcement mechanism that is autonomous and not subject to the calculus of geopolitics.

Globalizing Citizenship

The relationship of individuals to governance remains primarily bounded by the limits of territorial sovereignty. Yet the economic, political, and cultural matrix of human experience is essentially planetary in scope. At present, identity patterns are being reshaped in contradictory ways, moving toward the realities of globalization and affirming the particularities of religious and ethnic identity—both tendencies that withdraw authority from the state as the focus for identity, community, and allegiance. Given the growing intermingling of peoples on the planet, it is especially important to oppose those exclusivist images of identity that underlie genocidal impulses. It is not necessary from this perspective to support secularism, but it is necessary to conceive of citizenship and civic responsibilities as extending to the protection of all peoples from any concerted effort at abuse.

Such an ethos, if extended to governing coalitions, would overcome narrow realist worldviews, which conceive of interests territorially and materially, and which draw a sharp distinction between interests and values. The mind-set being proposed for the future would conceive of mutual tolerance among peoples as a primary global interest and would help to close the gap between interests and values.

CONCLUSION

It may still be too early to draw definitive conclusions about the genocidal features of the Bosnian conflict, but there is little doubt that much can be learned from the failure of Europe, the United Nations, and the United States to do more to stop genocide. If the international political community is to be better prepared to prevent genocide, transnational social forces will have to make a greater effort. Liberal democracies and intergovernmental institutions can only be helpful in this effort if pushed hard from below; to rely solely on governmental actors to carry out an antigenocide campaign, whether in Bosnia or in general, is to misunderstand the pattern of international relations over the course of the last two hundred years.

In the following chapter, the focus on genocide will be shifted somewhat to interrogate the underlying causal role of globalization. To what extent is globalization responsible either for inducing the sort of ethnic extremism that leads to genocide or for eroding the collective political will to act in response?

The Challenge of 10
Genocidal Politics in
an Era of Globalization

HUMAN WRONGS AS A WORLD ORDER CHALLENGE

Every phase in the history of international relations and world order can be identified by its distinctive achievements and failures. Much as Tolstoy observed with reference to families, all historical moment resembles each other in their moral achievements, but it is in their failures that each becomes distinct. Yet, as Ken Booth observes in an influential essay, there has been a systematic refusal on the part of academic specialists and diplomats to acknowledge moral failure with respect to the organization of international political life, that domain of political behavior called international relations or world order.[1]

With some notable exceptions, world order has been analyzed for centuries as if human suffering were irrelevant, and as if the only fate that mattered was either the destiny of a particular nation or the more general rise and fall of great powers, the latter being regarded as an inevitable consequence of the eternal, natural rivalry of self-serving states competing for territory, wealth, influence, and status.[2] Even such an egoistic moral aperture is generally misleadingly large, as it is rare indeed that the whole of a given people share in power and authority sufficiently to be regarded as effectively included in the self; that is, "self-serving." The struggle in constitutional democracies to extend tolerance and suffrage to minorities and women reminds us that even in societies committed in principle to equality of rights, the representation of the self by the state is partial, at best, and by no means complete. In fact, one impact of globalization seems to have been to marginalize the participation of those victimized by the discipline of regional and global capital, as well as to undermine the capacity of the electoral process to serve the interests of society as a whole and of territorial interests in particular.

At most, international morality is reduced to lame "realist" claims that peace is a public good achieved mainly through the rational calculations of the privileged, reflecting the dynamics of political will and relative power, and given direction by a set of predatory assumptions about human nature. This realist mode of perceiving morality is rarely turned inward, and is quite comfortable with a hypocritical but politically convenient division between the benevolent sense of self and a malevolent vision of the other. This radical dichotomy between the general assessment of world order and the specific enactments of foreign policy has been particularly pronounced in this century—perhaps most brazenly in the mythic self-image of the United States, which sees itself as a world leader in unflagging pursuit of noble ideals.

This pattern of posturing allows that master practitioner of realist statecraft, Henry Kissinger, to contend that the United States has been so captivated by Wilsonian moralism that in its pursuit of a just world order it has dangerously overlooked the protection of its own national interests.[3] Such a false rendering of America's role as world leader confuses, perhaps deliberately and with the help of compliant media, propaganda with policymaking. It is a message that enjoys little credibility abroad, even in Western Europe, where the American outlook is generally regarded, at best, as a compromise between moral pretensions and dangerous naïveté about how things really work in international life. Indeed, it has been the role of the most influential realists to instruct the American people on how things really work, especially in view of the alleged failure of Wilsonian policies to provide responsible world leadership after World War I, and the perceived success of a realist foreign policy throughout the cold war era.[4]

In recent decades this realist way of conceiving the world has gained unchallenged ascendancy in policymaking circles and has been most prominently associated in this period with the ideas and practice of "containment," "deterrence," "balance of power," and "credibility."[5] Such a self-satisfied orientation toward a bipolar image of world order was perversely captured by John Lewis Gaddis' notion of "the long peace," a phrase that resonated with the moral pretensions of Americans, while showing monumental insensitivity to the bloody ordeal of many non-Western peoples during the last half-century. It is a "peace" marred, and partially sustained, by more than 125 wars and upward of forty million war-related deaths.[6] The widespread acceptance of such a terminology in academic circles, especially in the United States, also exhibited the persisting Eurocentrism of mainstream intellectual approaches to matters of war and peace, and of living and dying.[7]

Wars are endlessly explicated as defining moments in international history, especially those involving the leading states, with scant regard to the existential consequences for the peoples engaged.[8] The avoidance of war among the rich and powerful is merely a matter of "deterrence," a brutish balance of virtually unlimited destructive capacity. Such violence-laden arrangements are, then, equated with peace. Even among allies, espionage is habitually practiced and shifts of alignment are never ruled out in the inner circles of statecraft. Such a peace is never peaceful.

In addition to mounting an attack on the realists, and their ideological forebears, Clausewitz and Machiavelli, Ken Booth assigns much responsibility for "human wrongs" to the Westphalian conception of world order that underpins contemporary diplomacy, including its internationalist embodiments in the United Nations and the European Union. Booth vividly notes, "[T]he international system—in the guise of the society of states— has not been normatively successful for 350 years. . . . In terms of spreading the good life, Westphalia is another of the West's failures."[9] At the risk of getting mired in an argument about the state system, it seems diversionary to attribute the normative failures of world order predominantly to the Westphalian conception of a world of sovereign, territorial states. Any sweeping condemnation of Westphalia tends to smooth out the ups and downs of history and overlooks the extent to which the idea of the secular state was a significantly successful response to the torment of religious warfare in the seventeenth century; it was the state system that indirectly fostered ideas of self-determination for colonial peoples and allowed coexistence between ideological adversaries in the twentieth century. In fact, it could be argued that the reempowering of the state as a true expression of its citizens and their territory would provide the best hope in the near future for mitigating the current cruelties and inequities of economic globalization. Add to this the fact that, despite its gross shortcomings, the state system has not given way to a viable alternative, be it a system of augmented global governance or a market-guided libertarian anarchism that promotes intergovernmental demilitarization.[10] The constructivist outlook is also relevant; it sees the state not as a real entity with particular features, but as a social construction of the mind that reflects biases, perceptions, historical circumstances, aspirations, and shifting priorities and values. In this respect, Westphalia as a construction of international reality retains a vast domain of unexplored normative potential, which will remain unexplored unless morally sensitive and forward-thinking political forces gain far greater access to policymaking and succeed in promoting a new image of reality that challenges prevailing economistic and geopolitical world pictures.[11] To sum up, the realist construction of world order should not be confused with the range of world order constructions that are possible within a Westphalian framework.

A sense of responsibility for human wrongs was weakened by two widely shared features of the Westphalian orientation: First of all, it promoted the exclusion of religion from the affairs of state, thereby opening the way for exclusivist political conceptions of community that were based on race, nation, civilization, and secular ideology, but which did not relate to humanity as a whole, and which discouraged the sentiments of human solidarity inherent in the main religious traditions.[12] Second, the impact of the Enlightenment, especially in the aftermath of the Industrial Revolution, gave rise to a civilizational consensus that modernity was synonymous with material progress in relation to human circumstances. It was thought that applying science and reason to social reality would produce an improved quality of life; modernity became the underpinning of both a new conception of happiness and a belief in progress. The most fundamental moral challenge for the Enlightenment was to extend these benefits universally, to all classes and peoples—though not necessarily to non-Western peoples, especially those of Africa and of pre-Columbian societies in the Americas, who were widely considered "barbarians" not suited for the benefits of "civilization." The political challenge was to ensure that the spread of material benefits was consistent with other goals, namely preserving domains of privilege for elites or, at the other end of the political spectrum, encouraging revolutionary transformations through mass action—a right-left split precipitated by the French Revolution and one that has given shape to Western politics ever since. Liberalism in different forms emerged as a centrist compromise that offered enough to those currently disadvantaged to discourage recourse to revolution while providing essential stability for existing social and economic hierarchies.[13] As long as this belief in progress was shared there was an underlying conviction that evolutionary change would in time by its own natural dynamic overcome human wrongs, and that responsible political debate should concentrate upon the most appropriate means to achieve such results.

Today, such a discussion of human wrongs takes place in a world where the project of progress and emancipation, at least in the West, has virtually collapsed—a signature of the postmodern age. There is a sense of despair in the popular culture, with its anger and obsession with violence, and its absence of hope about the future. This pattern is especially evident in, among other things, the lyrics in the songs of the most widely acclaimed rock and rap groups.

Statism, like democracy, is in many respects a normative failure—unless it is compared with likely alternatives. Globalization is weakening state structures, especially their capacity to promote global public goods, their traditional function of enhancing the quality of life within the boundaries of the state, and their most recent role of assisting and protecting vulnerable populations within their borders. Such trends, in turn, encourage disruptive ethnic and exclusivist identities that subvert modernist secular and territorial commitments to tolerance and moderation. Globalization also is unwittingly nurturing transnational social forces and encouraging the reconceptualization of democracy along cosmopolitan lines, but these tendencies (here identified as globalization-from-below, as opposed to market/media forces) appear to be mainly a rearguard tactic of minimal resistance that is only able to challenge globalization-from-above at the local level, and then only on rare occasions in special situations.[14] Offsetting the harms of globalization-from-above is exceedingly difficult, as the forces of resistance are too weak. The best hopes for the future seem to depend on the formation of new coalitions between grassroots initiatives and selected governmental authorities, coalitions forged by the ever weakening support for public goods, a process with potentially disastrous social and ecological consequences, as is already evident in some of the human catastrophes that have plagued sub-Saharan Africa in the 1990s.[15] Given such an analysis, the emergence of counterpolitics in any serious form will involve reinvigorating and reconstructing, rather than discrediting, the Westphalia legacy.

A serious inquiry into the cause and cure of human wrongs must cast its net wider than Westphalia. It needs to consider the question of human evil in all of its biological, neurological, cultural, psychological, and historical trappings, including the surprisingly robust reemergence of religion as a political force.[16] A disturbing dimension of current human wrongs is the extent to which severe forms of human suffering increasingly enjoy populist and democratic backing, whether at a safe distance (the Gulf War) or within the confines of intimate proximity (Bosnia, Rwanda). Put differently, if Gandhianism, not Machiavellianism, was the defining cultural frame within which influential inter- and intragovernmental narratives emerge, our normative appreciation of a Westphalian world would be different, and far more positive. Of course, Westphalia is a cause as well as an effect, and it is safe to say that sanctifying national flags and other symbols of nationality contributes to hostile stereotypes of "the other," encouraging violence and militarism, validating hierarchy, domination, and inequality, and providing an overall ethical facade for virulent, xenophobic patriotism. But even nationalism is an ideology of choice within a spectrum of possibilities implicit in the Westphalian framework, and there exist a wide range of nationalist orientations, some of which are receptive to strangers and neighbors.

Against this overall background, two interrelated contemporary developments have been responsible for the most widespread and acute human suffering in the world: genocidal politics and economic globalization. In both settings the fundamental ordering arrangements of international society and prevailing realist mentality seem unable and unwilling to protect vulnerable peoples. Human wrongs of horrifying magnitude result. Of course, the root cause of such abusive behavior is often local and national, with deep historical roots, and the responsibility of international society is primarily associated with the failure to provide an effective, mitigating response.[17]

GENOCIDAL POLITICS

International society has exhibited little capacity to address the supreme moral challenge of genocidal behavior. Despite decades of hand-wringing, the international response to Nazi atrocities remains the paradigm for most international policy. As long as the Nazi persecution of the Jews (and others) was differentiated from an expansive German foreign policy, the leading governments and authority structures practiced a diplomacy that was a combination of denial, indifference, and accommodation. The 1936 Olympics were held in Berlin despite abundant evidence of severe human rights abuses taking place within Germany at the time, and there were no boycotting states. And it has been recently confirmed that Swiss banks accepted deposits of gold and other assets that they knew had been confiscated from victims of Nazi persecution. The liberal democracies reinforced their indulgence with generally restrictive immigration policies that often turned the emigration of Jewish refugees into a second nightmare. Even when the war came, and the moral dimension was invoked to mobilize civic support, little effort was made to destroy the infrastructure of the Nazi extermination campaign.

There were supposedly two lessons drawn from the Nazi embrace of genocide: the first is the realization that genocide, as such, does not engage the strategic sensibilities of most political leaders; the second is encapsulated in the Nuremberg trials and the pledge "Never again," which implied a geopolitical promise to impose criminal accountability on political leaders in the future for crimes of state, as well as to mount some sort of interventionary response in the face of any future genocide, or its credible threat. As these two seemingly contradictory readings of the past and present evolved in the years after World War II, weak efforts to achieve reconciliation were fashioned. By widely ratifying the Genocide Convention, states seemed to acknowledge the strategic significance of genocide without making any specific commitment to take action in response to it.[18] At the same time the reluctance of governments, continuing to this day, to establish an international criminal court with jurisdiction over crimes of state, suggests the extent to which "victors' justice" sets limits on the accountability of leaders. The identity of the victors can be blurred, as was the case in Bosnia, where the Serbs appeared to be victorious in their campaign of ethnic cleansing, while their primary leaders, Radovan Karadicz and Radtko Mladic, were made formally subject to arrest and prosecution; in a sense, the clearest victors in this end-game diplomacy were the geopolitical forces that dictated the terms of peace.

Ethnic cleansing in Bosnia provided the reality test for contemporary genocidal politics, exhibiting for many the abiding strength of strategic indifference and the weakness of the commitment by the organized international community to avoid a recurrence of genocide. Actually, this geopolitical pattern had come to light earlier with the diplomatic response to genocidal politics in Cambodia during the period of Khmer Rouge rule in the mid-1970s. The United Nations sustained for years the diplomatic credentials of the Khmer Rouge regime after it had been replaced by the essentially liberating intervention of neighboring Vietnam, which, incidentally, was more concerned with the extension of Vietnamese influence than with controlling the practice of genocide. The Vietnamese seem to have been primarily motivated by security concerns, and secondarily, by the desire to protect the Vietnamese minority in Cambodia, but the effects of their intervention were generally positive. And yet, extensive aid to the Khmer Rouge from the Western alliance continued to flow through Thailand for years. The West was simply playing its "China card"—that is, it was supporting some of China's regional policies, among which was an intense anti-Vietnam posture, in order to increase pressure on the Soviet Union. The fact that as many as one-third of the Cambodian population either died or endured traumatic deprivations was treated as an incidental feature of a geopolitically beneficial stance. Even the golden propaganda opportunity to emphasize the cruelty of a Communist regime during the cold war was subordinated to the strategic assessment that "containing" Vietnam and accommodating China took precedence over protecting the Cambodian people against genocide. If Western diplomacy had prevailed, Vietnam would never have invaded Cambodia in the first place, or if they had, their forces would have been withdrawn immediately, leaving Cambodia in all likelihood to be again governed by the Khmer Rouge. It was only through the dedicated initiatives of a small number of individuals in the human rights community and by Cambodians themselves that the genocidal pattern was fully exposed and documented. Cambodia made it clear that, whatever else, the pledge of "Never again" did not apply to Asians.

What made Bosnia shocking was the stunning revelation that this same pledge did not even apply to Europeans. Of course, the principal victims in Bosnia were Muslim, and this fact undoubtedly eroded the moral and political response to overwhelming evidence of massive ethnic cleansing. Although there were pretenses of humanitarian concern expressed by leading European countries, the United States, and the United Nations, the diplomatic responses exhibited an unwillingness to mount a credible interventionary challenge to the Serbian operations. Instead, a series of marginal initiatives were taken, with the objective of disguising the extent of strategic indifference: sanctions, medical and humanitarian assistance, food drops by air to beleaguered communities, pin-prick NATO bombing, ill-defended safe havens, and an underfunded war crimes tribunal. The marginality of this commitment became fully manifest when the Serbs refused to respect the safe havens established under UN auspices, launching brutal attacks and civilian massacres in Gorazde and Srebrenica. The Security Council imposed an arms embargo that principally victimized the Bosnian government, and the United Nations was severely limited by its mandate of impartiality, an astonishing posture in view of the genocidal behavior on display.[19] Only after the real stakes of the war had been settled on the ground did the diplomatic initiative of the United States succeed in imposing "peace" in the form of the 1995 Dayton Agreement, which essentially ratified the main contours of genocidal politics. The core strategic interest in securing peace was the containment of the conflict, avoiding a dangerous spillover to other parts of the Balkans and Greece, as well as stemming the tide of war-generated refugees that were causing serious problems in several European countries, especially Germany.

The events in Rwanda and Burundi also confirm this pattern of indifference: only minimal efforts were made by the international community to protect the targets of genocide or to punish the main perpetrators.[20] No strategic interests were at stake. Even the usual concern with containment and refugee flows was not a big factor. The weakness of the UN response was partly a reflection of the failed humanitarian intervention in Somalia in 1992–94, and the consequent shift in outlook by the U.S. government from an attitude of "assertive multilateralism" to a posture of evasion and avoidance. This latter stance was highlighted by a directive within the Clinton administration instructing officials to avoid characterizing the events in Rwanda as genocidal because it would arouse public pressures to take some sort of action. Shashi Tharoor, a special assistant to UN Secretary General Kofi Annan, recently referred to "that dreadful summer of 1994," when the Security Council wanted to send 5,500 soldiers to Rwanda with the hope of saving many civilians from the genocidal onslaught. All nineteen governments that had previously pledged a total of 31,000 troops for various peacekeeping missions around the world refused to take part on this occasion, and no strengthened UN response was forthcoming.[21]

The prevention of genocide is not, in the best of circumstances, a simple matter.[22] In most cases, the passions of ethnic politics are unleashed, and intervention might be vigorously resisted as a form of neocolonial abuse, making success extremely problematic. The logistics of interventionary diplomacy are difficult under contemporary circumstances, given the resolve and desperate tactics of indigenous opposition forces and the tangled perception of motives and deeds on all sides. But the focus of concern here is on the low priority accorded to moral dimensions of foreign policy by the governments and elites of leading states—a problem all too evident in the weak commitments that have thus far been made in response to genocidal politics. Such weak responses would appear to confirm the inadequacy of a statist world order in redressing wide-scale human wrongs, and yet some circumstances seem to provide moderate evidence to the contrary. Human rights pressures on the Communist regimes in Eastern Europe, the anti-apartheid movement, and opposition to military government in the Western Hemisphere all seem to indicate a normative dimension of world order that can be politically effective under certain conditions, especially if linked to geopolitical projects (for example, opposition to strategic adversaries, or the containment of aggression) or to mobilized transnational ethnic forces (for example, the role of African Americans in exerting pressure on the U.S. government to impose sanctions on apartheid-era South Africa).[23] Such ambiguity gives rise to two lines of interpretation. It can be argued, on the one hand, that humanitarian intervention, even if given strong support, might fail for logistical reasons, which could help explain the reluctance of potential intervenors to endorse such projects. On the other hand, this reluctance might be little more than a lame rationalization. This latter line of interpretation seems more convincing in light of the absence of comparable reluctance when important geopolitical interests are perceived to be at stake.

Is this reluctance to intervene and establish accountability primarily structural or ideological? If structural, it seems mainly a result of the weakness of relatively autonomous institutions of global governance with respect to the implementation of fundamental norms of human rights. If ideological, it is the result of a Machiavellian orientation toward political reality that dominates the policymaking domain of states, an orientation that encourages xenophobia and discourages empathy, altruism, and sacrifices for the sake of the afflicted stranger or foreigner. Undoubtedly, given the evolution of the state system over the past three and half centuries, there is a tight interrelationship between statist structure and realist ideology, a relationship built on the dual pillars of appeasement (World War II) and deterrence (the cold war), the former an acknowledged failure and the latter a perceived success. It is no wonder, then, that despite the end of the cold war and a general geopolitical détente the states constituting international society are reluctant to contemplate serious demilitarization and disarmament initiatives. Even in countries with deep civic and democratic traditions, it has become indispensable for politicians, especially those suspected of antiwar sentiments, to demonstrate their credibility as leaders unafraid to rely on force to promote national interests. The behavior of Bill Clinton, a most cunning political animal, has been revealing in this regard: he has tried to erase any societal memory of his adolescent opposition to the Vietnam War, has then boasted about his commitment to the development of new weapons systems, has showed up at war memorials and events organized by war veterans, and has made a point to praise George Bush for his management of the Gulf War. Militarist credentials seem crucial as a qualification for political leadership in a leading constitutional democracy even during a time of international calm.

Is this indulgence of genocidal politics simply inherent to world order, or can it be overcome by a series of reforms such as establishing an enforcement capability under the control of a financially independent UN or regional auspices, thereby weakening the ties to geopolitical calculations;[24] creating an international criminal court with competence to address genocide;[25] strengthening transnational civic capabilities to issue early warnings of incipient genocidal dangers; and increasing public revulsion and media concern? In other words, can reformist measures reorient geopolitical calculations, or better, establish capabilities for effective action independent of geopolitical endorsement? There is little basis for short-term optimism. Whatever reforms might be feasible in the near future are almost certain to be subordinated to geopolitical control, by way of either a political or financial veto. What is more, the ethos of neoliberalism, as reinforced by "third wave" technologies, a postmodern cultural outlook, and the influence of cyberpolitics, is likely, if anything, to weaken existing societal impulses toward compassionate politics on a global scale, especially as expressed under the control of governmental institutions.[26] This is a time of so-called "compassion fatigue," the tightening of boundaries to stem refugee flows, a revival of capital punishment for serious criminals (not to mention chemical castration for sex offenders), and the denial of welfare benefits to illegal immigrants.

Additionally, as the next section argues, to the extent that geopolitics is being deterritorialized and the state internationalized in response to economic globalization, the indulgence of genocidal politics is likely to persist unless particular instances of its occurrence are regarded by policymakers as seriously detrimental to the interests of global market forces or to other strategic concerns, or unless countervailing political pressures emerge to challenge the economic priorities of governing elites. A special consideration arises if the domestic constituencies of a leading state identify with the victims of genocidal policies, and are well enough organized to exert effective political pressure for an interventionary response.

Over time, moves toward integrated markets may possibly reorient geopolitical calculations in favor of maintaining conditions of moderation and stability throughout the world, thereby making the eruption of genocidal politics anywhere assume the character of a strategic threat, but the prospects for such a process seem remote with regard to the peoples currently most at risk, namely those in sub-Saharan Africa and the Balkans. As matters now stand, genocidal activity has mostly occurred in settings (Cambodia, Bosnia, Rwanda, Tibet, Burundi) that are not notable for market opportunities, and therefore not strong candidates for costly international efforts at prevention, mitigation, and restoration.

Can non-Western influences in international life provide a new normative momentum? What of the emergence of the Asian/Pacific region as the epicenter of the global market? What of Buddhist, Confucian, Hindu, and Islamic ethics? It is difficult to offer convincing responses at this stage. The prevailing tendencies lead to pessimistic expectations about the future. It seems unlikely that sovereign states will be induced to accept even minimal procedures of external accountability. What seems more promising is the emergence of regional zones of civilizational autonomy that resist Western external modalities of exploitation and genocidal abuse, but remain relatively insensitive to both their own internal patterns of abuse and those abuses situated outside their own orbit of civilizational and regional identity. For instance, the Malaysian government is active in support of Muslim peoples whether their victimization is in Kashmir, Chechnya, or Bosnia, yet it is simultaneously guilty of abuses toward indigenous peoples located within its own territorial boundaries.[27] Thus a world of plural civilizational identity does not seem likely to provide the foundations for the sort of effective world community needed to discourage genocidal politics and protect its targets. The only hope is the deepening and expansion of democratizing tendencies, making leaders more consistently receptive to international law, and to the guidelines spelled out in the main human rights instruments. However the interrogation of human rights proceeds on the basis of cultural differences, there is present now a universal acceptance and understanding on the part of elites and public opinion of norms of tolerance in relation to others. There is also an acceptance of the view that genocidal practices are criminal. Implementing these shared normative attitudes in a consistent manner is a major challenge facing democratizing tendencies in a variety of settings. The assumption here is that the human wrong of genocide needs to be addressed, to the extent possible, by preventive modes, including education and through the inclusion of tolerance as an integral element of democratic theory and practice. For the reasons argued earlier, reactive modes of response to genocide are likely to be ineffectual unless, as in the case of Cambodia in the late 1970s, it provokes a major response that reflects security priorities of strong neighboring states (in this instance, Vietnam) or regional and global actors. In this regard, humanitarian intervention is a sham, either being cosmetic or a cover for a geopolitically motivated undertaking. To call such intervention "geopolitical" is not necessarily to condemn it outright, but such labeling at least discourages "false advertising," and the tendency of politicians to exaggerate the strength of genuine humanitarian concerns.

ECONOMIC GLOBALIZATION

Economic deprivation that results in the gross inability to satisfy basic human needs afflicts more than one billion persons on the planet. Such a condition is accentuated by the failure to allocate the modest resources required to overcome a range of childhood diseases that take the lives of millions of children each year.[28] The international financial system continues to exert effective pressure on many governments of indebted poor countries to maintain fiscal austerity and abandon policies designed to subsidize the poor. There are many mutually reinforcing explanations for this turning away from the welfare-oriented consensus that had existed nationally and globally since the time of the Great Depression. Some cite the collapse of a socialist alternative; others emphasize the weakening of organized labor as a progressive social force, still others point to the ideological hegemony of neoliberalism and supply-side fiscal policies. The list goes on: the ineptitude of large, long-lasting governmental bureaucracies, the adverse fiscal consequences of a lengthening average period between retirement and death, citizen disillusionment with welfare approaches, societal greed that resists tax burdens associated with redistributive policies, the cold dynamics of international competitiveness, or even a generalized postmodern malaise.[29] These are the types of issues associated with economic globalization, which in its myriad forms and with its elusive and often concealed mechanisms becomes all the more difficult to address through political action. Global market forces operate as an impersonal agency for the infliction of human wrongs, constantly eroding territorial means of redress.

Economic globalization, notwithstanding the vagueness and ambiguity of the term, has some positive normative effects. It has enabled a number of societies to make rapid economic progress, most spectacularly those on the Pacific Rim. For various reasons relating to land tenure and social structure, the benefits of rapid economic growth have reached a large proportion of the peoples living in these societies, greatly reducing the ranks of the impoverished and allowing the enjoyment of a more satisfying material existence for a significant proportion of society. In effect, the mobility of capital encourages a leveling up in certain settings and a leveling down in others, with the overall benefits and burdens of polarization becoming more pronounced and reordered. Thus it is possible to report that while economic globalization has had a homogenizing effect on the relations between the North and certain parts of the South, it has also accentuated differences elsewhere, most notably in the gap between the richest and poorest countries, and in many settings, between the upper and lower classes. Furthermore, globalization, in conjunction with neoliberalism, accentuates polarization within the countries of the North as territorial interests are subordinated in the face of superior investment opportunities abroad. Similarly, the challenge of "the dangerous classes" (those that play the role in a given historical period of challenging the established order) is being increasingly discounted, ignored, and addressed coercively, helping to explain the displacement of welfare concerns by a focus on prisons, police, and punishment.[30]

Despite the stress on territorial sovereignty, the Westphalian framework has facilitated the establishment of an elaborate normative architecture of human rights during the last half century. The dynamics of economic globalization are definitely undermining the will and capability of many states to fulfill their obligations, especially with respect to economic and social rights. Although the liberal democracies were always reluctant to include economic and social claims within the framework of human rights, preferring to limit the idea to political and civil rights, the de facto commitment of these governments to a welfare ethos assured high degrees of compliance. But with the reduction of "social dividends" in capitalist countries of the North and the persistence of externally imposed fiscal austerity in the poorest countries of the South, the economic and social deprivations are mounting at an alarming rate.

Globalization appears to inhibit efforts to devote resources to the alleviation of poverty and other forms of social distress. Of course, if those newly victimized were to become mobilized in a new political undertaking that proved effective in postindustrial settings, then one could imagine the possibility of a new global social contract that offered a compromise sufficient to contain, or even end, transnational class warfare. At present, the depoliticized ethos of cyberpolitics, combined with neoliberalism and militarism, makes it almost impossible to implement that portion of human rights concerned with economic and social issues. Governments take refuge in supply-side approaches that supposedly will spread the benefits of economic growth to all societal sectors, thereby deflecting calls for direct action. Concerns about competitiveness, especially a fiscal preoccupation with the reduction of trade and budgetary deficits, taxes, and inflationary pressures, add to the downward pressure on public goods. When large companies cut their employment rolls the price of their stock-market shares tends to rise, while news of a drop in unemployment tends to arouse fears of interest rate increases, sending stock prices plunging. Such patterns are characteristic of an era of globalization, with its logic dictated by the well-being of capital rather than of people.[31]

Economic globalization, then, weakens the overall capacity and will of governments to address human wrongs either within their own society or elsewhere. Furthermore, by undercutting the basis for supporting most categories of global public goods, economic globalization also weakens the resource base of those international institutions with a mandate to alleviate human suffering. Such tendencies are currently abetted by an ideological climate that does not mount significant resistance on behalf of those being most acutely victimized by the discipline of global capital. For these reasons, it seems appropriate to link economic globalization with a high threshold of tolerance for human wrongs, at least for now.

BUT WHAT OF THE FUTURE?

How can we encourage more attentiveness to the redress of human wrongs? There are several lines of response, each requiring patience and a realization that the improbable is possible because so much of social and political reality is obscured by a conventional wisdom that has grown cynical about compassionate politics. One way to address this question is to reevaluate morally the character of world politics, to acknowledge that international relations is a social construction, and that its normative emptiness is not a necessity. Another approach is to point to the emergence of global civil society through the efforts of transnational social forces to promote democratization—globalization-from-below, or what has been called elsewhere "cosmopolitan democracy."[32] Still another line of reasoning envisions that the emergence of geopolitical tensions and ecological crises generated by globalization will give rise to overwhelming demands that governments be more inclusive and socially responsible. In this regard, it should be recalled that during the cold war sub-Saharan African countries counted in the geopolitical balance, and for a variety of reasons are beginning to matter again. For instance, such an awareness is present in reactive patterns that appreciate that the flow of unwanted migrant workers can be slowed by improving social conditions in their home country. Yet another view envisions the reempowerment of the socially responsible state as a result of a political climate that is less wedded to economic goals and fiscal austerity. Such a result could come about in a number of ways, but one promising avenue would be transnational agitation for the implementation of social, economic, and cultural norms on a regional and eventually interregional, basis.

Beyond these substantive imperatives lie a series of difficult questions pertaining to the reach of human rights, and the conditions associated with their further development. Of growing interest is a subject touched on in the opening chapter: the rights of future generations and the lingering grievances of past generations. In a strictly defined sense, neither constituency can directly represent itself. To what extent should human rights pertain to unborn persons? From one angle the unborn are completely vulnerable to certain present abuses such as excessive global warming. The next chapter explores the vulnerability of future generations, while chapter 12 considers whether the unhealed wounds caused by past abuses can vest rights and remedies in members of the present generation.

PART 3

The Future Prospect

The Extension of 11
Human Rights
to Past and Future
Generations

A POINT OF DEPARTURE

The fiftieth anniversary of the Universal Declaration of Human Rights was both a moment of celebration for achievements well beyond reasonable expectations in 1948 and a time of renewed resolve to address the varieties of acute deprivation of fundamental rights that remained widespread at the end of the twentieth century. There is little doubt that the early impulses to put human rights on the global agenda were rather faint efforts to satisfy segments of public opinion without any serious expectation that the relationship between state and society could be effectively regulated by limits imposed in the name of international human rights. Too many UN member states in 1948 were themselves authoritarian and oblivious to the social responsibility of the state to make the implementation of human rights seem as if it were a genuine political project. Global statecraft was, and still is, firmly in the hands of a political leadership that overwhelmingly embraced a realist or Machiavellian ethos with respect to international law and morality. As the cold war unfolded, security was considered the core national interest in the countries of both the East and West, which left little room for the independent promotion of humane values in intergovernmental settings.

Despite this unfavorable set of defining circumstances, the evolution of human rights surprised skeptics and pleased advocates. Several factors help explain this evolution. First of all, soon after 1948 citizens in Western Europe and North America formed voluntary associations that pushed hard to expose patterns of human rights violations. This grassroots activism, which over the years has spread to all parts of the world, made effective use of its capacity to use information in a trustworthy manner. It took advantage of the concern of many governments about their international image and reputation, and was assisted by the increasing willingness of the media to highlight dramatic patterns of human rights violation. A second development of importance was the high-profile move by the Carter administration in the United States to make a commitment to human rights a cornerstone of its foreign policy as of 1976. The U.S. government, as the leader of the non-Communist world, appeared to add for the first time a genuine moral dimension to its strategic concerns and to its global rivalry with the Soviet Union. This Carter initiative exerted a lasting influence on the role of human rights in the internal bureaucratic structure within the U.S. foreign policy establishment, and indirectly helped to upgrade the role of human rights elsewhere. This enhanced role for human rights also influenced the pattern of debate on many issues of global policy. Quite unintentionally, the prominence of the Carter advocacy sent a foreign policy signal that was interpreted as a green light to political movements around the world that the U.S. government would no longer necessarily oppose, and would certainly not intervene against, political struggles against anti-Communist authoritarian governments.

A third step in this evolution was the role of human rights in major transformations of internal political situations, especially their salience in the movements against oppressive conditions in Eastern Europe in the 1980s. Human rights also were at the center of the global anti-apartheid campaign that seemed to have contributed to a remarkable, peaceful reversal in South Africa in the early 1990s. A fourth development was the gradual elaboration of more obligatory and specific human rights standards in the form of a series of lawmaking treaties that established norms for the treatment of refugees, the status of women, the prevention of racial discrimination, and the protection of children and civilian victims of war. A fifth and final factor was the impressive regime for the active protection of human rights that was successfully operating in Western Europe. Within this European setting individuals were given the right to challenge alleged abuses by their own governments in an external judicial arena. Challenged governments pledged themselves to carry out the external court's ruling even if it meant changing national law in sensitive areas of domestic policy such as treatment of alleged terrorists, the cultural rights of minorities, and the balance between secular commitments and the freedom of religion. If one test of the acceptance of the rule of law in international life is whether it is respected by a state whose interests and practices run counter to its mandate, then European regional support of human rights is by now a convincing rebuff to those ultrarealists who continue to believe that international law is not really law.

Of course, each of these five domains of achievement is complex, exhibiting certain contradictions, and each is interactive with the others. There is an ebb and flow of progress and setback, of according priority to human rights and then subordinating their relevance, a slow process that gives rise to conflicting interpretations. Among those who refuse to believe the claim that support for human rights has had a beneficial impact on the quality of governance in the world, there are two camps. One is closely associated with the writings of Noam Chomsky. Chomsky produces much evidence to the effect that the real foreign policy of the United States, as distinguished from its diplomatic posturing, has been consistent in its effort to reinforce oppressive regimes. In fact, says Chomsky, its foreign policy has often deliberately undermined the stability of those governments that were seeking to alleviate the suffering and injustices of their societies. In this view, the weight of strategic interests has led powerful governments to act generally in opposition to human rights. The other camp of critics, those in the mainstream of realism, takes an entirely different tack; their complaint, directed especially against Carter's approach to the Iranian Revolution, was that the promotion of human rights as a matter of foreign policy represented a serious failure of understanding which had a self-defeating and dangerous impact on the pursuit of strategic interests. It was argued that the human rights approach of the Carter administration perversely contributed to the downfall of the Shah's government in Iran, which had been a faithful and crucial strategic ally of the United States. The result was to bring to power a new elite that was intensely hostile to Western interests—and which was, incidentally, even more repressive than the outgoing regime. The immediate effect of this shift in the governing process in Iran was a serious weakening of the U.S. geopolitical position in the Middle East. According to these critics, a definite tension existed between active support for human rights and the successful pursuit of strategic interests on a global level. Furthermore, they argued, any sensible political leader understands that Westphalian logic required the abandonment of support for human rights under these circumstances, except as a propaganda tool useful against adversaries.

Even among those who do not accept this dominant realist critique, however, there is a feeling that it may be too early to celebrate the achievements of the last half-century. It became clear that the normative framework of the Universal Declaration, even if one includes the two subsequently negotiated human rights covenants, had serious deficiencies if it was meant, as claimed, to address the full spectrum of human rights concerns. As representatives of indigenous peoples began to make abundantly clear, the mainstream human rights tradition did not speak to their general circumstances. It was especially insensitive to their view that human rights had to include the protection of traditional ways of community life in the face of state- and market-driven modernization. Somewhat more controversial were the various contentions that non-Western civilizations did not participate fully in the standard-setting process, making the human rights tradition both insufficiently responsive to non-Western values and lacking in any truly global legitimacy. Islamic and Confucian scholars have both complained about the excessive individualism and permissiveness of the human rights tradition as written into international law. They have also complained about its failure to balance the rights of the individual against responsibilities to the community, and about the selectivity of emphasis in which civil and political rights are privileged over economic, social, and political rights. Always lurking in the background of this debate, as many non-Western critics point out, is the gross one-sidedness of interventionary diplomacy. Many of the countries of the South feel that their sovereign rights have been infringed by the North's championing of human rights, especially when support for human rights has taken the form of imposing conditions that interfered with priorities of economic development. Arguably, such priorities were of the essence of human rights for these governments in the South. It is hardly surprising that there is a backlash in the South that identifies human rights initiatives from the North as a neocolonial instrument that deserves resistance rather than acceptance.

Add to these geopolitical obstacles the rapid rise of global market forces and neoliberalism. In an era of economic globalization, human rights of an economic and social character are subordinated to varying degrees to fiscal criteria of sound economics. In effect, governments with insufficient revenues should not subsidize the poor even for the most basic necessities of life. This outlook acquires a global character when it is endorsed by the structures of global economic governance, including the IMF, World Bank, and the World Trade Organization. The contributing forces of globalization are not monolithic, however: some neoliberal economists believe that constitutional government, and civil and political rights, are essential ingredients of a dynamic market, and that they are ultimately ingredients for favorable conditions for investment. What is incontestable is that the full impact of globalization on the international protection of human rights is likely to be a major concern in the decades ahead.

It is against this complicated background that another line of critical comment becomes relevant, especially when considering the form that support for human rights is most likely to take in the twenty-first century. The human rights undertaking, with its modern origins in the American and French Revolutions, aspired to universality with respect to space and time. Even the civilizational critiques were generally based on an idea of ahistorical validity within a given region, civilization, or religion. The dimension of time has only recently become explicitly linked to the articulation and implementation of human rights. It was implicitly part of the critique by indigenous peoples, whose main contention was that the Universal Declaration embodied a false universalism, as it presumed a modernist and modernizing frame of reference, and thereby failed to mediate between the premodern and modern or to offer protection to the premodern (or traditional). Such a consideration of history is also implicitly present in the secondary claim of non-Western critics that their views and representatives did not play a sufficient role in the evolution of the human rights tradition.

The notion of time as an explicit embodiment, however, has only recently become a part of the human rights discourse, primarily in the form of the increasing focus on the rights of future generations. This attention, nurtured mainly by the inspirational efforts of Maltese scholars and statecraft in the United Nations and elsewhere over the last two decades, is now generally regarded as having achieved the status of a customary norm of international law. It is closely linked with a more visionary approach to international environmental law, with its far-reaching temporal horizons, its call for early-warning responses, and its attack on sovereignty-oriented views that insist that states can authorize whatever has not been explicitly forbidden to them. The idea of future generations is not limited to survival or even health concerns; it is also a matter of preserving the cultural, recreational, aesthetic, and spiritual heritage of the planet so that the descendants of those who are currently alive will not be deprived. The emergence of future generations as a focus of concern undoubtedly reflected the accelerated pace and greater depth of change, the dire implications of current trends in consumption, the realization that states acting on their own could not form effective global policy, and the awareness that preemptive approaches to adjustment were indispensable, since reactive modes would result in too little, too late. Environmental law's emphasis on the precautionary principle and on the protection of the global commons is responsive to these concerns about future generations. In this respect, the Maltese-led effort has achieved first-order results; that is, it has generated new norms widely acknowledged to be valid and binding. The second-order challenge remains: translating the normative imperative into an enforceable regime that implements these goals with specific undertakings.

There is another way in which the ahistorical view of human rights has come to be questioned, although not as systematically. It involves fairness to prior generations. To what extent should past injustices be acknowledged and rectified? Some have referred to this process as "the redress of history" (for example, Peter Van Ness), but it has not yet been championed as a domain of human rights by either scholars or diplomats. At the same time, specific efforts at redress are under way in many settings, some of them seeking symbolic results such as a formal apology, others a monetary payoff, and still others a combination of both. This type of backward-looking intergenerational justice seems to enjoy even less widespread attention than do forward-looking claims. We know that many efforts are under way, ranging from moves to punish the past crimes of the Khmer Rouge in Cambodia to extended battles over so-called "Holocaust gold" deposited in Swiss banks to apologies for a variety of injustices, including slavery, colonialism, and the abuse of indigenous peoples.

It seems important to incorporate time-oriented approaches to human rights into the global pattern of discourse, partly to increase sensitivity to the deep cultural wounds inflicted by past practices and to strengthen anticipatory approaches to the future. It is clear that these wounds of the past will seldom fully heal with the passage of time, and may actually become aggravated by continuing efforts to cover up and deny past abuses. Turkish officials have over the years repeatedly attempted to deny the 1915 genocide against the Armenian community, which has fanned the flames of indignation rather than extinguishing them.

It is admittedly extremely difficult to give concrete meanings to the obligations of the present to the future or the present to the past and thereby establish policy relevance. At the same time, the failure to include these concerns within the policy-making orbit of human rights is a serious limitation. The emphasis on future generations has had some positive effects; it has sensitized political consciousness and has widened the scope of policy debate. And by acknowledging injustices done to past generations, a striking achievement of the last decade, the universal need for healing and reconciliation has come to be recognized as fundamental.

A major challenge of the next fifty years is to incorporate and expand both the past and future dimensions of intergenerational equity. Affirming the validity of such perspectives raises many issues, including the costs to present generations, millions of whom are experiencing deprivation in the here and now. Still, it seems essential to begin moving beyond the mere acknowledgment of intergenerational rights and to start considering the problems of definition and implementation.

ADVANCING HUMAN RIGHTS
IN INTERGENERATIONAL CONTEXTS

There are some important distinctions to be made when considering questions of justice for past and future generations. The past supplies an image, however contested, of the magnitude of the injustices committed. The risks to the future, by contrast, are inherently speculative and difficult to agree upon given the varying identities and priorities of experts and the various possibilities that technological solutions will be found as the threshold of danger is approached. Still, at this stage of conceptualization it seems useful to treat past and future together as part of a broader effort to free people from the purely spatial constraints of the nation-state so they can embrace a temporal relationship that is part of the broader task of establishing humane governance for the peoples of the world.

Given this outlook, the image of the "citizen pilgrim" is suggestive, evoking a journey from past to future, a journey fueled by a belief that a moral and spiritual reorientation can help address the various challenges of an era of globalization. These challenges include the indispensable tasks of preserving the human environment, including the global commons. There is also the matter of reconciling cultural diversity with scientific debates about threats to human well-being in societal settings in which diverse peoples are increasingly mixed. In summary, the citizen pilgrim is committed to the process of establishing some form of humane governance for the planet as a whole, which presupposes the ethos of species solidarity across space and through time. Making this ethos operative depends on dealing seriously with the entire range of claims concerning injustice, including those of both past and future generations. To be credible, such species solidarity has to be responsive to the unresolved ordeals of history and to the ethical implications of high-risk social and economic practices. The journey of the citizen pilgrim follows several paths:

Clarifying the Normative Boundaries

A first step, already partially taken, involves acknowledging claims of past and future generations in formal settings. So far this has been done in very general terms with respect to future generations, especially in the context of global environmental protection. A follow-up to the basic affirmation of the "rights" of future generations has been set forth in the Declaration on the Responsibilities of the Present Generations towards Future Generations, a document approved by the General Conference of UNESCO at its twenty-ninth session in 1997. It is difficult to know whether such documents will attain a practical relevance with respect to such fundamental matters as slowing the process of global warming or ensuring the maintenance of biodiversity. But having greater clarity in relation to normative boundaries is both an invitation to specify policy implications and a call to further specification and application.

With respect to the past, grievances have been formulated around past historical occurrences ranging from the systematic abuse of native or indigenous peoples to the violent persecution of particular ethnic or religious identities. So far claims emanating from these grievances have been specific in scope and have not demanded material rectification from present generations (e.g., slavery or colonialism). In many cases, justice claims have arisen during convulsive periods of political transition, when past crimes of state are frequently brought to light. The Truth and Reconciliation Commission in South Africa and the Ad Hoc International Criminal Tribunals in The Hague are powerful examples of efforts to confront the past as a means of moving more successfully to embrace a different future. These are difficult undertakings, as victims of past crimes may make harsh demands for accountability that can upset the forward movement of a newly democratic state; for their part, past perpetrators often retain enough power to threaten the polity with bloody consequences if they are taken to task for their past crimes. It is worth recalling that the effort after World War II to hold German and Japanese leaders responsible for their crimes occurred in the context of their unconditional defeat and the temporary occupation of their country by victorious military forces. These contextual factors, including the extent to which the various constituencies are mobilized and the nature of the moral outlook of the new leadership, make it difficult to adopt a generalized approach. Justice for past generations needs to be conceived in highly contextualized terms, while still keeping in sight the universal objectives of reconciliation and restored human solidarity and community.

Tangible or Symbolic Acknowledgment?

To deal symbolically with the well-grounded concerns of future generations provides only the coldest comfort. To safeguard the rights of future generations requires tangible action directed at controlling adverse trends or dangerously high levels of risk. The same cannot be said for past generations, whose core grievance is often the sense of wounded dignity, and whose claims are softened by the passage of time. A particular complexity arises when the grievance has a compensatory mercenary element, as with respect to international banking practices during the Nazi era or the deprivation of natural resources from indigenous peoples. Shall the past be rectified by later normative assessments that were not made at the time that the wrongs occurred? Should morally suspect behavior be later punished and reimbursed by concerted political action on behalf of the victims?

These questions suggest that the struggle for justice for victims of past crimes can easily produce a widening rupture in the present that defeats the aims of reconciliation, community, and solidarity. This rupture can take the form of a backlash of denial and a defensive reflex to defend belligerently current strongholds of wealth and privilege. It is a delicate matter to find the formula that ensures redress of past wrongs without inflaming the resentments of present generations.

In relation to the future, the issue of tangibility is also relevant. It is easy to endorse the soft rhetoric of sustainability and the vague ideas about justice to future generations, but it is difficult to find a way of taking tangible steps to ensure such justice, especially given the unequal capacity and willingness of states to bear adjustment costs. What is a reasonable allocation of burdens? Should there be a sliding scale based on income per capita or based on the relative size of a country's contribution to the perceived environmental threat? Just how far into the future should these calculations project? Native Americans have a strong temporal consciousness. They often speak of a range of concerns that stretch backwards and forwards for seven generations, but the articulation was undertaken in contexts where life expectancy was much shorter and the pace of change far slower than in our contemporary circumstances. These matters of the proper time zones for accountability are difficult to decide upon. A balanced judgment must also consider the impact of the burdens assumed toward the future on those currently alive. Also, it is relevant to take into account the potential benefits to future generations of new technological innovations. Making such projections is always risky, but whatever effort is made will help prepare global society for the sort of normative orientation that will be most beneficial in a globalized, postindustrial future. The mere discussion of such issues opens the way for a more enlightened policy debate about the use of resources and the conservation of the natural and cultural heritage of humanity.

Interpreting the Level of Responsibility for Past Injustice and Future Risks

Further progress in the domain of intergenerational justice will rely on increased intercivilizational and intracivilizational discussion and reflection. In this regard, a world forum on these themes every five years would seem to be a useful consciousness-raising initiative, and could be tied to the work of a Peoples' Assembly that would operate within or outside the United Nations. The quality of such a forum would undoubtedly be enhanced by a more technical approach, possibly an annual publication on intergenerational claims, with factual narratives of claims and counterclaims, prepared under the independent auspices of a transnational citizens association or conceivably by a commission set up under the authority of the UN Economic and Social Council—or possibly under a restructured Trusteeship Council. Regional efforts could also be undertaken. Finally, it might be helpful to have a Council of Guardians—possibly composed of living Nobel Peace Prize laureates or of recipients of the Right Livelihood Award—that would consider intergenerational grievances and offer evaluations and recommendations. A preliminary initiative might be to constitute an independent world commission on the theme of intergenerational justice, one that would be expected to issue a report after three years. The commission could be spontaneously established by an organizing conference and planning committee, and its initial membership would be composed of individuals enjoying a stature of moral authority within a particular cultural or civilizational space.

CONCLUSION

The main idea explored in this chapter is the means by which to make time more creatively relevant to the quality of world order, both time past and time future. In many respects, time has been neglected in inquiries into the nature of justice, and justice itself has generally been philosophically conceived at the level of society and state, and not in relation to species and world. Globalization and accelerating change, as well as ecological hazard, the resurgence of historical memory, and a growing sense that there is a human stake in the conservation of genetic diversity and cultural heritage, give a practical urgency to this concern with intergenerational justice. Such a vision of justice represents one aspect of what political identity is coming to mean in this early phase of the era of globalization; it is a vision that is undermining the generally spatial connotations of obligation, loyalty, and citizenship. The incorporation of these concerns into the ongoing process of providing international protection for human rights is an important way to make sure that the one-hundredth anniversary of the Universal Declaration has as much historical resonance as does the fiftieth anniversary.

The next chapter considers duties toward victims of past human rights abuses in the specific setting of the Nanking Massacre that took place more than sixty years ago. By considering responsibilities to past generations, there is a further deepening of this rather new idea that "justice" is temporal as well as spatial. Such an idea may seem banal, but it should be appreciated against a background of international relations in which territorial boundaries were the major defining reality, and where the strongest cosmopolitan impulses were associated with responses to injustices occurring elsewhere, in the purely *geographic* sense of the word. What this idea of rights and duties toward past and future contributes to our conception of international justice is a *temporal* sense of elsewhere.

The Redress 12
of Past Grievances

The Nanking Massacre

WHY NANKING 1937?

In recent years, there have been many efforts to redress past grievances, at least symbolically, and in some instances, substantively. Among the more prominent examples are efforts by Holocaust survivors and victims' heirs to recover looted gold and art, calls on the part of the Organization of African Unity for Western governments to pay reparations for slavery, and some modest material and symbolic compensation for the wrongs committed against a number of indigenous peoples. These initiatives, along with others, represent essentially voluntary moves that seek to soften the harsher aspects of past injustice.

During Japan's war of aggression, its armed forces were guilty of numerous atrocities directed at the Chinese population. The most notable and dramatic of these occurred during the Japanese siege and subsequent occupation of the major Chinese city of Nanking in 1937. An inquiry into the Nanking Massacre fits within this wider setting of redressing historical wrongs, and reflects an overall surge in concern about intertemporal justice. There are also more particular explanations for the inquiry: recently discovered evidence of what happened during those fateful weeks in Nanking, widely read and discussed books reconstructing the events, and a mutual interest on the part of the governments of Japan and China to move forward into the new century free from the darker shadows of their shared past, especially the period between 1930 and 1945.

Beyond this, however, reconsidering Nanking represents an example of a still broader feature of the present: responsiveness to the acceleration of history—the sheer speed of change—which seems to be making our political consciousness more sensitive to various aspects of the dimension of time. As we seek to grasp a future that is emerging before our eyes from an ever more rapidly receding present, we are also becoming more aware of the temporal dimension of our experience, especially of what preceded. And of these past recollections nothing seems so vivid these days as the unhealed wounds of history. The mere passage of time often does not by itself achieve healing. It requires a deliberate, visible effort.

Some action was taken in the immediate aftermath of World War II that appeared to acknowledge the wrongs committed at Nanking. Above all, the Japanese commanding general at Nanking, General Iwane Matsui, was sentenced to death by the Tokyo War Crimes Tribunal for his role in the atrocities committed by his soldiers, and specifically for his failure as the responsible officer on the scene to take effective preventive action during those weeks of brutality against the inhabitants of the city.[1] But such an initiative did not achieve healing. For one thing, it was redress imposed by the victors in the war, and not volunteered by the Japanese government or by the Japanese people. For another, unlike the Nuremberg trials, the parallel Tokyo trials were not widely noted, made little impact on world public opinion, and remained characterized in Japanese society as little more than a kangaroo court.

Perhaps most important of all of these background considerations is the conviction that past and present crimes against humanity are becoming occurrences of universal relevance, not to be confined to the political and moral imagination of the countries and peoples who experienced the horrific events. As such, the activation of historical memory is both cathartic and potentially risky. It can be risky if the side of the perpetrator is seen to be attempting to deny or downplay the gravity of the past crimes. Such behavior seemed to be at the heart of the November 1998 visit of China's head of state, Jiang Zemin, to Japan, at which time the Japanese Prime Minister Keizo Obuchi refused to issue an apology in written form for Japan's wartime atrocities in China. Evidently, an oral apology was perceived by the Chinese government as being too ephemeral and ambiguous, especially considering that Japan had recently issued a written apology to Korea. On the Japanese side, Hiromu Nonaka, the chief cabinet secretary, confirmed the problematic character of the Japanese posture with respect to China when he tellingly declared in apparent exasperation, "Isn't this a finished problem?"[2]

These concerns form a complex tapestry that is very much part of the contemporary scene. This chapter seeks to examine some of these general international developments as a context in which to better appreciate the complex significance of delving anew into the human and historical reality of Nanking. It should be noted that this inquiry goes beyond what might be considered the standard academic scope—that is, merely setting the historical record straight. A conventional academic analysis, by most accounts, should be exclusively devoted to providing as objective and accurate an account of the events as possible, and to unearthing what is known about the participants and their motivation as part of an exercise in historical reconstruction. And indeed, such objectivity is important as an expression of sincerity, and it is an appropriate academic task to improve the accuracy of our interpretation and presentation of past events. Such professionalism should always guide a scholarly investigation of past events. Yet there is no reason why such an academic investigation cannot go further and seek to derive from the facts lessons for the future, and exhibit expressions of meaningful solidarity with the victims. This inquiry could produce a demand by the surviving victims and their families for one or more forms of redress for past grievances, which is especially likely if Japan as the perpetrating side does not sufficiently acknowledge the severity or wrongdoing, including the failure to seek forgiveness and reconciliation.

As recent intergovernmental encounters seem to indicate, conditions are still far from ideal for official reconciliation between China and Japan on the subject of Nanking. China's leaders evidently feel disappointed, if not dismayed, by Japan's unwillingness at this point even to formalize an apology as a way of closing the book on the past. Japan's current leaders, perhaps afraid to upset the unrepentant ultranationalists in their ranks, appear reluctant to do more than offer a casual and abstract oral acknowledgment of the wrongs committed, and would obviously much prefer that the matter be dropped altogether. In view of this apparent stalemate at the government level, transnational civil initiatives may be more successful in creating a better climate of awareness, even in creating movement toward reconciliation at a people-to-people level. Eventually, in an altered societal climate, the leaders of the two dominant countries in the Asia/Pacific region may be able to respond by adopting a common position that wipes away misunderstandings on both sides, acknowledging the past ordeal in its various dimensions, and expressing remorse in a form that seems credible.

There is another background factor that merits attention in any analysis of the events at Nanking. It involves the relative lack of attention given in Western, and specifically American, circles to the suffering endured by the Asian societies that were the main victims of Japanese military expansionism in the 1930s and 1940s. Such indifference contrasts with the high-profile attention devoted to the suffering of European peoples, and especially Jews, under German occupation. Also, Japan was not made to repudiate its past to nearly the same extent as was Germany after the war. Japan was allowed to keep its Emperor system intact, while Germany was forced to abandon its political past altogether, and reconstitute itself as a liberal democracy. The list of Japanese war criminals was considerably abridged for cold war reasons. The comparative superficiality of political reconstruction in Japan during the years of American occupation undoubtedly

adds to the bitterness of these newly resurrected memories and simultaneously makes redress all the more important.

There are mitigating factors as well. Unlike Germany, Japan's expansionist aggression was in part a response to a genuine security challenge in
the form of a deliberate policy of economic strangulation by Europe and
America that endangered its viability as a resource-poor state. Indeed, some
neutral analysts even endorsed Japan's recourse to military expansion; such
a view was expressed in the celebrated dissent of the Indian member of the
Tokyo War Crimes Tribunal, Judge Radhabinod Pal.[3] Furthermore, the use
of the atomic bomb on Hiroshima and Nagasaki at the end of World War
II evoked widespread sympathy for Japan as a victim of an international crime
of the greatest magnitude, a victimization that has never been the subject
of apology or regret by its perpetrator.

Japan's history aside, the West bears some responsibility for not being
more sensitive all along to the suffering experienced by the Chinese people
during the course of the Japanese invasion and occupation. This tendency
to overlook the Chinese ordeal was reinforced by political developments,
especially the 1949 Communist victory in China, which tended to preclude
any positive feelings in the West toward the country and its people. Of
course, this distancing pattern was further reinforced by cold war alignments
that created a strong relationship with Japan and a very hostile and adver-
sarial relationship with China, one that erupted into a direct military
encounter in the Korean War (1950–52).

With these considerations in mind, the illumination of such events as
the Nanking Massacre points to the fact that Western leadership and public opinion was morally complacent due to its failure to take more seriously
the Japanese record of atrocity in China.[4] In the new setting of international
relations, with the cold war over and China now an important trading partner and a more assertive global presence, the atmosphere has become conducive to fully bringing to light the horror of the Chinese experience under
Japanese occupation. It is notable, in this regard, although hardly surprising, that much more attention was given by the popular media in the West
to the sixtieth anniversary of Nanking than to any earlier anniversary. A
number of developments help account for this late awakening. For one
thing, a changing strategic equation put China and Japan on a more equal
basis in the eyes of the West; for another, there was a growing tendency
worldwide to air past injustices. The publication of Iris Chang's book *The
Rape of Nanking* and the documentary materials on which her research relied
also generated interest and controversy, motivating a clarification and reinterpretation of the events at Nanking.

Evoking these memories in an American setting may subtly reopen
another unresolved chapter from the same era, namely the dropping of atomic

bomb on Japanese cities. American society has generally been reluctant to confront its own past narratives of injustice, especially in relation to African Americans and indigenous peoples. Such an encounter would complicate an historic American identity based on benevolence and innocence. Even the traumas of defeat in the Vietnam War were quickly and effectively swept under the rug of forgetfulness. The success of the Reagan presidency in the 1980s included its success in restoring American moral pride, which involved overlooking the dark shadows cast by past practices and policies, shadows that in many respects extended to the present.[5]

Perhaps there exists a somewhat greater receptivity in the post–cold war setting for Americans to reexamine its ambivalent relationship to Japan's past. These opportunities should not be exaggerated, however, as these issues remain extremely sensitive. American leaders are not at all ready to accept any moral and legal responsibility for the consequences of their World War II military strategy, which relied heavily on strategic bombing and weapons of mass destruction. Both of these tactics of war remain deeply embedded in current American military doctrine and practice. Nuclear war is not being widely challenged even in its post–cold war expressions. It is virtually impossible to know whether greater attentiveness by the United States to Japan's past partial victimization would encourage a corresponding willingness by Japan to be more forthcoming in acknowledging its own past wrongdoing.

As earlier suggested, the international climate is increasingly conducive to multifaceted concerns on many fronts in relation to unresolved grievances of earlier eras. Previously, claims deriving from such grievances were dismissed as irrelevant, as cries in the wilderness. The prevailing approach was to view the injustices of the past as finished business for which an insistence on redress could serve no useful purpose except to reawaken angry feelings of resentment and frustration, to reopen wounds that had begun to heal. Although general trends are evident, attentiveness to the distinctive features of each object of inquiry is essential. It is useful to consider contextual factors that help determine whether a past grievance is likely to be constructively raised, and if so, what can be done to ensure that such a reexamination creates a spirit of resolution and reconciliation rather than hostility and bitterness.

This introductory discussion has been an attempt to contextualize a reevaluation of the Nanking Massacre. The next section discusses the recent emergence of a normative dimension in international relations that is expressed partly through the quest for intergenerational justice. The final section contends that the Nanking Massacre, as a particular occurrence situated in time and space, warrants this increased attention that it is receiving both because of its intrinsic character and because of this trend toward recognizing and seeking to rectify unresolved intergenerational grievances.

A NEWLY SUPPORTIVE GLOBAL SETTING

There are a number of ideological and structural obstacles that have long stood in the way of all transnational actors who rest their claims on grievances of an *international* character, whether arising from war or in a period of peace. My contention is that the evident weakening of some these obstacles already represents a sea change in the international status of moral concerns, and that this weakening may be most generally understood as an expression of stronger normative impulses in an increasingly integrated world.

Sovereignty and the Realist Tradition

The history of global politics contains many instances of brutal behavior that violates minimal standards of morality and, more recently, positive rules of international law. The system of sovereign states that has been the foundation of world order since at least the middle of the seventeenth century contains two defining properties appropriate to this discussion: first, the territorial supremacy of governments representing sovereign states, and second, the affirmation of "military necessity" as the governing principle for the conduct of war. On this basis, the role of moral and legal restraints in wartime has been minimal (and even more so during episodes of internal civil conflict). As such, there have been no international procedures to assess accountability, beyond those which the victor could exact from the vanquished—and those used by strong countries in the North to protect their nationals abroad against abuses allegedly committed by the territorial government.[6]

This condition has been reinforced intellectually over many years by a series of influential thinkers who stress the primacy of state power as the fundamental basis for order in the relations among states, and who counsel against a sentimental and allegedly self-destructive reliance on the enticements of law and morality. Machiavelli, Hobbes, and Clausewitz are among those writers of the past whose realist assessments of international society have exerted an extraordinary influence on the thought and action of states. In our own time Hans Morgenthau, Reinhold Niebuhr, George Kennan, and Henry Kissinger have in various ways applied this tradition of thought to contemporary circumstances, particularly since the end of World War II. A dominating consensus in support of a realist orientation toward policy issues has been guiding U.S. foreign policy. A valuable softening of the realist outlook, however, can be found in the work of Hedley Bull, who conceived of a modest form of international society in which territorial sovereignty of weaker states was generally respected (nonintervention norms) while dominant states, often self-styled "great powers," assume additional roles in sustaining overall moderation and stability.[7]

The ideological dominance of realism has also been reinforced by conventional accounts of the history of this century. Such accounts stress heavily the supposed failures of idealist approaches to world order in the period after World War I, approaches that managed neither to provide stability in international relations nor to meet the challenge posed by aggressive, expansionist powers in Europe and Asia. The complacency of the liberal democracies after 1918, realists say, was characterized by a reliance on an impotent League of Nations, on misleading moves toward disarmament, and most of all, on a diplomacy of appeasement in the face of the Axis challenge; such complacency shaped the most generally accepted understanding of the reasons for the onset of World War II. Drawn from this experience were what the West called "the lessons of Munich," the highwater mark of the failed diplomacy of appeasement.

What resulted in the postwar context was a realist thinking based on countervailing power, continuous war preparations, and a vigilant diplomacy of containment toward potential adversaries. Such thinking became a widely endorsed foundation for world order after 1945, and hardened into geopolitical doctrine during the cold war. The approach taken by the West during this period between 1945 and 1989 is generally regarded as a success story. World War III was avoided by the policy of brinksmanship and deterrence on the part of the two superpowers. Warfare occurred with frequency and intensity during these years, but it was "safely" confined throughout the cold war to interventionary uses of force in various "peripheral" countries of the South. The realist path is thus credited, though with monumental insensitivity to the magnitude of violence during this period in the South, with maintaining world peace, and with achieving a generally bloodless victory for the West in the cold war. John Lewis Gaddis has bestowed on this period the misleading but ever popular label, "the long peace," "peace" being a distinctly Western privilege. Apparently the war zones in Asia, Africa, and Latin America in the aftermath of colonialism were thus treated as "acceptable" arenas for geopolitical competition, even though the resulting political violence in a large number of Third World countries was no doubt considerably less "acceptable" to the people living there.

Ever since the founding of the modern state, there have existed various counter-traditions to realism, especially those associated with a persistent moral dimension of political thought associated with foreign policy in the United States, a moral edge perhaps best, and first, articulated by Thomas Jefferson. Jefferson's basic antirealist formulation contended that a state should respect moral guidelines as fully in its international relations as individuals should in their personal relations. This orientation was initially the dominant American view as the country emerged from its own revolution as an independent state determined, above all else, not to emulate the European powers in their external relations, which seemed driven by great-power rivalry and geopolitical calculations. In contrast, the United States, as a matter of fixed principle, would remain aloof from "entangling alliances," avoid the seemingly continuous cycle of war among the European states, and seek to exemplify its claimed moral exceptionalism. In this way the new nation, the world's first victor in an anticolonial war, could exert a positive moral influence on the conduct of international relations, which in the late eighteenth century meant the avoidance of international warfare.

There is no doubt that a large part of this early quest for a distinctive American identity on the global stage involved a desire on the part of American leaders to distance themselves from their European forebears, whose approach to international relations was perceived to be decadent, cynical, and needlessly war-prone. Of course, a more realist reading of American exceptionalism would stress the special security benefits enjoyed by the United States from such a policy. The United States had the great geopolitical advantages of having weak neighbors, two vast oceans separating its territory from the stronger states of the world, and a weakly defended continental expanse within which to realize its great-power destiny. Revealingly, the United States broke its isolationism and joined the European system of "internationalism" only after its sense of peacetime invulnerability was shattered by the attack on Pearl Harbor in 1941.[8]

Nevertheless, the idea of exerting a benign influence has never entirely disappeared in American thinking about world order. It reached the climax of its influence in the last years of the presidency of Woodrow Wilson at the end of World War I with the failed effort to supplant balance-of-power conceptions of global security. As suggested earlier, to the extent that they were projected outwardly, such moralistic and legalist views later became discredited, especially among policy elites and within academic circles, due to what was perceived to be their disastrous applications during the leadup to World War II.[9] Whether this was a proper historical judgment about the causes of Nazi expansionism and World War II remains somewhat contested in scholarly circles to this day, but there is no doubt that a strong consensus supports the view that departures from the canons of realism contributed to the terrible failures of foreign policy in Europe during the 1930s.

The Normative Dimension of International Relations

World War II had a strange, contradictory impact on thought and policy relating to international relations—and more specifically on the political landscape of the United States. As indicated, the events leading up to World War II, especially the appeasement of expansionist powers, led the United States to abandon once and for all its historic stand of noninvolvement outside the Western Hemisphere. This shift was also prompted by the evolution of long-range military technology that nullified the benefits of geographic isolation. As a result of these factors, the United States conceived of itself from 1945 onward as global power, an alliance leader, and as a power continuously prepared to engage in major warfare.

But the picture is incomplete without also taking into account the ambiguous ending of World War II, especially the atomic bomb attacks on Hiroshima and Nagasaki. The scale of devastation, combined with the sense that any subsequent large-scale war would likely be fought with improved weapons of mass destruction, led to a public outcry against "the war system," even while victory in what was generally regarded as a "just war" was being celebrated. In effect, despite "the lessons of Munich," there was a new idealistic pressure to revive the Wilsonian vision of a world order based less on the interaction and political will of sovereign states and more on the collective responsibility of these states to keep the peace in order to avoid disappearing in a final orgy of annihilation.

Thus, despite the emergence of a realist consensus, elements of the earlier moral orientation continued to function, sometimes quite effectively, as a counterpoint to realism. Such attitudes contributed strongly in the mid-1940s to the initial American enthusiasm for the United Nations as a partial guarantor of global security. The UN Charter appeared to be premised on international law and the collective responsibilities of the organized international community. The charter prohibited all uses of international force other than those that could be justified as self-defense against a prior armed attack or those that were authorized by an explicit UN Security Council decision. As such, the United Nations did seem to offer an alternative to statist ideas of global security, which rested on calculations of countervailing power and alliance arrangements, although the UN vision was not seriously implemented by real transfers of sovereignty or allegiances. Also expressive of a renewed normative approach to U.S. relations with the world was the move to make human rights an integral part of international law, a shift that actually began to affect policy as NGOs became more active and then as the Carter administration began to put human rights on the foreign policy agenda. Not insignificantly, by the way, it was the United States government that most strongly advocated a war crimes tribunal to try the leadership of the defeated Axis countries in 1945. Without this American insistence, the likelihood is that the victorious powers would have organized mass summary executions of large numbers of high-ranking German and Japanese military officers and civilian officials without being troubled by the niceties of indictment, prosecution, and assessment of individual cases.

Despite these normative initiatives, however, realist thinking most definitely carried the day. The United States exercised its leadership role mainly by way of military, diplomatic, economic, and ideological pressure. The United Nations, for its part, was rendered more or less impotent during the prolonged geopolitical stalemate of the cold war. But even in the last decade, in the absence of a central rivalry among states, the continuing marginality of the United Nations confirms the extent to which the realist world picture remains ascendant. Today, European countries seem more inclined to address seriously normative concerns, while the United States behaves as if international relations are entirely reducible to self-serving power/interest calculations.

Beyond Realism and Global Reform

Throughout the twentieth century there has also been evident a more transformative view of world order that has enjoyed some support in civil society, but which never achieved much resonance in leadership circles. It is a vision that has become more manifest as civil society has become more vocal in matters of policy, and it may be part of the explanation of why intertemporal justice has begun to engage the political imagination of many societies. From time to time prominent thinkers have proposed some form of world government as the essential foundation for a peaceful world in which war ceases to exist as a social institution. Such advocacy peaked in the aftermath of each of the two world wars in this century, enjoying considerable backing in civil society. For some, the advent of nuclear weapons represented a conclusive argument in favor of drastic disarmament at the level of states, with security functions being transferred to global institutions. Jonathan Schell's *Fate of the Earth*, a worldwide best seller in 1982, argued with great eloquence the thesis that human survival depended on making a profound stand against nuclear weapons. Such concern for the future inevitably prompted parallel concern about unacknowledged grievances from the past. As soon as time future is brought into political focus, time past becomes relevant.

Persisting Realism in an Era of Globalization

At present, with the end of the cold war and the absence of superpower confrontation, concerns about nuclear war have receded from public consciousness, at least temporarily. The focus is now on nonproliferation rather than disarmament or deterrence. Realist approaches to global security remain the basis of policymaking in major countries, and remain the principal justification for not renouncing the nuclear option. At the outset of the twenty-first century the main preoccupation internationally is how to adjust realist views given the heightened importance of economic integration at regional and global levels—in other words, how to usher geopolitical realism into what has come to be called the "era of globalization."

Even more at odds with this rise of global market forces is transnational civic activism, which is primarily driven by ethics and values. Yet, despite the dominance of realist thinking, and despite the market-driven orientation of globalization, the interest in intertemporal equity has over the last few years become more powerful than ever on the international scene. A number of hypotheses may help explain this phenomenon, of which the revived interest in the Nanking Massacre is but a small, yet telling, illustration.

The rapidly increasing pace of change in the electronic age seems to have heightened our sense of the time dimension as it relates to perceived justice and injustice. In this sense, notions of both future and past become more active in the political consciousness. The recent scholarly efforts to extend the protection of international law to future generations exhibit the futurist side of intertemporal equity.[10] Environmental decay and resource depletion have become cause for concern that the lifestyle of present generations, in addition to increasing demographic pressures, is creating a situation in which the life prospects of future generations may be in dire danger. And with global warming and ecological collapse greater threats than ever, an ethos of responsibility that emphasizes a temporal perspective of human solidarity seems entirely appropriate. Anticipatory redress seeks to restrain present activity by invoking what has come to be called in international environmental law "the precautionary principle." The idea here is that restraint should be imposed in a precautionary spirit without waiting for a judgment of scientific certainty as to the risks posed. This approach, in effect, sounds a note of caution with respect to long-range risk-taking. It remains to be seen whether such guardianship of future generations is a genuine political project, or merely lip service to an ethos of temporal responsibility. From the vantage point of the present, a skeptical appraisal seems in order. Those forces that favor maximizing the benefits to present generations remain firmly in control of market and governmental outlooks. It is undeniable, however, that the temporal dimension has definitively entered the discourse about international justice.

As the temporal dimension gains ascendancy, the spatial dimension of international justice seems to be in decline. There is a direct opposition between market pressures and any concerted effort to rectify by direct action relations between rich and poor countries. This trend is visible in the dramatic decline in direct foreign economic assistance on the part of rich countries in the North, especially the United States. Such assistance was earlier partly supported as an effective means of overcoming human suffering and income inequalities in North/South relations. The idea of distributive justice with countries also seems to be losing importance to the extent that territorial boundaries are being eroded by globalization—and by its backlash, fragmentation, and localization. These opposed tendencies both diminish the centrality of the state as the defining unit in the existing world order, and as the principal guardian of human well-being. To look back in time, however, is to resurrect the relevance of identities associated with the state, and with the ideology of nationalism.

The Challenge and Relevance of Global Civil Society

A further development is the awakening of global civil society to a broad normative agenda. As states and markets are shaped primarily by self-interest, it is primarily movements and initiatives organized by voluntary associations that are raising issues of moral significance and global scope. Whether the issue is compensation for victims of the Holocaust, the grievances of indigenous peoples, the injustice of slavery or colonialism, or official recognition of the atrocities of Nanking or Hiroshima, the motive force for such activism is situated in civil society.

This civic activism is encouraged by two additional factors. First of all, the global media provides vivid images from scenes of popular activism and makes the struggles in one setting suggestive to potential activists in another. Such a global learning process is greatly aided by way of television and the Internet, which convey in real time to all parts of the world various struggles for justice. The second factor has to do with the increased intermixing of the peoples of the world through various forms of transnational migration, including the flow of students across national and civilizational boundaries. In these post-migration settings there may emerge a particularly strong motivation to communicate deeply felt grievances, including anguish associated with past injustices.

Trends toward democratization and internationalization are also helpful. There is an increasing variety of arenas within which to raise consciousness and pursue specific forms of redress, thereby creating practical outlets for suppressed feelings of hurt and resentment. The United Nations has provided a number of suitable arenas that allow such claims for recognition and redress to be pursued. Women, indigenous people, and environmentally aggrieved groups have made particularly effective and creative use of such arenas. This process reached its high-water mark in the early 1990s at a series of UN conferences that provided a space for transnational civic activists to press their claims, and which combined democratizing and internationalizing features.[11] Other important arenas include a variety of educational forums around the world, including international academic meetings.

The emergence of human rights as an important dimension of world politics has also buttressed the cause of civic activism and intertemporal rights. This emergence is a complex story that has been narrated many times in recent years, especially during celebrations organized around the fiftieth anniversary of the Universal Declaration of Human Rights in 1998.[12] The idea that rights exist on an international level and deserve protection by regional and global institutions automatically allows past and present abuses to be brought to light. The human rights movement started a half-century ago as an exercise in exhortation, with assurances to governments that there would be no intention to seek enforcement mechanisms, and thus no implicit threat to the territorial supremacy of the sovereign state. It was thus left to civil society to cast such political expectations in a new light, to question sovereign rights, and to confront authoritarian rule with a legitimated basis of resistance. Transnational human rights NGOs took the norms seriously, gathered information on violations, and used the media to exert leverage on governments. Opposition movements were encouraged to believe that their goals were legitimate, and enjoyed international support. This dynamic converged with geopolitics in the latter stages of the cold war as Western governments mounted pressures, based on human rights norms, that greatly strengthened the position of internal resistance movements, especially in the countries of Eastern Europe during the 1980s. The global anti-apartheid campaign lent historical weight to the claim that the prolonged denial of human rights could ultimately result in an international movement to uproot deeply entrenched injustice.

This evolving "human rights culture," as Richard Rorty has called it, has become part of a whole new mode of thinking and speaking about global rights issues. One of the most fertile, powerful, and germane terms in this new lexicon is Ken Booth's notion of "human wrongs" as a corollary to "human rights."[13] Booth criticizes the whole tradition of thought and practice in international relations that had for centuries sanitized human wrongs behind the protective screens of sovereignty and war. In effect, a legitimate world order must not provide such mechanisms for insulating human wrongs from accountability, and in due course, must provide the means to correct existing abuses. In this new world order, the ongoing quest for the future redress of past grievances would no longer be necessary, because present modes of redress would be sufficient. Securing such effective channels of redress is a principal goal of a well-functioning constitutional democracy. Booth's perspective would reinforce this democratic process with mechanisms to ensure the responsible and humane exercise of sovereignty by states.

The War Crimes Experiment

Perhaps the strongest element of all in this series of normative developments involves the push toward accountability for crimes of state. As mentioned earlier, the Nuremberg/Tokyo breakthroughs grew out of the special circumstances of a world war in which the defeated countries surrendered unconditionally, and in which their surviving leaders were available for indictment and prosecution in criminal tribunals set up for such a purpose. Although the human wrongs being addressed were of the greatest severity, the enterprise remained controversial because of its one-sidedness (the exemption of legal scrutiny for the alleged crimes committed by the victorious side) and its retroactivity (the post-facto nature of the delimitation of the crimes and the contention of individual criminal liability). This negative impression was reinforced by the failure to transform the Nuremberg/Tokyo framework into a more enduring foundation for accountability by establishing a permanent criminal court and setting forth a code of international crimes and punishments that would in the future bind all governments. The cold war decades precluded most forms of international cooperation that rested on shared normative commitments, especially if the nature of the cooperation might lead to legally mandated accusations across the East/West ideological divide.

But in the last twenty years the outlook for international accountability has been steadily improving. One reason for this has been the experience of a series of Latin American societies, most notably Argentina and Chile, that experimented with various means of imposing some sort of closure on past abuses of power. The initial effort to prosecute the representatives of the former regime as war criminals was abandoned due to fears of provoking a backlash. Instead, established impunity arrangements in which the project of imposing individual criminal liability on past political and military leaders were given up, and instead procedures of inquiry into the past that expressed and documented "the truth" were established. Such arrangements were never entirely satisfactory to either side, especially to those who had been the direct victims of unforgivable crimes, but the disclosure of the past was at least a symbolic form of redress. Such a compromise was characterized by the slogan "Rather peace than justice." The issues have achieved worldwide salience recently partly due to the 1998 reports of South Africa's Truth and Reconciliation Commission. The South African approach granted amnesty to the perpetrators of past human wrongs if they fully cooperated as witnesses legally bound to tell the whole truth.

The political violence that accompanied the breakup of the former Yugoslavia in the 1990s also created a special set of circumstances that prompted the revival of the Nuremberg idea. Accordingly, the UN Security Council established an ad hoc tribunal in The Hague for the prosecution of those indicted for war crimes, and due to pressures not to ignore African abuses added a second tribunal in the same location to address charges against those accused of genocide and crimes against humanity in Rwanda.[14] The former tribunal has made notable progress, despite initial skepticism, and despite the inability to arrest the most prominent of the Serbian wrongdoers, especially Radovan Karadzic and General Ratko Mladic, who were the architects of ethnic cleansing in Bosnia. The arrest in 1997 of Major General Radislav Krstic, the commander responsible for the 1995 massacre at the UN-designated "safe haven" of Srebrenica, represented a breakthrough; the first high officer among those indicted at the Hague had been apprehended.[15] Another dramatic development occurred in March 1999 when Yugoslav president Slobadan Milosevic, a sitting head of state, was indicted, in the midst of the NATO war over Kosovo, by the Hague tribunal for alleged crimes against the people of Kosovo.

The Yugoslav/Rwandan initiative has also stimulated widespread support among governments and in global civil society for the establishment of a permanent international criminal court. This transnational coalition, though opposed in essential respects by the U.S. government, succeeded in organizing a 1998 intergovernmental conference in Rome that produced a treaty in support of establishing such a court as soon as ratification by sixty countries occurs. It remains to be seen whether the coalition that provisionally approved the treaty can now mount enough pressure to obtain widespread ratification that results in meaningful implementation. If such an institution is established, it could strongly reinforce efforts to invoke international law to seek redress and accountability in an international global setting. It would be important that such a tribunal apply the authority of law to representatives of all states, both strong and weak, but it's not a likely prospect in the decade ahead.

A dramatic development pertaining to accountability was the 1998 detention of General Augusto Pinochet, the former dictator of Chile, in Britain pending an extradition request from Spain, where he would be subject to prosecution for crimes against humanity committed in the 1970s during his time as head of state in Chile. The central question is not whether Pinochet enjoys immunity due to his former status as governmental leader, but whether such immunity, granted as part of the deal by which Pinochet relinquished power, should be respected on an *international* level if that is what the Chilean Government formally requests. In this instance, the Government of Chile has requested Pinochet's release from British detention and his return to Chile, supposedly to face pending charges arising from cases in Chilean courts. The alternative to deferring to Chilean domestic law by returning Pinochet to Chile is to assert that by international legal standards the character of the crime engages the whole world and thereby confers a universal jurisdiction to prosecute, as in the case of piracy. Even if Pinochet is eventually not prosecuted in Spain or elsewhere, his detention has generated a very important debate about the accountability of political leaders and the redress of grievances.[16] In early 2000 the Pinochet case took a different turn through a British decision that he was unfit to stand trial and should be returned forthwith to Chile.

For all of the reasons summarized above, the theme of redress for past grievances has generated unprecedented interest, though a developing backlash may cause this prominence to recede. There is a growing argument that it is unnecessary for subsequent generations to be overly apologetic about past human wrongs, which should only be morally and legally evaluated in the temporal context of their occurrence, and not in the present, when other considerations can be brought to bear. Such a contention has been advanced in the debate over holding banks in Europe materially accountable for unjust practices carried out over a half-century earlier—that is, applying a 1990s morality to a 1940s context. Another argument is that certain forms of redress assume a mercenary character and cheapen the historical memory by giving a cash value to past injustices.[17]

On a different level, many governments, despite their endorsement of democracy on a state-society level are very threatened by the growth of transnational democratic institutions and forums such as global conferences on world issues held under UN auspices. In fact, a backlash has ensued such that this UN conference format is soon likely to disappear, or at least lose substantial momentum, an occurrence that will probably be explained as a result of bureaucratic downsizing and cost efficiency. The real reason for such a retreat is that these conferences were a mechanism of empowerment for those seeking redress in a series of high-profile media-sensitive arenas. Such media access created an opportunity for aggrieved groups to magnify their overall influence and mount a campaign for redress.

The real opposition to democratization on a global level was motivated less by the substantive issues at stake than by a feared power shift, a loss of control by the state. This prospect was especially troubling at a time when state capacity was already being redefined and diminished by the rise of global market forces. As matters now stand, there exists a series of unresolved tensions between the priorities of an emergent global civil society and the defensive, and still formidable, power of the state to dominate world order in the face of intensifying globalization.

REDRESS IN THE SETTING OF THE NANKING MASSACRE

The preceding discussion depicts the context in which the unresolved character of the Nanking Massacre needs to be viewed. An awakening of political consciousness accompanied the sixtieth anniversary of the ordeal endured by the citizens of Nanking, and disclosed a lingering sense of grievance and misunderstanding. That the issue of Nanking remains contested political terrain is evident at intergovernmental diplomatic levels. Leaders of Japan and China seem unable to close the book on the past in a mutually satisfactory manner. At the level of civil society, preliminary efforts to engage the Japanese scholarly community in the dynamics of shared inquiry into the historical reality of Nanking has achieved only a preliminary and partial success, and has generated its own tensions. Japanese scholars tended to question the scale of the massacre and victimization being alleged by Chinese scholars. Such a controversy was about the meaning of the inquiry as much as it was about the accuracy of the historical narrative. On one side, Japan's hairsplitting over the statistical reliability upon which the allegations was perceived as a diversion from the calls for emotional and political redress. On the other side, the perceived exaggeration of the occurrences in terms of the scale of victimization is seen by Japan as a way of unfairly deepening that country's responsibility beyond its factual reality.

The minimum achievement resulting from films, books, and conferences of the last several years has been to extend to Nanking the spirit of serious remembrance, not to mention valuable historical clarification.[18] Carolyn Forché has aptly said that "[t]he resistance to terror is what makes the world habitable."[19] And certainly part of this resistance is activating the memory, even if belatedly, of past human wrongs, especially those that have been allowed to be forgotten, drained of their full meaning, or presented in a distorted fashion. As mentioned earlier, many believe that, especially in the United States, there has been far greater compassion and concern for the survivors of Nazism and their descendants than for Asian victims of Japanese military expansionism. True, nothing done by Japan, including its predatory behavior at Nanking and elsewhere in the region, approaches the sheer horror of the Holocaust. But on another level each experience of acute victimization deserves our most sensitive concern. In reality, much of the long-standing neglect of redress for Japanese atrocities seems to be partly explained by a series of secondary factors. For one thing, China moved soon after World War II into the camp of America's ideological and strategic adversary; for another, racial, ethnic, religious, and cultural factors made most Americans feel more affinity with European victims than they did with Asian victims. Also, postwar efforts to impose criminal accountability on surviving leaders were far more prominent in Europe through the Nuremberg trials than were the rather obscure parallel efforts in Tokyo. Finally, the American reliance on the atomic bomb in its war against Japan appears to have made the U.S. government somewhat reluctant to press the Japanese too hard on the war crimes front, especially as the Japanese elite were solicited very soon as allies in the quickly developing standoff with the Soviet Union and the newly communist People's Republic of China.

Attending the issues of memory and various interpretations of historical fact is the question of appropriate redress. There appears to be a sort of natural division of labor in the search for justice for unresolved grievances. For the government representing the victims and their descendants, there is the search for formal recognition, whether by apology or some kind of material restitution. For the victimized society, the work of memory involves a kind of collective psychotherapy that centers on rituals of acknowledgment on a less official, civilian level. If the opposing sides can engage constructively on the civilian level, there ensues a collaboration that helps overcome the accusatory/defensive interaction and tone that will otherwise mar this work of excavating such a painful past. It seems that the inquiry into Nanking 1937 seeks to proceed on this basis, with a grassroots effort calling for reflection and remorse, but not necessarily material restitution or public humiliation.

This effort also has implications outside China. Locating some of the Asian memory work within the United States is a way of seeking to overcome the persisting Eurocentricism in America that continues to regard human wrongs more seriously if they occur in the West than if their locus is elsewhere, as in this instance in China. Furthermore, such an inquiry undoubtedly helps to awaken Japanese society from its official and societal forms of denial, which have often kept the past in darkness for the Japanese, despite some brave and notable exceptions. There are several Japanese individuals of conscience who have taken steps on their own to verify the accusations and to give them currency in Japan. It remains doubtful that the minimal goals of redress for the crimes at Nanking have been yet realized, but at least a start has been made.

In a broader sense, the Nanking inquiry resonates globally, sending a clear message that this process of recalling painful past memories and properly acknowledging past wrongs is a collective human responsibility. It needs to engage people as people and exhibit an ethos of human solidarity, one that could ultimately help deter future crimes against humanity and encourage timely global responses to such profound challenges. The world community's ineffectual and tepid responses to ethnic cleansing in Bosnia and to genocide in Rwanda suggest that much work needs to be done, and the NATO intervention in Kosovo, although responsive, reveals the dangers of a vengeful form of humanitarianism.[20]

What is ultimately needed is not only an emphasis on redress of past wrongs, as in the case of the Nanking Massacre, but also a sense of shared human commitment to the pledge of "Never again." The past has intrinsic importance, partly because it inevitably informs the present, but also because it can teach us how to prevent future repetitions of criminal behavior by governments and by their militarist undertakings.

The final chapter broadens the human rights inquiry by addressing the profound challenge of how to ground the pursuit of global security upon a terrain of moral principles. In this regard, morality and human rights are reciprocally related, and both bear on an unfolding debate about the changing character of security for states and peoples in an ever more integrated world order. Both provide the essential features of an aspirational world order that qualifies as the first historical realization of humane governance for the peoples of the world, and offer one scenario of stable politics and global security in the emergent era of globalization.

Morality and Global Security 13

A Human Rights Perspective

PRELIMINARIES

The topic of morality in the global sphere of politics is complex, confusing, controversial, and in the end, unavoidable. It is unavoidable because the undertaking of war is inconceivable in the modern world without an attendant chorus of justifying and discrediting arguments; even nondemocratic governments do not in modern times generally embark upon war without elaborate public efforts to legitimate their actions. But whether these moral and legal debates are more than mere reiterations of the rhetorical diplomacy that has evolved over the course of several centuries remains inherently uncertain and is subject to contradictory conceptual and historical modes of interpretation.

Recently the relevance of morality to international or global security has been further problematized by the fact that security can no longer be simply defined in a purely statist context. Human factors must be considered: the right to freedom from fear, for example, and the satisfaction of basic survival needs. One must consider the conditions of domestic political order that shape attitudes toward war in foreign policy, and the role of international institutions in specifying limits on the permissible, and most recently, the demographic, environmental, and resource dimensions of sustainable development. International security becomes, then, a synonym for whatever is valued in international life.[1]

There are, in turn, two interpretations of this broader conception of security: one is to regard security, quite simply, as the state of individual and collective existence that is free from threat of harm in all its forms. The more restricted conception defines international security as the elimination of threats arising from the use of force across international boundaries. The narrow conception of international security is concerned only with the military means and material capabilities relied upon by states to uphold the relative position of their country in the world, and more important, to sustain sovereignty in relation to people, resources, and territory. An important reformulation of the narrow conception would include military initiatives mandated or undertaken by the United Nations or regional actors such as NATO in places like Bosnia. In any case, it is important to understand that the choice to use the term "global security" is a deliberate one, as it encompasses the widest possible range of interpretations, as opposed to "international security," which refers essentially to a narrow statist conception.

Of course, the complexity doesn't end here. There is, above all, a fundamental distinction between the security of the state or unit and the security of the system as a whole. For instance, the elected leaders of France are presumably sincerely persuaded that France will be more secure as a result of its controversial series of nuclear tests in the Pacific during 1995–96, but the very same tests may create profound insecurity on the international scene, either because other states will feel encouraged to follow suit or because of harm done to health and environmental conditions in the affected region. Global security encompasses both discourses, that on behalf of particular states and that on behalf of the past, present, and future of global society as a whole.

This raises the question of whose authority shall be respected in decisions of international scope. Major states have long regarded it to be an element of their sovereignty to determine their national security policy with virtually no duty of external accountability. Thus, the French state has the last word with regard to French security even if its decisions are widely regarded as wrong. Minor or outlaw states have more restricted discretion to define their own security, as they are subject to geopolitical constraints and unilateral enforcement of nuclear nonproliferation norms; in particular, countries such as North Korea, Iran, and Iraq are perceived as threats to established regional orders and are subjected to various constraints on their exercise of sovereign rights with respect to security. These constraints are set and enforced by hegemonic states and their allies.

One source of widespread confusion is the indeterminate relationship between law and morality as it bears upon our thinking about global security. It is quite possible for these two sources of normative authority, which are commonly treated as mutually reinforcing, to point in divergent, even contradictory, directions. For instance, a lawful peace treaty can validate an immoral outcome in warfare—quite clearly the case with the 1995 Dayton Peace Agreement, which failed to reverse the effects of ethnic cleansing in Bosnia. Also, international law for decades lent an aura of legality to colonial relationships and exploitative foreign investment arrangements.

At the same time, there is a continuous moral pressure to make law into a vehicle for the realization of moral goals. There is growing pressure, for example, to impose strict international limits on the use of force on the part of all states and political actors, implying that these actors have a *moral* duty to uphold international law, and that the law, in effect, embodies authoritative standards of morality that confine use of force to "defensive" modes. But even if the authority of law is affirmed in such circumstances, the nature of the guidance provided is often vague and unsatisfactory, allowing multiple self-serving interpretations of the doctrine of self-defense. For decades prominent diplomats labored to agree upon a definition of "aggression," which when finally achieved, turned out to be useless, given its abstractness and vulnerability to loopholes. Law on such fundamental matters as the right of states to use force is subject to limitless manipulation due to the authority retained by governments to interpret its meaning in each context and with respect to the proper delimitation of the right of self-defense.[2]

Problems of legal interpretation of the use of force become even more daunting in a political order in which authority is dispersed and decentralized. Generally, sovereign states have been reluctant to refer interstate disputes to third-party mediation. Even on the rare occasions when a global arena for decision is available in disputes relating to security policy, as was the case with the Nicaraguan government's complaints about U.S. efforts during the 1980s to destabilize the Sandinista government, dominant states rarely avail themselves of these arenas. The U.S. government did its utmost to prevent the World Court from reaching a decision, and then when its policies were held in violation of international law, defied the decision.[3] After the decision, U.S. officials attacked the integrity of the World Court as "Marxist and third-world oriented," and argued that, in any event, a country was not obliged to sign a suicide pact in deference to international law. Capitulation to geopolitics by an international institution should not have been surprising, but what may have been less expected was the degree to which distinguished international law specialists of realist persuasion came rushing to the defense of the U.S. position, which denied the relevance of international law to the use of force. In the same breath, these jurists urged the U.S. government for pragmatic reasons to restore its adherence to the compulsory jurisdiction of the World Court.[4]

The proper application of morality to international political behavior is far from self-evident even when the relevance of morality is affirmed. Its application is conditioned by various assumptions about human nature, both as it happens to be intellectually conceived at a given moment, and as defined by decisive historical experiences. Cynical perceptions of war and morality abound; they are influenced by the various decontextualized readings by international relations specialists of the "Melian dialogue." Thucydides' immortal account of the Peloponesian Wars is virtually reduced to a single aphoristic assertion, "The strong do what they will and the weak do what they must," which is then generalized to validate a cynical view of the role of moral constraint in warfare, at least in the relations between unequal entities.[5] This is a narrow reading of Thucydides' that is most misleading. If anything, Thucydides seems to be arguing that a decent respect for moral restraint is as much, if not more, of a necessity for the strong as for the weak, and that the decline of Athens was linked to an abandonment over time of such limits.

Another relevant debate over the interpretation of recent world history is centered upon the prescriptive link between morality and international security; various types of realists insist that moral sensitivity (including deference to international law) and international security are negatively cor-related in all situations of strategic conflict. Because realism has been ascen-dant in most elite circles since the end of World War II, autonomous claims about adherence to norms, whether moral or legal in nature, have been gen-erally disregarded whenever serious security objectives have been at stake. In this view, morality is for the naïve, whether weak or strong; the perceived failure of Wilsonianism in the years leading up to World War II is fre-quently invoked by proponents of this realist outlook. Such a realist read-ing of this historical debate—the lessons of Munich, the rejection of appeasement, moralism, and legalism—has dominated political conscious-ness and has dampened the assertion of moral claims as serious constraints on behavior as distinct from providing helpful rationalizations for recourse to force by powerful states.[6] The realists' domination of foreign policy dis-course has been reinforced by an exaggerated dichotomy between domestic and international contexts. This distinction between the orderly hierarchy of a territorial state and the anarchy of international space underlies struc-tural arguments that are usually traced back to Hobbes. Such an orienta-tion resurfaced in recent decades in various forms, perhaps most influentially in the phrase of Reinhold Niebuhr ("moral man in immoral society") and the parallel self-serving assertion generally made by American liberals that the United States is "a Lockean nation in an Hobbesian world."

It is against this ideological and historical background that the role of morality in global politics comes to light. It seems useful to distinguish three types of moral relevance in the domain of global security, and to treat them for the sake of analysis as distinct, while recognizing their interrelat-edness in the minds of leaders and citizens:

- Type I: morality as a constraint on the use of force as a source of security in international society;
- Type II: morality as a means by which to realize the security goals of sover-eign states;

- Type III: morality of ends by which one exerts control over the role of force in world politics through a combination of disarmament, demilitarization, and an ethos of nonviolence.

Inherent in this delineation is a Habermassian outlook in that it takes as essential for the full realization of democracy that the role of political violence as a basis for global security must be drawn into serious question by a process of comprehensive reflection and debate, and that moral perspectives (a concern for what is right and proper) are integral to this process; but the policy outcome of such a moral inquiry is inherently ambiguous, as it depends more on "which morality" rather than on the essentially false question of "whether morality?" Without a dynamic of continuous and unconditional democratic accountability (an undertaking made difficult by the use of secrecy and media manipulation, especially with respect to national security); the overall benefit of bringing moral considerations explicitly to bear on the global security policy of states and other actors is questionable. Type I, or realist, morality tends toward apologetics, while transcendent, or Type III, Kantian morality tends toward utopian irrelevance.[7] It would be a mistake to regard moral considerations as responsible for a declining reliance by states on the use of force. Rather, such a decline reflects the impact of the narrowing of strategic interests in the current phase of global politics.[8] This strategic narrowing has been evident in recent debates about humanitarian intervention under the auspices of the United Nations in Bosnia, Burundi, Rwanda, and elsewhere. In some respects, it was the avowedly Type I moral pressures to use force that were being deflected by reference to an amoral calculus of geopolitical factors at stake.[9]

Given the current situation, it is easy to share the outlook of Gabriel Kolko, author of *Century of War*, a powerful study of wars since 1914, that the societal arrangements that caused so much human suffering through the recurrence of wars remain in place and cast a very dark shadow across the future prospects of humanity.[10] In this regard a people-oriented approach to global security, as distinct from statist or market-oriented approaches, proceeds from a transpolitical moral claim, namely, that the social institution of war must be repudiated, as must its cultural, social, economic, and political support structures. From such perspectives, clear actions taken in self-defense and recourses to force by the United Nations and regional institutions might no longer seem morally acceptable even if the behavior in question conforms to international law as impartially understood.

To consider this line of argument more fully, the historical dialogue on war must be considered in relation to the present global setting. As it stands, the human predicament seems Sisyphean in nature as there is no enduringly satisfactory reconciliation between morality and global security available for application to concrete circumstances, and yet there is a permanent need to search again and again for alternatives to violence in the setting of international disputes or humanitarian catastrophes. And yet our inability to know what are the limits of the possible in political life validates a balancing of the imaginative faculties against the assessments of the rational faculties.[11]

HISTORICAL FRAMING

Our understanding of the connections between morality and global security is framed by our collective short- and middle-term historical memory, occasionally reinforced by longer-term classical references to Athens and Rome. In this regard, the way the narrative of the past is most authoritatively understood by elites and the media, especially through interpretations of historic failures of political leadership, exerts an enormous influence on policy and decision in the present. With respect to the place of morality in global security policy, such a narrative for the United States is heavily conditioned by the interpretation of the two world wars and the cold war.

World War I was a disillusioning experience for the citizens of Europe. The war was far more devastating and traumatic in its societal impacts than had been anticipated at the time by military and political elites. The war was widely condemned as the necessary consequence of an amoral approach to international relations by the rulers of Europe; in its aftermath was left a space for those who called for a more morally oriented approach.[12] In years following World War I, various conditions of acute alienation existed, most dramatically in Russia, where the Bolshevik Revolution soon filled the vacuum. Elsewhere in Europe, liberal democracies found themselves hamstrung by their suppression of political opposition during the upswell of wartime patriotism, and thereby forfeited the opportunity to reconstitute the established order.[13]

A less discernible impact of World War I was its effect on opinions about the maintenance of global security, a consequence made far more salient because of the happenchance of Woodrow Wilson's moralizing, crusading leadership role. If a less visionary leader had represented the United States during the years 1918–1920 the effect on subsequent debates about global security would almost certainly have taken a different turn. If the United States had not rescued the victorious powers from the quagmires of a disastrous war, Wilson's influence as U.S. president would have mattered far less. And if Wilson had been Italian, or even British, his voice would have not counted. The diplomats representing the great powers of Europe, however cynical their actual convictions, were obliged, given the outpouring of enthusiasm by the peoples of Europe for Wilson, to listen and even to proffer a nominal acquiescence. Georges Clemenceau expressed vividly the European skepticism of his era with his witty response to Wilson's celebrated "Fourteen Points": "Even the Good Lord had only ten!"

But Wilson was the bearer of an antirealist view of international security that was expressly couched in moral rhetoric and which sharply criticized Europe's deeply entrenched power relations, especially in relation to the breakdown of peace in the period leading up to World War I. Wilson's fervent plea centered on an insistence that it was possible and necessary to do better than realist geopolitics (to which he gave no Type II moral credence to whatsoever), and that "doing better" entailed the establishment of a global institutional authority that would substitute for the ever-shifting, ever-scheming alliances that characterized prewar Europe. The League of Nations was made responsible for upholding peace and security on the basis of the abstract rules set forth in the League Covenant. In essence, the rule of force would be superseded by the rule of law, and the pursuit of security by states acting on their own would be replaced by collective procedures. Such an approach was interpreted by critics and advocates alike as an antiwar orientation that was to be complemented by drastic disarmament and a strict regulation of arms sales (arms dealers were then being widely defamed as "merchants of death").

There is here a far most complex and multifaceted story, however. The treatment of Germany as a defeated state was significant, as was the Euro-American opposition to the Russian Revolution, as well as the isolationist refusal of the United States, despite Wilson, to join the League. But the essence of the relationship between morality and global security had to do with the insistence that flexible alliance arrangements designed to sustain balance among major states in earlier decades could not be relied upon to avoid destructive and useless wars; such a Wilsonian disposition toward power also tended to be wary about buildups of national military capabilities, especially given the pre-Keynesian reluctance to devote public revenues to defense given the depressed economic conditions that prevailed in the 1930s.

As we know, what resulted was the rise of fascism as a political force, one determined to revise the established international order to the benefit of Germany, Japan, and Italy. The leaders of these states believed that military might was the basis of all forms of power and prosperity in the world, and that war was an honorable and indispensable means to improve the relative position of a given country. Against this onslaught, European countries were psychologically and politically unprepared, and fascist leaders, especially Hitler, resorted to a variety of coopting and delaying tactics at the diplomatic level. As fascism grew in Europe, the United States was once again descending into isolationist slumber. In light of what ensued, particularly the horrors of the Holocaust, this diplomacy between the two world wars was savagely attacked for its support of appeasement, its idealistic moral-

ism and legalism, and its utopianism. The critical focus of these various realist readings of history was that by neglecting the logic of power and self-
interest as the proper foundation for global security, liberal Western leaders
invited catastrophe; the established order, realists argued, can be protected
only by military means, and in this sense, legal and moral rules of prohibition are futile, and even dangerous to the extent that they induce complacency. The American realist response, which invoked America's supposed
innocence, was characterized by bouts of excessive engagement followed by
irresponsible withdrawal. Such withdrawal was presented as a corrective to
grandiose pretensions of global reform and universalizing idealism. It
reflected the pronounced realist stress on narrow national interests, as defined
by reference to broad strategic goals. This retrenchment was most influentially articulated by Morgenthau, Kennan, Acheson, and Lippmann. Each
of these interpreters were seeking to discredit the American impulse to do
everything (Wilsonian idealism) or nothing (isolationism); instead, they
wanted to establish a middle road, grounding policy on purely rational and
selfish premises, and not on the grandiose imaginings associated with the
alleged Wilsonian insistence on changing the world.

Against this background of experience and ideas, a realist consensus
reemerged after World War II, especially given the widely shared conviction that the war against fascism was both a necessary and a just war, and
not, like World War I, an essentially meaningless orgy of death and destruction. In this regard, the cumulative learning process of peoples and their
leaders with respect to two great wars of the century emphasized the constructive role of military capabilities and preparations for war. These realist tendencies were reinforced by the strategic impact of nuclear weapons,
which shifted attention from battlefield outcomes to deterrence capacities.
In this security setting, mind games, decision logics, and rational choice
theory came naturally to the fore, and Type I morality, inasmuch as it existed
at all, was ideologized as an instrument to be deployed in an essentially
geopolitical encounter between East and West. Such a marginalization of
morality doesn't imply that there were not crucial moral issues at stake in
the cold war, or that there was some sort of equivalence between the pre-
ferred public order systems of the two superpower rivals.[14] It does suggest,
however, that global security was being safeguarded by essentially military
means, including threats of nuclear retaliation, which necessarily trans-
gressed the most minimalist conceptions of Type I, but not necessarily of
Type II, morality, resting as they did on the extreme assumption that the
security of a single country was worth threatening the extinction of the
human species and the breakdown of the biosphere.[15]

As with World War II, the cold war ended with a triumphalist mainstream reading of the security policies of the preceding decades. As a result,
despite the absence of strategic conflict, no determined effort to promote

even nuclear disarmament has occurred in the years since 1989. There was the momentary pseudo-Wilsonian interlude associated with George Bush's efforts to mobilize support for the Gulf War by calling for "a new world order," which would essentially rely on the collective security procedures of the United Nations Security Council to meet threats of aggression directed at vulnerable countries. Officials, not surprisingly, were quick to compare the robust response to Iraq's attack upon Kuwait to the feebleness of the 1930s responses to Japan's aggression against Manchuria, Italy's against Ethiopia, and Germany's against its neighbors. But this flash in the pan for Wilsonian ideas was clearly opportunistic, rather than principled, and was rapidly abandoned by the United States to the detriment of the United Nations, whose reputation suffered from a shattering of raised expectations.

Such broad strokes do not purport to recast historical experience; they serve merely to illuminate the role of morality in the pursuit of global security by states and their representatives. There are two features of this narrative that warrant special critical comment. First of all, Wilson's conception of an alternative to traditional balance-of-power geopolitics was not sufficiently comprehensive and drastic to be credible; sovereignty and national military capabilities were to by retained by states with no enforcing authority vested in the League. In this sense, realist attitudes and structures were not actually being challenged by Wilsonian ideas, except for the rhetorical and symbolic role of the League as either constitutional vision or political actor.[16] And second, despite the repudiation of the alleged utopianism of the pre-1945 period, the essential Wilsonian stand on outlawing war, and the institutionalization of security policy at the global level, prevailed, and was carried several steps forward in the conception and incorporation of the United Nations. Articles 2(4) and 51 of the United Nations Charter incorporated the central moral idea that force is an illegitimate and illegal instrument of statecraft unless used in self-defense against a prior armed attack in a manner that is adjudged, and then approved, by the Security Council.

But again, the United Nations was never psychologically, constitutionally, financially, or politically empowered to become an alternative to traditional geopolitics. Franklin Roosevelt's main expectation was that the United Nations could provide a framework for the continuation of the alliance that had won the war, and could now act to safeguard the peace. From the time of United Nation's inception, the cold war undermined and fractured the great-power solidarity that was embedded in UN decision procedures in the form of the veto given the permanent members of the Security Council. As fifty years of experience has now demonstrated, the United Nations cannot fulfill its moral/legal mission of preventing aggression and protecting weak states unless there happens to be a convergent geopolitical consensus among its leading members. Such a consensus has existed only twice in UN history: in the Korean War as a result of the fortuitous

Security Council boycott by the Soviet Union, which enabled a creative interpretation of the Charter that treated the Soviet "absence" as satisfying the requirement of Article 27(3) that decisions of the Security Council be supported by the concurring votes of the permanent members; and then in the Gulf Crisis when oil, Israeli security, and nonproliferation provided the strategic justification and there was no longer a political will on the part of the Soviet Union or China to block collective action (although again the constitutional status of the undertaking depended on counting China's abstention from the crucial Security Council vote as a concurrence). China, incidentally, foresaw the outcome in the Gulf War and, unlike decades earlier with the Korean War, accepted the compromise as a way of establishing a new global identity—as neither partner nor adversary.

As subsequent developments have underscored, when strategic interests are absent or marginal, as was essentially the case in Bosnia, Rwanda, Burundi, Haiti, and Somalia, the normative commitments of the Charter are ignored, or at best, thinly acknowledged. In these circumstances, the self-interested nature of international society has not been altered, and aggression against weaker states is tolerated so long as it does not infringe upon strategic interests of regional or global actors. To similar effect, the basic legal expectation that equals will be treated equally has not characterized UN responses to such salient questions as Israeli/Arab relations, where double standards have been the order of the day.

What, then, is the historical conditioning for the relevance of morality to global security as the world enters the new millennium? The next section explores the extent to which security policy remains largely in the domain of the Type II realist morality of geopolitics—retaining nuclear weapons and military capabilities, implementing the nonproliferation regime, and resisting calls for financially autonomous international institutions with major responsibilities for the maintenance of global peace and security. In this regard, reliance on NATO rather than the UN in establishing normalcy in Bosnia, and even more so in Kosovo, revealingly discloses the current disposition to prefer an alliance arrangement, a renovated relic of the cold war, to a community-based peacekeeping initiative even of regional scope.

WHICH MORALITY?

In a number of respects, the dichotomizing of morality and power has been profoundly misleading. It has encouraged the impression that realists are amoral or immoral with respect to force, when in reality the realist contention is simply that a *different* morality is appropriate when questions of global security are at issue. Furthermore, to associate morality only with Wilsonian moralizing, and to pass moral judgment on the existing world order without clearly comprehending the depth of adjustment required, is to misconceive, and in the end discredit, the claims of any authentic antiwar morality. The role of morality is to guide behavior toward principled ends while understanding the characteristics of the relevant societal order; morality as a decontextualized template can never itself be transformative. Even Shelley's famous assertion that poets were the unknown legislators of the world rests on the unspoken premise that poetry articulates the specific unconscious strivings of peoples in both their national and universal aspects—in this respect even a poet's morality is a rooted morality.

Any genuine alternative, then, to realist morality must be predicated upon a comprehensive vision of global security. It must also satisfy the political preconditions for a transition from one security framework to another. Any prescriptions for transformative initiatives with respect to global security must take into account several emergent trends: globalization in many aspect of international life; the alleged nonviability of war as a resolution of strategic conflict; the growth of global civil society; the declining problem-solving capabilities of states; and the potency of ethnic, civilizational, and religious identities.

But before considering alternatives to realism with respect to global security, it is important to grasp why different variants of realism exerted such a powerful impact on the political imagination in this century, and to appreciate that realists never advocated the abandonment of morality, but only its adjustment to the actualities of international political life. The prior section emphasized the relevance of historical conditioning, a process that goes hand in hand with cultural conditioning. Western cultural development since the Renaissance has exhibited a cumulative tendency toward secularization and materialism that has marginalized religion, and with it, any self-referential form of moral discourse, leaving morality as a bone for official and unofficial propagandists. The most influential practitioners of realism could be understood, in effect as the rediscoverers of a moral discourse appropriate for a statist geopolitics that operates in secularized cultural space.

It was never E. H. Carr's intention to discard morality as irrelevant to statecraft, but only to refocus attention on its proper, and admittedly marginal, role in relation to global security. In Carr's words, "In the international order, the role of power is greater and that of morality is less."[17] Indeed, Carr points out that intellectual inquiry into political activity is inherently guided by an implicit sense of moral purpose. He relies on the metaphor of "the body politic" and suggests that the inquirer is like a doctor seeking to cure the body's ills.[18] With his rousing use of language Carr wanted to reorient the discourse about security as it relates to self-interested states, which regard their own well-being as the highest moral end, the pursuit of which would take precedence over other considerations such as the avoidance of war or the upholding of legal commitments. Carr was also clear that the juridical equality of states was misleading in view of their political and military inequality; such inequality, Carr suggests, doomed efforts to treat states equally and, therefore severely confined the domain of law, and more generally, of rule-guided behavior. Carr invites confusion to some extent by discussing morality exclusively in its Kantian, Type I connotations—that is, governance in relation to right action—and fails to incorporate into morality the Machiavellian Type II connotations of right action as determined by systemic properties.[19]

Martin Wight once wrote that E. H. Carr essentially restated Hobbes for his time, which in a sense is what Hedley Bull did in relation to Carr. The strength of Bull's achievement was to be very clear about what kind of morality applies to the use of force, and to the status of war, given the existence of a society of unequal, sovereign, states. While Carr was concerned with utopianism, really a special case associated with the Wilsonian phenomenon in his era, Bull emphasized more nuanced issues that related to the appropriate degree of cooperation among states. In this regard, Bull was skeptical of efforts to promote what he called "a Grotian conception of international society," which he felt exaggerated the existing strength of sentiments of solidarity among states. In this sense he questioned efforts to outlaw war, to punish political leaders for war crimes, and to use the United Nations as a peacekeeper. Bull believed that raising expectations above the capacities for performance unwittingly resulted in a lessening of the specific morality of international relations: a shared commitment by great powers to keep conflict limited and the overall system stable, moderate, and durable. Passing harsh moral judgment on states and leaders, Bull believed, merely encouraged the erosion of limits and injected a conflict-magnifying insistence on the unconditional surrender of the defeated side in international conflicts and on the criminal accountability of its leaders.[20]

Bull favored benevolence by the great powers as an aspect of their stake in systemic stability; accordingly, he also favored meeting some of the equity demands for reordering international life that had been made two decades before by the newly independent states of the Third World. He also explicitly realized that sentiments of solidarity could strengthen over time in such a way as to sustain more ambitious forms of international cooperation among states than was presently possible, although he rejected the role of globalization-from-below and the potential agency of transnational democratic forces.[21] Of course, Bull was writing in the 1960s and 1970s, that is, before the surge of transnational activism, but whether he would have allowed these developments to alter his statist assumptions about world order seems doubtful.

In this regard, the realist view of global security is heavily oriented toward ideas of balance, deterrence, and containment, but also prudence and accommodation to minimize risks and to avoid conditions that are likely to radicalize oppressors or disenfranchised groups. John Mearsheimer has given a logical, if severe rendering of global security in the aftermath of the cold war, a rendering that contrasts with Bull's stress on addressing the grievances of challengers. Mearsheimer replaces this concern with the geopolitician's anxiety about unchecked power and power vacuums; in this extreme realist spirit, Mearsheimer, without Bull's emphasis on philosophy and history, actually suggests that denuclearization of security would be the worst imaginable future for Europe, and that an optimal security setting would include controlled proliferation that resulted in German acquisition of nuclear weapons.[22]

Of course, there are many variations on the realist theme, but all rest on the proposition that what morality means for international relations is privileging the part over the whole and regarding the configurations of power as the operative structures of order and as the limits of meaningful cooperation. In these regards, rules, international institutions, and transnational social movements are all categorized as more or less epiphenomenal when it comes to global security.[23] The deficiency in this conception of Type II morality is that it foreshortens normative horizons with its ahistorical conservatism about political potentialities. By purely realist reasoning, the transformations of the Soviet Union and South Africa in the 1990s simply couldn't have happened. And indeed they wouldn't have happened, had not a morality of ends been treated as a necessary political project.

TOWARD A TYPE III MORALITY OF ENDS

The argument up to this point has been based on two broad ideas: (1) A moral template, Type I morality, cannot be effectively superimposed on global politics to improve the quality of security; this was the Wilsonian fallacy and the many variants of nonstructural reformism.[24] (2) Realism provided a morality of means, Type II morality, by which political behavior could be adopted to the characteristics of an international society constituted by sovereign states and incorporating war as the ultimate means of conflict resolution. But this morality of means has many problematic aspects with respect to global security, including an accommodation of war, a failure to anticipate the extent of globalization from above and below, a disregard of ecological and equitable requirements for sustainable development, and an inability to foresee the emergence of an inchoate global civil society grounded on a human rights culture. To incorporate these dimensions of international political reality at this stage of world history requires a morality of ends, a Type III morality, and as a consequence, a drastically revised conception of global security that includes a depiction of normative horizons. Such an encompassing vision relies on social activism, oppositional tendencies, and transnational initiatives to give political weight to moral aspiration. Admittedly, the prospects for political implementation and intellectual acceptance in academic and policy constituencies are not currently favorable for a variety of reasons.[25] Global security seems effectively entrapped in the neorealist paradigm, which stresses great-power hegemony and displays a high tolerance for abusive arrangements of state-society relations, including ethnic cleansing and genocide, so long as strategic interests are not seriously encroached upon. The tendency of such violent eruptions to generate massive refugee flows to countries unwilling to offer asylum may generate crises of perceived strategic interests. Indeed, such a perception seems to have largely accounted for the U.S. willingness in 1994 to restore Jean-Bertrand Aristide to power in Haiti and dislodge the military junta that had been brutalizing the Haitian people for many months. But where such factors are not present, as in Burma, or even Chechnya, the tendency is to embrace a politics of accommodation, euphemized as "constructive engagement."

What, then, is the moral factor in such a context? In recent decades, it has been principally conceived as a systemic focus on stability and moderation, as specified by the dominant state actors, with a certain display of humane concern for severe patterns of abuse. What is not drawn into question is the continuing dominance of self-interest-based security, which includes the military option, and which accepts limits imposed only by great power initiatives or prudence. The current absence of strategic conflict among leading states creates a sense of geopolitical calm, a complacency that ignores the historic opportunity posed by the end of the cold war to champion ambitious forms of demilitarization and denuclearization—comparable, say, to regional free trade negotiations or the step taken toward global economic governance by the establishment of the World Trade Organization. Indeed, pressures to achieve governance of a globalized world economy are currently far more formidable and controversial than pressures to transform the global security system.

To avoid rootless utopianism, a variant of the superimposed moral template, a serious and useful morality of ends with respect to global security must address the question of political agency at the outset. Accepting this mandate immediately suggests a consideration of the Kantian political revival in which a democratic peace is established by the spread of democracy to all countries. The claim being made is that democracies do not engage in wars against each other and that if democracy could be universalized, then the security rationale for militarism of current varieties would be severely eroded.[26] The Clinton administration in its early period proposed a doctrine of enlargement, whereby it would use its influence to encourage a peaceful world by promoting the spread of market-oriented democracies. Others foresaw that the rapid growth and the ubiquity of the global market would inevitably generate a democratizing spillover as a byproduct of prosperity and an expanding middle class. Among the likely benefits of such a world order scenario would be the disappearance of peacetime arms races arising from secrecy, the security dilemma, and the fear of disabling surprise attacks. Also, a democratic political culture, in its present phase, is widely believed to be less war-prone under most circumstances and more inclined toward compromise and negotiation—and disposed to regard "progress" more as a function of market shares and export opportunities than as a result of successful military expansionism.

This current popular democratizing scenario is quite different from its Kantian antecedent, and it overlooks several serious problems: the political culture of leading democracies has become more violent and war-prone; strategic conflict is likely to reemerge in the next decade (perhaps in the form of a renewed Sino-Russian alliance against a nonaligned Japan, creating one of several possible formats for a new cold war more plausible than the Huntington "clash" thesis); the disparities in world political and economic conditions is growing, both in terms of nuclear capability and in terms of technological and financial empowerment; and the conditions of economic and technological globalization are likely to generate "enforcement" missions against potential challengers to the global order (for example, the Gulf War).

A more coherent and credible democratization scenario, especially as developed in the recent work of David Held, couples domestic democratic patterns with ambitious and cumulative regional and global democratizing developments.[27] In effect, this scenario envisions a democratic structure of global, or as Held prefers, "cosmopolitan," governance, with participatory procedures for the peoples of the world and effective accountability extended to sites of economic, as well as political, power. Would cosmopolitan governance qualify as a Type III morality of ends such that global security would be reembedded in a nonrealist framework? It would depend, it seems, on whether leading political actors, including international institutions, effectively renounced war as their major instrument for achieving security. It needs to be noted that a morality of ends does not escape the moral dilemma arising from the character of knowledge as necessarily situated within a complex and ambiguous context, thereby being dependent on interpretation. A morality of ends reflects a variety of ontological, epistemological, anthropological, and historicist assumptions, and thus an array of alternative candidates for the selection of ends is always present, including those advocating retention of the war option, and even nuclear weapons, on moral grounds. This debate between contending moral claims can never be resolved through argument or analysis.[28] What is called for, then, is dialogue and a politics of conviction; the latter being fraught with danger as a general position because it cannot be assumed to imply a renunciation of instrumental violence by all participants.[29]

Another approach to the issue of political agency is to emphasize another threat posed by globalization: the possibility that technologically disempowered groups will become radicalized. Robert Cox enumerates some potentially oppositional social forces: "National capital, those sections of established labor linked to national capital, newly mobilized nonestablished workers in the Third World, and social marginals in the poor countries are all in some way or another potentially opposed to international capital, and to the state and world order structures most congenial to international capital."[30] From such tensions Cox envisions as "remotely possible" the emergence of "a counterhegemony based on a Third World coalition against core-country dominance and aiming toward the autonomous development of peripheral countries and the termination of the core-periphery relationship."[31] Such a development doesn't imply anything more than a realignment of relative forces in relation to global security, but elsewhere Cox looks sympathetically at the emergence of what he calls "the new multilateralism," the power of transnational social movements to give birth to a rudimentary global civil society, one that calls militarism into question but that may not be clearly abolitionist with respect to the war system.[32]

CONCLUSION

Realist morality continues to underpin global security, providing widely acceptable moral rationalizations along Type II lines for recourse to force and for stretching the law opportunistically in the relations among states. Such behavior is characteristic for both hegemonic leading states and dissident states. These rationalizations for the use of force include opposing aggression, preventing nuclear proliferation, upholding a balance within a given region or protecting a particular state, containing or promoting the spread of Islam, ending Western domination and secularization, resolving ethnic and territorial grievances, and promoting independence and justice. Humanitarian morality, embodied in various ways in different Type I constructions of a "human rights culture," exerts only a marginal influence, one that is uneven, media dependent, and generative of shallow commitments; in this regard global security structures and processes give only lip service to humanitarian morality.

For humanitarian morality to underpin global security it would be necessary for drastic shifts in world order to occur, principal among them a reining in of state/market forces and a rise of transnational social forces that embody a nonviolent ethos. Tendencies in this direction cannot be ruled out, although their present prospects appear to be in virtual eclipse. It is possible, however, that within the next decade or so, the economic, ecological, and cultural pressures of inadequately regulated globalization-from-above will generate acute alienation of sufficient magnitude as to create new revolutionary opportunities, including those that would mount a Type III challenge to realist morality as the basis of global security. Although unfocused and primarily agitated by fears of environmental and health concerns, the widespread grassroots protests against French nuclear tests in the Pacific (1995–96) bear witness to the existence of human constituencies that reject statist authority to manage world order on the basis of realist morality. Whether such resistance will turn into a Type III movement dedicated to the drastic reform of global security and an insistence on humanitarian morality, will perhaps be the most profound question of the next hundred years.

Notes

INTRODUCTION

1. See Torbjørn L. Knutson, *The Rise and Fall of World Orders* (Manchester, England: Manchester University Press, 1999), 11–13.
2. For a preliminary sketch of these desired outcomes see R. Falk, *On Humane Governance: Toward a New Global Politics* (University Park, Penn.: Penn State University Press, 1995).
3. On the arbitrariness of geopolitical practice associated with self-determination, see Falk, "The Cruelty of Geopolitics: The Fate of Nation and State in the Middle East," *Millennium* 20 (1991): 383–93.
4. See John Lewis Gaddis, *The Long Peace* (New York: Oxford University Press, 1987); Gaddis, *We Now Know* (New York: Oxford University Press, 1997).
5. That is, Covenant of Economic, Social, and Cultural Rights and Covenant of Civil and Political Rights. For convenient texts, including the Declaration, see Burns H. Weston, Richard Falk, and Hilary Charlesworth, eds., *Supplement to Basic Documents to International Law and World Order*, 3rd ed. (St. Paul, Minn.: West Publishing, 1997), 375–79, 428–45.
6. Fukuyama, *The End of History and the Last Man* (New York: Free Press, 1992).
7. David Held has written extensively on this theme, perhaps most comprehensively in *Democracy and the Global Order* (Cambridge, England: Polity, 1995).
8. For wide analysis of the eroding Westphalian threshold see R. Falk, *Law in an Emerging Global Village: A Post-Westphalian Perspective* (Ardsley, N.Y.: Transnational, 1998).
9. Falk, *On Humane Governance*.

CHAPTER 1

1. The most influential considerations by Plato are contained in *The Laws* and *The Republic*, both texts contained in Edith Hamilton and Huntington Cairns, eds., *Plato: The Collected Dialogues* (Princeton, N.J.: Princeton University Press, 1961), 575–844, 1225–1513; and in Trevor J. Saunders, ed., *Book III: The Politics of Aristotle* (Middlesex, England: Penguin Books, 1981), 167–232. Both philosophers considered justice to be the result of a citizen's personal virtue, although Aristotle connects justice with ideas of distributive equity and with "the golden mean" of moderation between extremes. John Rawls, *A*

Theory of Justice (Cambridge, Mass.: Harvard University Press, 1971), provides a contemporary rearticulation of the character of justice as pertaining to organized society rather than to the human condition. See also Derek L. Phillips, *Toward a Just Social Order* (Princeton, N.J.: Princeton University Press, 1986). In more recent writings, Rawls has given a global dimension to his views about political benevolence. See John Rawls, "The Law of Peoples," in Stephen Shute and Susan Hurley, eds., *On Human Rights: The Oxford Amnesty Lectures 1993* (New York: Basic Books, 1993), 41–82. Rawls draws strongly on the emergence of a universally endorsed human rights framework for establishing conditions of political legitimacy in state-society relations. For a view of global justice based on the promotion of "equality of capabilities," see Amartya Sen, *Inequality Reexamined* (Cambridge, Mass.: Harvard University Press, 1992).

2. Thomas Hobbes, *Leviathan: Or the Matter, Forme and Power of a Commonwealth Ecclesiasticall and Civil*, trans. and ed. Michael Oakshott (New York: Collier, 1962). For an exposition of this central theme in Western thought, see Francis H. Hinsley, *Power and the Pursuit of Peace* (Cambridge, England: Cambridge University Press, 1963). For an illuminating discussion of how sovereignty was linked to a conception of international political life as essentially a war zone, see R. B. J. Walker, *Inside/Outside: International Relations as Political Theory* (Cambridge, England: Cambridge University Press, 1993).

3. For a useful survey of this evolution, see Frank Parkinson, *The Philosophy of International Relations: A Study in the History of Thought* (Beverly Hills, Calif.: Sage, 1977).

4. For natural law countertraditions, see Otto van Gierke, *Natural Law and the Theory of Society*, 2 vols. (Cambridge, England: Cambridge University Press, 1934); and E. B. F. Midgley, *The Natural Law Tradition and the Theory of International Relations* (London: Paul Elek, 1975).

5. For a favorable assessment along these lines, see J. B. Scott, *The Spanish Origin of International Law, 1, Francisco de Vittoria and His Law of Nations* (Oxford, England: Clarendon Press, 1934). For a skeptical presentation of Spanish contributions, see Arthur Nussbaum, *A Concise History of the Law of Nations*, 2nd ed. (New York: Macmillan, 1954).

6. The initial edition of 1646 was published in Amsterdam, translated to English from Latin, and published in Francis W. Kelsey, ed., *Classics of International Law*, vol. 1 and 2 (Oxford, England: Oxford University Press, 1925). For a useful overview of Grotius's life, work, and influence, see Charles S. Edwards, *Hugo Grotius, The Miracle of Holland: A Study of Legal and Political Thought* (Chicago: University of Chicago Press, 1981).

7. Two extremely valuable interpretations of the contemporary relevance of Grotius are contained in Yasuaki Onuma, ed. *A Normative Approach to War: Peace, War, and Justice in Hugo Grotius* (Oxford, England: Oxford University Press, 1993); and Hedley Bull, Benedict Kingsbury, and Adam Roberts, eds., *Hugo Grotius and International Relations* (Oxford, England: Oxford University Press, 1990). I have argued that Grotius is peculiarly relevant to our own era because we are in transition from a world of states to a globalized order assuming some as yet undetermined structure of authority and influence. I identified this indeterminacy as "a Grotian moment"—awaiting a Grotius capable

of synthesizing the Westphalian legacy and the emergent globalism. First articulated in Richard Falk, preface to Edwards, *Hugo Grotius*, viii–xxi.

8. Bodin, in his *Les Six Livres de la République*, published in 1577, was primarily
concerned with rationalizing the rise of the centralized state against the more
local claims of autonomy by feudal lords. Vattel, in *Le Droit des Gens* and other
works, carried the analysis into the relations among sovereign states, arguing
that the sovereignty of the state was the final authority, making international
law rest exclusively on the consent of the state. Both authors were very helpful in providing justifications for behavioral trends and dominant political projects in their distinct historical circumstances. Such views gave rise to the
jurisprudential tradition of legal positivism that remains predominant. Vattel's views were also consonant with realist views of international relations, in
which the security of the state was posited as the highest obligation of those
acting on behalf of the state. See Emmerich de Vattel, *The Law of Nations in
Carnegie Classics of International Law*, trans. and ed. Charles Fenwick (Washington, D.C.: Carnegie Institute, 1916).

9. Compare Hersch Lauterpacht, "The Grotian Tradition in International Law,"
British Yearbook of International Law 8 (1946): 1–53, with Hedley Bull, "The
Grotian Conception of International Society," in Herbert Butterfield and Martin Wight, eds., *Diplomatic Investigations: Essays in the Theory of International Politics* (Cambridge, Mass.: Harvard University Press, 1966), 51–73.

10. Bull, "The Grotian Conception," 51–73. See also R. John Vincent, *Nonintervention and International Order* (Princeton, N.J.: Princeton University Press,
1974); and several of the contributions to Hedley Bull, ed., *Intervention in World
Politics* (Oxford, England: Oxford University Press, 1984).

11. Such is the thesis of Richard Falk, *Law in an Emerging Global Village: A Post-
Westphalian Perspective* (Ardsley, N.Y.: Transnational, 1998), especially chap. 1.

12. For a very fertile and influential formulation of the minimalist position, see
Hedley Bull, *The Anarchical Society* (New York: Columbia University Press,
1977). See the important book by Kenneth Waltz, *Man, The State, and War*
(New York: Columbia University Press, 1959), which explores the main proposed pathways of escape from the war system. The thinking about justice in
international society has for centuries been almost exclusively preoccupied with
the problem of war until the recent preoccupation with the world economy.
For two of the most helpful studies see Michael Walzer, *Just and Unjust Wars*
(New York: Basic Books, 1977) and W. B. Gallie, *Philosophers of War and Peace*
(Cambridge, England: Cambridge University Press, 1978). My own assessment is set forth in Richard Falk, *Legal Order in a Violent World* (Princeton,
N.J.: Princeton University Press, 1968).

13. Sylvester John Hemleben, *Plans for World Peace Through Six Centuries* (Chicago:
University of Chicago Press, 1943). For a survey of such proposals since 1945,
see Wesley T. Wooley, *Alternatives to Anarchy: American Supranationalism since
World War II* (Bloomington, Ind.: Indiana University Press, 1968).

14. Perhaps the foremost example is Arthur N. Holcombe, *A Strategy of Peace in a
Changing World* (Cambridge, Mass.: Harvard University Press, 1967). For a
more recent example of this genre, see James A. Yunker, *World Union on the
Horizon* (Lanham, Md.: University Press of America, 1993).

15. There are also many suspicions, especially in the countries of the South, about

such grandiose proposals emanating from the existing Western power centers of the world. This "ethic of suspicion" is well articulated in Rajni Kothari, *Footsteps into the Future: Diagnosis of the Present World and a Design for an Alternative* (New York: Free Press, 1974), especially xix–xxiii, and Ali Mazrui, *A World Federation of Cultures: An African Perspective* (New York: Free Press, 1976), especially 1–15.

16. My attempt to propose drastic global reform in this vein is contained in Richard Falk, *A Study of Future Worlds* (New York: Free Press, 1975), especially 150–349.

17. Such a functionalist approach was initially developed in David Mitrany, *A Working Peace System* (London: Royal Institute of International Affairs, 1943). It was subsequently elaborated upon, and modified, in Ernst B. Haas, *Beyond the Nation-State: Functionalism and International Organization* (Stanford, Calif.: Stanford University Press, 1964).

18. Grenville Clark and Louis B. Sohn, *World Peace through World Law*, 3rd ed. (Cambridge, Mass.: Harvard University Press, 1966). Their proposals took the form of an article-by-article revision of the UN Charter. Clark and Sohn tackled the problem of attainability by offering incentives to the developing countries of the South in proposing the establishment of an equity fund, a peace force, disarmament, and constitutional guarantees about the limits of UN authority as a means to secure order on the basis of real collective security.

19. This view underlies a recent assessment that the United Nations continues to be subject to statist constraints. See Gene M. Lyons and Michael Mastanduno, eds., *Beyond Westphalia? State Sovereignty and International Intervention* (Baltimore, Md.: Johns Hopkins University Press, 1995).

20. Immanuel Kant, "Perpetual Peace," in Hans Reiss, ed., *Kant's Political Writings* (Cambridge, Mass.: Cambridge University Press, 1970).

21. The work that most directly inspired this intense renewal of interest in Kant's hypothesis was, of course, that of Michael Doyle. See Michael Doyle, "Kant, Liberal Legacies, and Foreign Affairs," *Philosophy and Public Affairs* 12, nos. 3 and 4 (Summer and Fall 1983): 205–54, 323–53. See also Michael Doyle, *Ways of War and Peace: Realism, Liberalism, and Socialism* (New York: W. W. Norton, 1997), especially 251–300, 474–84.

22. See Thomas Franck's influential article, "The Emerging Right to Democratic Governance," *American Journal of International Law* 86, no. 1 (January 1992): 46–91.

23. For a more complete exposition of this line of thinking, see various seminal writings by David Held. In particular, David Held, *Political Theory and the Modern State* (Cambridge, England: Polity Press, 1989); and Held, *Democracy and the Global Order: From the Modern State to Cosmopolitan Governance* (Stanford, Calif.: Stanford University Press, 1995). See also Daniele Archibugi, David Held, and Martin Köhler, eds., *Re-imagining Political Community: Studies in Cosmopolitan Democracy* (Cambridge, England: Polity Press, 1998).

24. Among the many studies of these developments, the following are important: Robert B. Reich, *The Work of Nations: Preparing Ourselves for the 21st Century* (New York: Knopf, 1991); Kenichi Ohmae, *The End of the Nation State: The Rise of Regional Economies* (New York: Free Press, 1995); Joseph Camilleri and Jim Falk, *The End of Sovereignty? The Politics of a Shrinking and Fragmenting*

World (Hants, England: Edward Elgar, 1992); and William Grieder, *One World, Ready or Not: The Manic Logic of Global Capitalism* (New York: Simon and Schuster, 1997).

25. Richard Falk, *Predatory Globalization: A Critique* (Cambridge, England: Polity Press, 1999).

26. See Kofi Annan's corrective proposals at the Davos World Economic Forum in 1998, where he proposed a dual partnership of the United Nations with the world of business and finance on one side and with representatives of civil society on the other. See Laura Silber, "UN Reformer Looks for New Friends in World of Business," *Financial Times* (London), March 17, 1998, 7.

27. For representative writings derived from WOMP in its three main phases, see Saul H. Mendlovitz, ed., *On the Creation of a Just World Order* (New York: Free Press, 1975); R. B. J. Walker, *One World, Many Worlds* (Boulder, Colo.: Lynne Reinner, 1988); and Richard Falk, *On Humane Governance: Toward a New Global Politics* (University Park, Penn.: Pennsylvania State University Press, 1995).

28. For an attempt to specify "humane governance" see Falk, *On Humane Governance*. For a somewhat parallel effort by The Commission on Global Governance, see their report *Our Global Neighbourhood* (Oxford, England: Oxford University Press, 1995).

29. See Bruce Rich, *Mortgaging the Earth: The World Bank, Environmental Impoverishment, and the Crisis of Development* (Boston: Beacon Press, 1994).

30. See symposium issue, "War Crimes Tribunals: The Record and the Prospects," *American University International Law Review* 13, no. 6 (1998): i–xi, 1383–1584.

31. Thomas Franck has made by far the most comprehensive and useful attempt to do just this in his impressive book, *Fairness in International Law and Institutions* (Oxford, England: Oxford University Press, 1995).

32. For a helpful explanation of global governance, see *Our Global Neighbourhood*, note 28, 2–7.

33. For an overall critique of this framework, see James N. Rosenau, *Turbulence in World Politics: A Theory of Change and Continuity* (Princeton, N.J.: Princeton University Press, 1990). On the idea of global civil society, see Richard Falk, "Global Civil Society: Perspectives, Initiatives, Movements," *Oxford Development Studies* 26, no. 1 (1998): 99–110. See also Ronnie D. Lipschutz, *Global Civil Society and Global Environmental Governance* (Albany, N.Y.: State University of New York Press, 1996).

34. See Franck, *Fairness in International Law and Institutions*, for appraisal in careful, yet generally positive terms. For a skeptical, statist backlash view of international institutions, see John J. Mearsheimer, "The False Promise of Institutions," *International Security* 19, no 3 (Winter 1994/95): 5–49. See also the response by Robert Keohane and Lisa Martin, "The Promise of Institutionalist Theory," *International Security* 20, no. 1 (Summer 1995): 39–51; Charles A. Kupchan and Clifford A. Kupchan, "The Promise of Collective Security," *International Security* 20, no. 1 (Summer 1995): 52–61; John Gerard Ruggie, "The False Premise of Realism," *International Security* 20, no. 1 (Summer 1995): 62–70; Alexander Wendt, "Constructing International Politics," *International Security* 20, no. 1 (Summer 1995): 71–81; and John Mearsheimer, "A Realist Reply," *International Security* 20, no. 1 (Summer 1995): 82–93.

35. For a balanced assessment of such harm even prior to the ravages wrought by

the 1997–98 Asian economic crisis, see United Nations Development Programme, *Human Development Report 1997* (New York: Oxford University Press, 1997), especially 82–93. On the effects of the economic crisis on Indonesia see Rawdon Dalrymple, "Indonesia and the IMF: The Evolving Consequences of a Reforming Mission," *Australian Journal of International Affairs* 52, no. 3 (November 1998): 233–39; and M. W. Brauchli, "Was the World Bank Part of Indonesia's Problem? Indonesia's Downfall Casts a Long Shadow over the World Bank," *Asian Wall Street Journal* (Hong Kong), July 15, 1998, 1.

36. Ken Booth, "Human Wrongs and International Relations," *International Affairs* 71, no. 1 (January 1995): 103–26.

37. It is correct that economic globalization has lifted millions from poverty, but there is no evidence that it can by its own dynamics reach those who are not able to participate productively in the market. See Reich, *The Work of Nations*; and for advocacy of "pro-poor growth," see United Nations Development Programme, *Human Development Report*, 94–116.

38. George F. Kennan, *American Diplomacy 1900–1950* (Chicago: University of Chicago Press, 1951); Henry Kissinger, *Diplomacy* (New York: Simon and Schuster, 1994); Barry Buzan, Charles Jones, and Richard Little, *The Logic of Anarchy: Neorealism to Structural Realism* (New York: Columbia University Press, 1993); and Bull, *The Anarchical Society*.

39. For a range of views, see Robert Keohane, ed., *Neorealism and its Critics* (New York: Columbia University Press, 1986). For an ultrastatist and geopolitically oriented view, see Mearsheimer, "A Realist Reply."

40. There are, however, realist arguments for the instrumental use of international institutions in relation to the foreign policy goals of the U.S. government. On the United Nations, for example, see Thomas M. Franck, *Nation Against Nation* (Oxford, England: Oxford University Press, 1985); and on the International Court of Justice, see Thomas M. Franck, *Judging the World Court* (New York: Priority Press, 1986), especially 53–76.

41. For an extraordinary claim that American foreign policy has tended to be Wilsonian in character, that is, insufficiently interest-guided and excessively value-oriented, see Kissinger, *Diplomacy*, especially 805–34.

42. For various formulations, see Neil Barrett, *The State of Cybernation: Cultural, Political, and Economic Implications of the Internet* (London: Krogan Page, 1996); Mark Dery, *Escape Velocity: Cyberculture at the End of the Century* (London: Hodder and Stoughton, 1996), especially 1–18, 227–319; and Mike Featherstone and Roger Burrows, eds., *Cyberspace/Cyberbodies/Cyberpunk: Cultures of Technological Embodiment* (London: Sage, 1995), especially 1–19.

43. Blair evidently borrowed the term "the Third Way" from Anthony Giddens's recent influential book with the same title. See Anthony Giddens, *The Third Way* (Cambridge, England: Polity Press, 1998). Giddens argues that the way forward politically is to borrow from both neoliberal and social democratic orientations to shape a new politics that is both business-friendly and socially empathetic, while avoiding the dogmatic extremes of either unconditional deference to market forces or an uncritical endorsement of the welfare state. The Third Way aims to minimize the intrusiveness of the state without overlooking the special needs of the poor and jobless. Whether this approach is genuinely new or merely masks a shift to the right by the old left-of-center is difficult to say.

44. The Internet is a complex technological revolution that is having many transformative effects of a beneficial character, including creating new democratizing opportunities. For the most comprehensive assessment of a generally favorable character, see Manuel Castells, *The Information Age: Economy, Society and Culture* (Oxford, England: Blackwell, 1996–98). My stress here is on the negative effects that arise from the ideological pressures on business and the market consistently being advocated by the most influential editorial cybervoice, that of *Wired* magazine.

45. The standard definition of crimes against humanity is that given in Principle VI(c) of the Nuremberg Principles as formulated in 1950 by the International Law Commission: "Murder, extermination, enslavement, deportation and other inhuman acts done against any civilian population, or persecution on political, racial or religious grounds, when such acts are done or such persecutions carried out in execution of or in connexion with any crime against peace or any war crime." Crimes against humanity have now evolved to the point where the connection with other crimes is no longer considered to be a necessary element of indictment and prosecution. Genocide is defined in Article II of The Genocide Convention of 1948 as follows: ". . . [G]enocide means any of the following acts committed with the intent to destroy, in whole or in part, a national, ethnic, racial or religious group, as such: (a) Killing members of the group; (b) Causing serious bodily or mental harm to members of the group; (c) Deliberately inflicting on the group conditions of life calculated to bring about its destruction in whole and in part; (d) Imposing measures intended to prevent births within the group; (e) Forcibly transferring children of a group to another group." For convenient texts see Burns H. Weston, Richard A. Falk, and Hilary Charlesworth, eds., *Supplement of Basic Documents of International Law and World Order* (St. Paul, Minn.: West Publishing, 1997), 197, 373.

46. The reference here is to Johan Wolfgang Von Goethe, *Faust* (London: Heron Books, 1970), in which Faust sells his soul to the devil in exchange for technological know-how.

47. For assessment along these lines see many of the contributions to Jerry Mander and Edward Goldsmith, eds., *The Case Against the Global Economy* (San Francisco, Calif.: Sierra Club, 1996).

48. Nancy Fraser, *Justice Interruptus: Critical Reflections on the "Postsocialist" Condition* (New York: Routledge, 1997), 11.

49. United Nations Development Programme, *Human Development Report*, especially 9–10.

50. Ibid., 94–116.

51. The idea of distributive justice is concerned with fair distribution among the relative membership of a community. Equality is one conception of fairness, but not the only one. The duty of the rich to ensure distribution sufficient to meet the basic needs of the poor would be one approach to the implementation of distributive justice. Distributive justice is often contrasted with retributive justice, which is concerned with appropriate punishment or rectification for prior wrongs. For an important effort to conceptualize a distributive justice imperative on a global level, see Charles Beitz, *Political Theory and International Relations* (Princeton, N.J.: Princeton University Press, 1979), especially 125–76.

See also Henry Shue, *Basic Rights: Subsistence, Affluence, and US Foreign Policy* (Princeton, N.J.: Princeton University Press, 1980).

52. For discussion along these lines, see Richard Falk, *Predatory Globalization*. For the view that globalization has been hyped in such a way as to convey the misleading impression that governments of states are losing their discretion to implement socially compassionate policies, see Paul Hirst and Grahame Thompson, *Globalization in Question: The International Economy and the Possibilities of Governance* (Cambridge, England: Polity Press, 1996).

53. For an influential depiction, see Edith Brown Weiss, *In Fairness to Future Generations* (Dobbs Ferry, N.Y.: Transnational, 1989).

54. Normative energies are meant to invoke the combined influence of law, morality, and religion, each of which is centrally concerned with realizing norms of human behavior.

55. Among the more important of these conferences were the UN Conference on Environment and Development (1992), the UN Conference on Human Rights and Development (1993), the UN Conference on Population and Development (1994), and the UN Conference on Women and Development (1995).

56. The internal U.S. debate on the usefulness of the United Nations is also revealing of two contending views on the utility of the United Nations as an instrument to pursue national interests. It has turned into essentially a debate between those in the executive branch, who believe the organization to be useful as a legitimating instrument of foreign policy, and conservatives in Congress, who regard the United Nations as superfluous, and on occasion obstructive, with respect to the pursuit of national interests. This latter view holds that unilateralism is preferable.

57. Such an achievement has been substantially compromised by maintaining the sanctions/inspection process over such a long period since the 1991 cease-fire, inflicting suffering on the people of Iraq without sufficient justification.

58. See Richard Falk, "The Complexities of Humanitarian Intervention: A New World Order Challenge," *Michigan Journal of International Law* 17 (Winter 1996): 491–513.

59. This latter tendency has some negative features, including demands for ethnic purification as the basis for political legitimacy, as in the states of the former Yugoslavia. It may, however, take the milder form of giving up moves to claim self-determination for "a people," and the acceptance of autonomy arrangements combined with participation in larger regional frameworks—a process that seems to be softening Basque and Irish ultranationalism, which had been responsible for years of civil violence and acute insecurity.

CHAPTER 2

1. Prior to World War II, practices associated with protecting aliens and their property could be considered in some respects antecedents to the emergence of the international protection of human rights. These practices, known as "diplomatic protection of aliens abroad" and "capitulations," were explicitly associated with the colonial era, in which colonial rulers provided interventionary support for individuals whose rights were endangered by the "independent" countries in Latin America. Under this policy, Europeans were

exempt from territorial applications of criminal law in Asia. Status of Forces Agreements that partially exempt U.S. military personnel from territorial application of criminal law have been criticized for these reasons. The main point here is that international law made some effort to uphold the economic, political, and social rights of individuals, and even if Eurocentric in its implementation, it initiated a rights discourse in international relations. Additionally, as such individuals were generally supported by their governments, enforcement capabilities existed, although their application was not a right of the individual but dependent on a policy assessment by the state. See Burns H. Weston, Richard A. Falk, and Hilary Charlesworth, eds., *International Law and World Order*, 3rd ed. (St. Paul, Minn.: West, 1997).

2. Of course, nationalism and statism are not identical, although the state has done its best to co-opt nationalist identities both by the embrace of secularism and through control over the status of juridical nationality. It is obvious that tensions persist between dominant and subordinate nationalisms caught within the boundaries of a given state. These tensions have strong human rights implications that will be discussed later.

3. Of course, the internal accountability of a government for abuses of the rights of its citizens goes back at least as far as the American and French Revolutions in the late eighteenth century. The French Revolution's rhetoric of "the rights of man," leaving aside its gendered formulation, most directly anticipates the thinking that underlies "human rights" as the foundation of external accountability. If even a conservative thinker such as Hobbes acknowledged a right of revolution in reaction to tyrannical government, the rationale for humanitarian intervention in response to genocidal practices and widespread crimes against humanity becomes more readily understandable as a limitation upon territorial sovereignty.

4. Over time this legal status has changed as a result of the widespread acceptance of the norms contained in the Declaration. The incorporation of the Declaration in the constitutions of many newly independent developing countries, its frequent citation, and its treatment by scholars as expressive of *jus cogens* gradually endowed the Declaration with an obligatory character in international law. Such an evolution occurred without little careful scrutiny by independent observers of its specific standards, and the degree to which they were accepted by states as obligatory. A second step in this evolution was the reformulation of human rights standards in a treaty form, and their broad categorization into civil and political on one side and economic and social on the other, thereby reflecting East/West ideological differences. See Burns H. Weston, Richard A. Falk, and Hilary Charlesworth, eds., *Supplement of Basic documents to International Law and World Order*, 3rd ed. (St. Paul, Minn.: West, 1997), 375–79, 435–45, 428–34.

5. Such concerns have united the U.S. Government and that of China in their resistance to the establishment of a truly independent international criminal court; major geopolitical actors, regardless of their apparent commitment to law and humane governance, are very worried about diluting traditional notions of sovereignty in relation to the external accountability of their own citizens.

6. The internalization of human rights is also an incomplete process even in states

that claim to be constitutional democracies. There are powerful cultural practices that may be difficult to overcome by reliance on law enforcement, especially practices relating to the treatment of women and children, and to social differentiations among classes, castes, and religions. See S. Kothari and H. Sethi, eds., *Rethinking Human Rights: Challenges for Theory and Action* (New York: New Horizons Press; Delhi: Lokayan, 1989).

7. These realities include the techniques, priorities, and dominant ideas associated with the theory and practice of economic globalization, and they rely on the pseudo-internationalist identity of the International Monetary Fund and other agents of global market forces.

8. Chandra Muzaffar, *Human Rights and the New World Order* (Penang, Malaysia: Just World Trust, 1993). Also, chapter 8.

9. To the extent that the mission of the state is to make the world more receptive to neoliberal ideas, the promotion of human rights in the sense of constitutionalism becomes a new type of "strategic interest." However, if upholding human rights interferes with important market access and investment opportunities, then pressure mounts to overlook the human rights abuses of trading partners. In the first context the state is acting on behalf of the overall neoliberal program, while in the second it is furthering the more mercantilist goals of its citizens.

10. The U.S. approach to human rights has exhibited various forms of contradiction over the years. Human rights began to assume a high profile role in American foreign policy during the early years of the Carter presidency, 1976–78, partly as an expression of liberal conviction, but also because at the time it served to restore national self-esteem in the aftermath of the Vietnam War. By highlighting human rights, whatever the initial motivations, the administration encouraged human rights activists throughout the world, given the U.S. leadership role. It also strengthened permanently the role of human rights within the federal bureaucracy of the United States. This convergence of political circumstances and support for human rights is what has periodically pushed implementation beyond the limits of earlier expectations.

11. This journalistic rephrasing pointed out that the critical side of engagement was muted, and over-ridden by the effort to exhibit friendship and respect, an unqualified acceptance of China's legitimacy. This contrasts with the view that a process of engagement by the West with China is justified because it is the best way to encourage a repudiation of the currently illegitimate modes of Chinese governance.

12. Jingsheng Wei, "The 'Brutal Cynicism' of the West's Defection," *International Herald Tribune*, June 20–21, 1998.

13. B. Gellman, "New U.S. China Ties Are the Fruit of '96 Shift in Policy," *International Herald Tribune*, June 23, 1998.

14. Richard Falk, *On Humane Governance: Toward a New Global Politics* (Cambridge, England: Polity, 1995).

15. Richard Falk, "The Haitian Intervention: A Dangerous World Order Precedent for the United Nations," *Harvard International Law Journal* 36, no. 2 (Spring 1995): 341–58.

16. This failure to include the human rights of the Iraqi people in the goals of the U.S./UN mission in Iraq since the ceasefire in 1991 is further aggravated by

the maintenance of sanctions over a period of more than nine years despite overwhelming evidence of their devastating impact upon the well-being of Iraqi civilian society, especially the very young. In this respect, the United Nations seems complicit in a policy that has had the effect on a massive scale of depriving innocent Iraqis of their most basic right to life, and in a setting where there is no evidence that the Baghdad government or its leaders have been weakened or significantly curtailed in their capacity to rule; indeed, by so alienating the people of Iraq, it has been argued that the sanctions have strengthened the government's grip on the society.

17. Even then, however, the difficulties of humanitarian intervention should not be underestimated, especially if the geopolitical incentives are not very pronounced, as was the case in Bosnia, or subsequently in Kosovo. Shallow humanitarian intervention may have the main effect of intensifying the internal conflict, and adding to the human suffering. See Richard Falk, "The Complexities of Humanitarian Intervention," *Michigan Journal of International Law* 17, no. 2 (Winter 1996): 491–513.

18. In each instance, a political leadership had come to power by constitutional means with a strong program of social reform that includes efforts to acquire greater control over the sources of wealth situated within the state. These governing elites were suspected of being unfriendly to Western strategic interests as defined by cold war parameters, but their unacceptability seemed most directly rooted in their hostility to foreign investment and their radical affirmation of a program of applied economic nationalism. This latter program adversely affected important vested foreign economic interests, which exerted pressure for intervention. Each case is different, involving different combinations of ideological, geopolitical, and economic interests, but in each instance the end result was to repudiate the democratizing tendencies of the state in question.

19. Thomas Franck, "The Emerging Right to Democratic Governance," *American Journal of International Law* 86 (1992): 46.

20. J. F. Harris, "Clinton's Message to China: Individual Freedom is Vital," *International Herald Tribune*, June 29, 1998, 1, 4.

21. Weston and others, *Supplement of Basic Documents*, 608–615.

22. W. Pfaff, "Gambling with Nihilo-Capitalism," *International Herald Tribune*, May 18, 1998.

23. Richard Falk, "An Inquiry into the Political Economy of World Order," *New Political Economy* 1, no. 1 (March 1996): 13–26; Richard Falk, "Resisting 'Globalisation-from-Above' Through 'Globalisation-from-Below'," *New Political Economy* 2, no. 1 (1997): 17–24.

24. M. W. Brauchli, "Indonesia's Downfall Casts a Long Shadow Over the World Bank," *Wall Street Journal Europe*, July 14, 1998, 1, 10.

25. It should be noted that most of the better-known human rights NGOs have also concentrated more than 90 percent of their energies and resources on the protection of civil and political rights, according virtually no attention to the developmental and antipoverty priorities within the broader domain of human rights.

26. Weston and others, *Supplement of Basic Documents*, 397–403, 553–61.

27. Ibid., 645–52.

28. Muzaffar, *Human Rights and the New World Order*; Kothari and Sethi, *Rethinking Human Rights*.
29. A. Sen, "Human Rights and Asian Values," Sixteenth Morgenthau Memorial Lecture on Ethics and Foreign Policy, Carnegie Council on Ethics and International Affairs, 1997.
30. Ann Mayer presents the reaction of Sudan to UN censure of its human rights record as deference that is not meant seriously. She also interprets the participation of representatives of the Islamic governments of Saudi Arabia at the 1993 UN Conference on Human Rights and Development as a matter of pretense. In effect, such governments acknowledge the authority of the norms, but argue that allegations of Islamic violations are either without substance and even slanderous, or claim that with appropriate interpretive freedom to take account of Islamic tradition, any semblance of a violation would quickly disappear. See A. E. Mayer, *Islam and Human Rights: Tradition and Politics*, 2nd ed., (Boulder, Colo.: Westview, 1995), 179–84.
31. Edward W. Said, *Culture and Imperialism* (New York: Knopf, 1993), xx–xxvii.
32. United Nations, *The United Nations and Human Rights (1945–1995)*, Blue Book Series, Vol. VII (New York, N.Y.: UN Publications, 1995).
33. Ken Booth, "Global Ethics," *International Affairs* 71 (January 1995): 103–26.
34. Weston and others, *Supplement of Basic Documents*, 375–79, Art. 25 and 28.

CHAPTER 3

1. The Helsinki Process refers to the annual review of human rights practices established by the Final Act of the 1975 Conference on Security and Cooperation in Europe, known as the "Helsinki Accords" because of the site of negotiation and signature. This signal East/West agreement stabilized the post-1945 borders of Eastern Europe, a concession to Moscow, in exchange for this process of accounting for human rights, a concession to Washington. For text see Weston and others, eds., *Documents on International Law and World Order*, 3rd ed., (St. Paul, Minn.: West 1997), 97–103.
2. Norberto Bobbio, *The Age of Rights* (Cambridge, England: Polity, 1996).
3. For consideration of Stoic perspectives see William L. Davidson, *The Stoic Creed* (Edinburgh, Scotland: T & T Clark, 1907).
4. See Robert A. Dahl, *Democracy and Its Critics* (New Haven, Conn.: Yale University Press, 1989), esp. 52–79; see also David Held, *Models of Democracy*, 2nd ed. (Cambridge, England: Polity, 1996), 28–35.
5. R. J. Vincent, *Human Rights and International Relations* (Cambridge, England: Cambridge University Press, 1986), esp. 111–52.

CHAPTER 4

1. Javier Perez de Cuellar, "Reflecting on the Past," *Global Governance* 1 (1995): 149–70, at 167.
2. Ken Booth, "Human Wrongs and International Relations," *Journal of International Affairs* 71 (1995): 103–26, at 120, 123.
3. For an important interpretation of the link between the political entities of

the colonial era and the failed states of postcolonial Africa see Jeffrey Herbst, "Responding to State Failure in Africa," *International Security* 21 (1996/97): 120–44.

4. See discussion of "the democratic entitlement" in Thomas M. Franck, *Fairness in International Law and Institutions* (Oxford University Press, 1995), 83–139; for a more skeptical perspective on humanitarian intervention see Richard Falk, "The Complexities of Humanitarian Intervention: A New World Order Challenge," *Michigan Journal of International Law* 17, no. 2 (Winter 1996): 491–513.

5. For creative exploration of these themes see Gidon Gottlieb, *Nation Against State: A New Approach to Ethnic Conflicts and the Decline of Sovereignty* (New York: Council on Foreign Relations Press, 1993).

6. The idea of nonintervention as applicable to the United Nations itself is enshrined in the Charter as a basic principle in Article 2(7): "Nothing contained in the present Charter shall authorize the United Nations to intervene in matters which are essentially within the domestic jurisdiction of any state. . . ." Of course, there is room for interpretation, as by reference to "essentially" as well as "domestic jurisdiction."

7. This deference is being questioned from a variety of perspectives, especially in response to genocide, the racism of apartheid in South Africa, the occurrence of severe violations of human rights, and in the context of a total breakdown of internal order. For exploration of many of these issues see Kevin M. Cahill, ed., *A Framework for Survival: Health, Human Rights, and Humanitarian Assistance in Conflicts and Disasters* (New York: Basic Books, 1993).

8. One rather equivocal affirmation of this feature of world order has been expressed by the former UN Secretary General, Boutros Boutros-Ghali, in a widely noted passage in *An Agenda for Peace* (United Nations, 1992), 9: "The foundation-stone of this work is and must remain the State. Respect for its fundamental sovereignty and integrity are crucial to any common international progress. The time of absolute and exclusive sovereignty, however, has passed; its theory was never matched by reality." For an academic interpretation see Jarat Chopra and Thomas G. Weiss, "Sovereignty is No Longer Sacrosanct: Codifying Humanitarian Intervention," *Ethics and International Affairs* 6 (1992): 95–117.

9. For exposition of the peace of Westphalia see Richard Falk, "The Interplay of Westphalia and Charter Conceptions of the International Legal Order," in Richard Falk and Cyril E. Black, eds., *The Future of the International Legal Order* (Princeton, N.J.: Princeton University Press, 1969), I, 32–70; and Antonio Cassese, *International Law in a Divided World* (Oxford, England: Oxford University Press, 1986), esp. 34–54.

10. For a general line of interpretation see Richard Falk, *On Humane Governance: Toward a New Global Politics* (College Park, Penn.: Penn State University Press, 1995); see also contributions to Yoshikazu Sakamoto, ed., *Global Transformation: Challenges to the State System* (Tokyo: United Nations University Press, 1994).

11. For one rationale of such a realist orientation by a leading international jurist see Thomas M. Franck, *Judging the World Court* (New York: Priority Press, 1986), 35–61; to the same effect, with reference to participation in the United

Nations, see Franck, *Nation Against Nation* (New York: Oxford University Press, 1985), esp. 246–72. This insistence on discretion contrasts with the willed acceptance of constraints on economic policymaking in the context of support for the establishment of the World Trade Organization.

12. Perhaps the most notable expressions of support for this transition from colonial status to full political independence were contained in a pair of General Assembly resolutions: "Declaration on the Granting of Independence to Colonial Countries and Peoples," UN General Assembly Resolution 1514 (XV), 1960, and "Resolution on Permanent Sovereignty over Natural Resources," UN General Assembly Resolution 3171 (XXVIII), 1973.

13. For a notable attempt from a philosophical perspective to be more inclusive in according political legitimacy to a state see John Rawls, "The Law of Peoples," in Stephen Shute and Susan Hurley, eds., *On Human Rights: The Oxford Amnesty Lectures 1993* (New York: Basic Books, 1993), 41–82.

14. For a comprehensive argument along these lines see Robert H. Jackson, *Quasi-States: Sovereignty, International Relations, and the Third World* (Cambridge, England: Cambridge University Press, 1990).

15. Adam Roberts, "Humanitarian War: Military Intervention and Human Rights," *International Affairs* 69 (1993): 429–49.

16. For an extreme portrayal of the future in these terms see Robert D. Kaplan, *The Ends of the Earth: A Journey to the Frontiers of Anarchy* (New York: Random House, 1996); see also Kaplan's earlier article, "The Coming Anarchy," *The Atlantic Monthly* (February 1994).

17. See Cahill, ed., *A Framework for Survival.* Also Thomas G. Weiss, "Rekindling Hope in UN Humanitarian Intervention," in Walter Clarke and Jeffrey Herbst, eds., *Learning From Somalia* (Boulder, Colo.: Westview, 1997), 207–28.

18. . For a more positive assessment of the Somalia undertaking as a whole see contributions to Walter Clarke and Jeffrey Herbst, eds., *Learning from Somalia.*

19. This tension is discussed at length in Falk, "The Complexities of Humanitarian Intervention."

20. Several contributions to Sakamoto, *Global Transformation,* explore this pattern.

21. The difficulties that strong governments have had in subduing determined internal adversaries has been confirmed over and over again in recent years. Among the most prominent recent instances have arisen in Northern Ireland, Sri Lanka, Kashmir, Chechnya, and Algeria.

22. This pattern of unwarranted deference to the regime in Baghdad was aggravated in many respects by imposing comprehensive sanctions under the auspices of the United Nations. The consensus of informed observers is that sanctions have not eroded the authority of the Iraqi government, but have added greatly to the torments of the Iraqi people.

23. For extreme expressions of this outlook see Kenichi Ohmae, *The End of the Nation State: The Rise of Regional Economies* (New York: Free Press, 1995); and John-Marie Guehenno, *The End of the Nation-State* (Minneapolis, Minn.: University of Minnesota Press, 1995); for a more balanced view see Hendrick Spruyt, *The Sovereign State and Its Competitors* (Princeton, N.J.: Princeton University Press, 1994).

24. See sophisticated and influential analysis in Joseph A. Camilleri and Jim Falk,

The End of Sovereignty? The Politics of a Shrinking and Fragmenting World (Hants, England: Edward Elgar, 1992).

25. As quoted in Ken Booth, "Human Wrongs," at 123.

26. There are many allegations that prospects for humane governance of such troubled countries is further undermined by the fiscal policies and approaches of the Bretton Woods institutions of the World Bank and the IMF. Structural adjustment programs have been blamed for impairing the capacity of such governments to devote public-sector resources to alleviating the sufferings of the poor.

27. It was the emergence of countervailing pressures in the form of threatening challenges by organized labor that led governing elites to negotiate historic compromises between the logic of the market and a social contract with workers and the poor. For a useful short exposition see John Gerald Ruggie, "At Home Abroad: International Liberalisation and Domestic Stability in the New World Economy," *Millennium* 24 (1995): 399–423.

28. For a sophisticated, yet still self-serving example of Western liberal refutation, see the otherwise illuminating essay by Michael Ignatieff entitled *Whose Universal Values? The Crisis in Human Rights* (The Hague: Foundation Horizon, 1999).

CHAPTER 6

1. See Burns H. Weston, Richard A. Falk, and Hilary Charlesworth, eds., *Supplement of Basic Documents to International Law and World Order*, 3rd ed. (St. Paul, Minn.: West Publishing, 1997), 375–79, 428–45.

2. "Lenin's Fourth Letter from Afar" (25 March 1917), quoted in Antonio Cassese, *International Law in a Divided World* (New York: Oxford University Press, 1986), 131.

3. For a helpful discussion see Cassese, *International Law in a Divided World*, 132–34.

4. This language is repeated in Article 55 in the setting of human rights.

5. UN General Assembly Resolution 1514 (XV), 14 December 1960. The vote was 89–0, with 9 significant abstentions, including Portugal, Spain, South Africa, United Kingdom, United States, Australia, Belgium, Dominican Republic, and France; note that Canada voted with the majority. For text see Weston et al., *Supplement of Basic Documents*, 404–05.

6. See also UN General Assembly Resolution 1541 (XX), for amplification.

7. This thinking is made manifest, and is expressed more authoritatively, two years later in the General Assembly Resolution on Permanent Sovereignty Over Natural Resources, UN General Assembly Resolution 1803 (XVII), 14 December 1962. Text in Weston et al., *Supplement of Basic Documents*, 695–96.

8. UN General Assembly Resolution 2625 (XXV), 24 October 1970. Text in Weston et al., *Supplement of Basic Documents*, 92–96.

9. Rosalyn Higgins, *Problems and Progress: International Law and How We Use It* (Oxford University Press, 1994), 122–23; see also Professor Higgins's discussion relating to the determination of the boundaries of Guinea-Bissau.

10. Higgins, *Problems and Progress*, 123.

11. Cassese, *International Law in a Divided World*, 134.

12. ICJ Reports, 1975. This decision considered the claims of the people of Western Sahara to exercise a right of self-determination in the broad historical context created by the assertions of sovereign authority by Morocco.

13. Ibid., 122.

14. Some of these issues will be discussed in later sections on the breakup of Yugoslavia and the Soviet Union; and the relevance of diplomatic recognition and admission to the United Nations is a major theme of Donat Pharand's study.

15. Higgins, *Problems and Progress*, 128.

16. For more detail on the Commission see note by Marizio Ragazzi introducing the texts of the opinions thus far rendered. *International Legal Materials* 31 (1992): 1488–1519, 1488–91.

17. See the devastating critique of the work of the Commission in Hurst Hannum, "Self-Determination, Yugoslavia, and Europe: Old Wine in New Bottles?" *Transnational Law and Contemporary Problems* 3 (1993): 59–69.

18. Ibid., 69.

19. Ibid., 68.

20. *Frontier Dispute (Burkina Faso v. Mali)*, 1986 ICJ 554 (December 22), at 565.

21. See Hannum, "Self-Determination," 66–67 for criticism; see also Benedict Kingsbury, "Claims by Non-State Groups in International Law," *Cornell International Law Journal* 25 (1992), 481.

22. "The Territorial Integrity of Quebec in the Event of Its Accession to Sovereignty" [herein after cited as "Pellet Report"], a study commissioned by the Committee of the Quebec National Assembly, but not officially presented to it.

23. Pellet Report, 2.

24. The Pellet Report itself confirms such an interpretation when it states that the questions put to it "are situated 'downstream' from accession to independence. That event is postulated, and it is a matter of determining the effect of international law after it has occurred"; Pellet Report, 7.

25. Ibid., 5.

26. Ibid., 24.

27. Ibid., 24.

28. Ibid., 28.

29. Ibid., 35.

30. Ibid., 40–42.

31. Ibid., 41.

32. Thomas Franck, "The Emerging Right of Democratic Governance," *American Journal of International Law* 86, no. 1 (1992).

33. Pellet Report, 55.

CHAPTER 7

1. For an excellent assessment of human rights from the perspective of group rights or collective identity see William Felice, *Taking Suffering Seriously: The Importance of Collective Human Rights* (Albany, N.Y.: State University of New York Press, 1996).

2. The American experience reflects an important understanding of the challenges

confronting multi-national states to achieve legitimacy. The idea and reality of citizenship must be experienced as a positive one, which probably includes both a record of achievement by the state and some degree of equality between regions and ethnic groups. The Soviet state was an example of failure on both levels. Aside from territorial security and global stature, the Soviet state fashioned neither economic well-being, political participation, nor social justice, and it perpetuated the sense of Russian nationalist hegemony. In countries such as South Africa, or in the territories occupied by Israel, the subordinated populations are more blatantly victimized, and there is no question whatsoever of achieving legitimacy within existing arrangements.

3. There are some interesting nonterritorial extensions of this basic statist conception of allegiance. Israel has been sustained, to a significant degree, by its capacity to inspire allegiance from overseas Jewish communities, especially among those in the United States. This pattern is repeated to various degrees within other ethnic groups, including Palestinians dispersed throughout the Arab world. An important example is the linkage between the Tamils in the Indian state of Tamil Nadu and the Tamil minority in Sri Lanka.

4. The image of "autonomy" for the Occupied Territories was never acceptable to Palestinian leadership on both substantive and symbolic grounds. For a range of views from a Palestinian perspective see Emma Playfair, ed., *International Law and the Administration of Occupied Territories* (Oxford, England: Clarendon Press, 1992); see also Stephen Bowen, *Human Rights, Self-Determination and Political Change in the Occupied Palestinian Territories* (The Hague, The Netherlands: Kluwer, 1997).

5. See D. Ronen, *The Quest For Self-Determination* (New Haven, Conn.: Yale University Press, 1979), 29–34; Arno J. Mayer, *Political Origins of the New Diplomacy, 1917–1918* (New Haven, Conn.: Yale University Press, 1959).

6. See I. Claude, *National Minorities: An International Problem* (Cambridge, Mass.: Harvard University Press, 1955); Thomas D. Musgrave, *Self-Determination and National Minorities* (Oxford, England: Clarendon Press, 1997).

7. In effect, was it possible to base security on a collective arrangement of global scope, or must it rest upon traditional mechanisms of alliances and balance of power?

8. Also, interdependence and the fragility of the state make it seem less beneficial for minorities to defer to central authority on practical grounds.

9. The vulnerability of minorities, as distinct from indigenous peoples, is of a more heterogeneous character. At one extreme, the circumstances of some minorities are virtually indistinguishable from those of indigenous peoples as described in the text. At the other extreme are minorities with international influence and access, whose victimization may nevertheless be severe—as has been the case with the Jews in Germany or the Tamils in Sri Lanka—but whose cultural orientation is modernist, even ultramodernist, rather than premodern.

10. See Richard Falk, "In Pursuit of the Postmodern," in David Ray Griffin, ed., *Spirituality and Society: Postmodern Visions* (Albany, N.Y.: State University of New York Press, 1988), 81–98.

11. *Declaration on Principles of International Law Concerning Friendly Relations and Co-operation Among States in Accordance with the Charter of the United Nations*, UN

General Assembly Res. 2625, UN Doc. A/8028 (1971); see Principle (e), the principle of equal rights and self-determination of peoples.

12. Ibid.

13. Ibid.

14. See Antonio Cassese, *Self-Determination of Peoples* (Cambridge, England: Cambridge University Press, 1995).

15. The prohibition on discrimination is meant to uphold the rights of an individual, but the character of the infringement arises because the individual belongs to a group that is perceived to be in a disadvantaged position. Hence, there is in the Covenant, and elsewhere in the human rights literature, a blurring of the distinction between individual and group. The United States' approach is to act as if what is at stake is the rights of the individual, but procedural devices such as class actions and proof-of-systematic-discrimination actions for individual relief accord significance to group identity.

16. As might be expected, the more militant representatives of indigenous peoples tend to object to this lumping of their grievances together with those of minorities. They contend that indigenous peoples are distinct nations with an incompatible set of cultural attitudes, and that this distinction is threatened, if not destroyed, by the economic and social policies of the state, even if (as is rarely the case) these are administered in a nondiscriminatory and equitable manner. On the other side, representatives of minorities rarely, if ever, regard their grievance as akin to those of indigenous peoples. Minorities do not, by and large, associate their identity with premodern practices and institutions. Their aim is to uphold a cultural experience distinct from that of the majority people or of other minorities, and to receive financial support from the state to enable separate schools, or to ensure the dissemination of a minority culture among its members.

   What emerges, then, are two quite different dimensions of group claims with few prospects for coalitions between indigenous peoples and minorities. Oddly enough, indigenous peoples seem more conscious of their common situation—confronting an erosion of identity through the long march of modernization—and more prone to manifestation of solidarity than are minorities. Minorities are more preoccupied with working out their particular destiny, and seem reluctant to record their plight as an aspect of a larger category of problems.

17. It should be stressed that most UN attention to group claims continues to focus on core, traditional violations (that is, murder, disappearances, prolonged detention, torture) rather than on encroachments upon group identity and a group's cultural and physical survival.

18. The genocidal approach taken by Paraguay to the Ache Indians is documented in Richard Arens, ed., *Genocide in Paraguay* (Philadelphia, Penn.: Temple University Press, 1976).

19. See Hurst Hannum, *Autonomy, Sovereignty, and Self-Determination: The Accommodation of Conflicting Rights*, rev. ed. (Philadelphia, Penn.: University of Pennsylvania Press, 1990).

20. See Ronen, *The Quest of Self-Determination*.

21. See Richard Falk, *Revolutionaries and Functionaries: The Dual Face of Terrorism* (New York: Dutton, 1988).

22. Other factors also produce an inherent tendency toward internationalization: bilateral patterns of assistance to governments and/or minorities, border violence and cross-border sanctuaries, transnational refugee flows, grants of political asylum, and exile communities. These factors interrelate with geopolitical circumstances, creating opportunities for coalitions, influence, and salience.

23. In this regard, and to note a certain positive evolution in normative thinking within the UN, compare Conventions 107 and 169 of the International Labor Organization on the rights of indigenous peoples. Also compare Convention No. 169 with the Draft Declaration on the Rights of Indigenous Peoples as adopted by the UN Commission on Human Rights Sub-Commission on the Prevention of Discrimination and Protection of Minorities. For respective texts see Burns H. Weston, Richard Falk, and Hilary Charlesworth, eds., *Supplement of Basic Documents to International Law and World Order*, 3rd ed. (St. Paul, Minn.: West Publishing, 1997), 397–403, 553–61, 645–52.

24. Thomas Franck, "Who Killed Article 2(4)? or: Changing Norms Governing the Use of Force by States," *American Journal of International Law* 64: 809 (1970) versus Louis Henkin, "The Reports on the Death of Article 2(4) Are Greatly Exaggerated," *American Journal of International Law* 65: 544 (1971).

25. Francisco Capotorti, *Study on the Rights of Persons Belonging to Ethnic, Religious and Linguistic Minorities* (New York, United Nations: UN Study E/CN.4/Sub 2/384/Rev. 1, 1979).

26. For useful overview see Wolfgang Danspeckgruber (with Arthur Watts), ed., *Self-Determination and Self-Administration* (Boulder, Colo.: Lynne Rienner, 1997).

27. For a survey of standard-setting see Ruth Thompson, ed., *The Rights of Indigenous Peoples in International Law* (Saskatchewan, Canada: Native Law Center, 1986). See also Independent Commission on International Humanitarian Issues, *Indigenous Peoples, A Global Quest for Justice* (London, England: Zed, 1987), 109–131.

28. Thompson, *The Rights of Indigenous Peoples*.

29. One consequence is to make counter-examples vivid and rending, as when South Korea crushed the student uprising in Kwangju or when China resorted to brutal violence to break up the prodemocracy demonstrations in Tiananmen Square. Television conveys the reality that stimulates feelings of outrage, but these feelings also relate to a growing sense that governments (and their leaders) are accountable internationally for failures to uphold minimum decencies in relation to their own citizenry.

30. See UN Doc. E/CN.4/Sub. 2/1987/22, at 4–5 (1987) for an enumeration of participating entities with consultative status.

31. For instance, the Independent Commission on International Humanitarian Issues, headquartered in Geneva, put the protection of indigenous peoples high on its agenda, issuing a useful report, *Indigenous Peoples,* which in turn was introduced and discussed by representatives of the commission at the fifth session of the Working Group in 1987. Social and political feedback mechanisms deepen the impact of group claims on world public opinion and, more generally, on normative consciousness.

32. See Ernst B. Haas, *Beyond the Nation-State: Functionalism and International Organization* (Stanford, Calif.: Stanford University Press, 1964), on the positive

effects of politicizing conflicts over rights and duties. It is arguable that UN successes in 1988 with respect to regional conflict (Namibia, the Iran-Iraq war) are moving the organization back in the direction of its original mandate.

CHAPTER 8

1. Of course, this orientation was hardly original with Huntington; it rests upon a civilizational exploration by many fine scholars, most notably the extraordinarily important depiction of civilizational reality in Fernand Braudel, *The Mediterranean and the Mediterranean World in the Age of Philip II* (New York: Harper Collins, 1972; France, 1949; 1966), 545–96; and the monumental achievement of Arnold Toynbee in *A Study of History*, 12 vols. (Oxford: Oxford University Press, 1961). For a negative perception of the impact of resurgent Islam see Adda B. Bozeman, *Politics and Culture in International History*, 2nd ed. (New Brunswick, N.J.: Transaction, 1994), esp. xix–xxi; for a view that is favorable to an Islamic orientation and perspective see Ahmet Davutoglu, *Civilizational Transformation and the Muslim World* (Kuala Lumpur, Malaysia: Mahir Publications, 1994).

2. Stephen C. Toulmin, *Cosmopolis: The Hidden Agenda of Modernity* (New York: Free Press, 1990). For other presentations of contemporary world order see James N. Rosenau, *Turbulence in World Politics: A Theory of Change and Continuity* (Princeton, N.J.: Princeton University Press, 1990); R. B. J. Walker, *One World/Many Worlds: Struggles for a Just World Peace* (London: Zed Press, 1988); Falk, *On Humane Governance: Towards a New Global Politics* (College Park, Penn.: Penn State University Press, 1995).

3. The character of "significant difference" is substantively complex, but procedurally rather simple, referring to relatively equal access, representation, and status in principal arenas of formal authority, as well as relatively equal treatment in the application of norms of behavior and regimes of prohibition, for instance, the regime prohibiting the proliferation of nuclear weapons. The qualification of a civilization as "major" is also potentially troublesome, raising the question of "what counts as a civilization?" The comparable question at the level of the state has occasioned much bloodshed under the banners of nationalism.

4. David Held, *Democracy and the Global Order: From the Modern State to Cosmopolitan Governance* (Cambridge, England: Polity, 1995), esp. 219–86; Daniele Archibugi and David Held, eds., *Cosmopolitan Democracy: An Agenda for a New World Order* (Cambridge, England: Polity, 1995).

5. The argumentative assertion here is the insistence on the word "essential," reflecting a psychopolitical, as well as a legal and moral, assessment. There is, of course, no implication that Islam (or any other civilization) is monolithic, but only that the collective identity expressed by the label "Islam" is a meaningful category in a manner analogous to the label "Britain" or "France."

6. An eloquent and persuasive Muslim perspective, both critical toward the West and visionary in relation to the Islamic contribution to an enhanced world order, is that of Chandra Muzaffar. See Muzaffar, *Human Rights and the New World Order* (Penang, Malaysia: Just World Trust, 1993); in his role as founder and director of Just World Trust, Muzaffar has convened a series of meetings

and issued many commentaries on world policy issues that react against the geopolitics of exclusion. A particularly notable effort was an international workshop, "Images of Islam: Terrorising the Truth," 7–9 October 1995, Penang, Malaysia; see also the publication of a collection of essays that is more geopolitical than intercivilizational in tone: *Dominance of the West over the Rest* (Penang, Malaysia: Just World Trust, 1995). See also various writing by Abdol Karim Saroush of Iran.

7. For rather enlightened examples of recent literature that invokes the deep historical roots of the encounter see Graham E. Fuller and Ian O. Lesser, *A Sense of Siege* (Boulder, Colo.: Westview/RAND, 1995); John L. Esposito, *The Islamic Threat: Myth or Reality* (New York: Oxford University Press, 1992); and Fred Halliday, *Islam and the Myth of Confrontation* (London: I. B. Tauris, 1996). In the context of human rights, the uncritical call for universal human rights, without reference to intercivilizational agency, is problematic; see Ralf Dahrendorf, *The Modern Social Conflict* (London: Weidenfeld and Nicolson, 1988), 181.

8. There is an important caveat relating to their contention that overlooking the interideological cleavages of the cold war was a dangerous instance of false universalism; see Harold D. Lasswell and Myres S. McDougal, "Diverse and Contending Public Order Systems," in McDougal et al., *Studies in World Public Order* (New Haven, Conn.: Yale University Press, 1960), 3–42.

9. These efforts involved trying to insist upon sovereignty rights as a balance against interventionary claims, and whose identity was associated with the jurist or diplomat responsible for the assertion, as, for instance, "the Calvo clause," "the Drago doctrine," as well as efforts to put foreign and domestic investors on a level of parity in relation to expropriation controversies.

10. The most prominent of these were the Declaration on the Establishment of a New Economic Order, the Program of Action on the Establishment of a New International Economic Order, and the Charter on the Economic Rights and Duties of States. For pertinent texts see Burns H. Weston et al., eds., *Basic Documents in International Law and World Order*, 2nd ed. (St. Paul, Minn.: West Publishing, 1990), 550–75.

11. For the most authoritative formulation see the Declaration on the Right to Development, adopted as UN General Assembly Resolution 41/128, December 4, 1986; text in Weston et al., *Basic Documents*, 485–88.

12. For a powerful argument that stresses the importance of the acceptance of the right to development as an integral element of human rights at the UN Conference on Human Rights held in Vienna, June 1993, see Upendra Baxi, *Mambrino's Helmet? Human Rights for a Changing World* (New Delhi: Har-Anand Publications, 1994), 1–17, 22–54.

13. See Rosanne Ortiz, *Indians of the Americas: Human Rights and Self-Determination* (London: Zed Press, 1984).

14. For a prime instance of paternalism, see ILO Convention No. 107, 1957, which bears the title "Concerning the Protection and Integration of Indigenous and Other Tribal and Semi-Tribal Populations in Independent Countries"; text in Weston et al., *Basic Documents*, 335–40. Compare ILO Convention No. 169, 1989, for a vastly improved formulation that reflects pressure from and participation by representatives of indigenous peoples; text in Weston et al., *Basic Documents*, 489–97. For a sensitive account of the consequences over a period

of centuries see James Anaya's contribution to the Report of the Canadian Royal Commission on Aboriginal Peoples, 1995.

15. For a helpful account of the obstacles in the path of acceptance within the UN system see the newsletter *Nouvelles Internationales HSD International News* 4, nos. 1–2 (January 1996): 2–5.

16. The comparison is meaningful in light of the stereotypical and demeaning images of "orientalism" and "occidentalism," especially if combined with relations of domination and subordination. Basic here, of course, is Edward Said's *Orientalism* (New York: Pantheon, 1978). Also insightful is Jean-Francois Lyotard, "The Other's Rights," in Stephen Shute and Susan Hurley, eds., *On Human Rights* (New York: Basic Books, 1993), 135–46. Also of relevance may be the shared element of antimodernism in both the indigenous/traditional and Islamic challenges; antimodernism may be one aspect of an explanation for their coemergence in the late twentieth century. For valuable, varying perspectives on Islamic attitudes, see Akbar S. Ahmed, *Postmodernism and Islam: Predicament and Promise* (London: Routledge, 1992) and Fatima Mernissi, *Beyond the Veil: Male-Female Dynamics in Modern Muslim Society*, rev. ed. (Bloomington: Indiana University Press, 1987).

17. See Abdullahi Ahmed An-Na'im, "Problems and Prospects of Universal Cultural Legitimacy for Human Rights," in An-Na'im and Francis Deng, eds., *Human Rights in Africa: Cross-Cultural Perspectives* (Washington, D.C.: Brookings Institution, 1990), 331–67; An-Na'im, *Toward an Islamic Reformation: Civil Liberties, Human Rights and International Law* (Syracuse, N.Y.: Syracuse University Press, 1990); An-Na'im, "Islamic Law, International Relations, and Human Rights: Challenge and Response," *Cornell International Law Journal* 20, no. 2 (1987): 317.

18. See conference proceedings, *Images of Islam: Terrorizing the Trust* (Penang, Malaysia: JUST, 1996); also Davutoglu, *Civilizational Transformation*, for a more systematic approach to the Islamic view of international relations.

19. Ibid., 101; see also discussion in immediately subsequent paragraphs.

20. Ibid., 103–104.

21. Ibid., 27.

22. Ibid., 114–17.

23. It should be noted that leading thinkers of indigenous peoples make similar claims.

24. It is true that the Bosnian government understated their Islamic identity throughout the war, emphasizing their pluralistic character and their own refusal to emulate the ethnic cleansing of their Serbian and Croatian adversaries.

25. On media bias see Edward Said, *Covering Islam* (New York: Pantheon, 1981).

26. For an excellent overall presentation of the nonproliferation regime see Michael Klare, *Rogue States and Nuclear Outlaws* (New York: Hill & Wang, 1995). Klare points out that Pakistan's strategic relationship with the West definitely moderated to some extent efforts to obstruct Pakistan's nuclear program. See Klare, 156–57. On the support of the Israeli weapons program by antiproliferation states see Seymour Hersh, *The Sampson Option* (New York: Random House, 1991).

27. For balanced analysis that supports this assessment, although not phrased in civilizational terms, see Janna Nolan, "Sovereignty and Collective Intervention: Controlling Weapons of Mass Destruction," in Gene M. Lyons and Michael

Mastanduno, eds., *Beyond Westphalia: State Sovereignty and International Intervention* (Baltimore, Md.: Johns Hopkins University Press, 1995), 170–87; Nolan's conclusion is pertinent: "The Achilles heel of nonproliferation initiatives, as such, is emerging regional powers' perception of discrimination in a system that continues to place a high value on weapons of mass destruction as an indicator of state power and prestige, even while trying to promote the global prohibition of such weapons" (187).

28. See the Harvard report based on field assessments by health specialists: International Study Team, *Health and Welfare in Iraq after the Gulf War: An In-Depth Assessment* (Cambridge, Mass.: Harvard University Press, October 1991). Also see the report prepared by Eric Hoskins, Calvin Bauman, and Scott Harding of the Gulf Peace Team Special Mission to Iraq: Health Assessment Team, Amman, Jordan, April 30, 1991. Francis A. Boyle, "Indictment, Complaint, and Petition by the 4.5 million children of Iraq for Relief from Genocide by President George Bush," distributed as an informal document, Sept. 18, 1991. A useful discussion is to be found in Sarah Graham-Brown, "Intervention, Sovereignty and Responsibility," *Middle East Report* 25: 2–12, 32; for a more general condemnation by way of international law see Hans Kochler, "The United Nations Sanctions Policy and International Law" (Kuala Lumpur, Malaysia: Just World Trust, 1995). An excellent overview, with useful chapters on the impact of sanctions on Iraq, is contained in David Cortright and George A. Lopez, eds., *Economic Sanction: Panacea or Peacebuilding in a Post–Cold War World?* (Boulder, Colo.: Westview, 1995); and Fred Tanner, ed., *Effects of International Sanctions* (Malta: Mediterranean Academy of Diplomatic Studies, January 1996).

29. Nolan, "Sovereignty and Collective Intervention," 175.

30. This impression is supported by the unquestionably hostile treatment of the scandal by two sophisticated books written by leading writers for *The Wall Street Journal* and *The Financial Times*; both make the striking point that many of BCCI's most dubious practices were in most respects identical to those of mainstream international banking. See Peter Truell and Larry Gurwin, *False Profits: The Inside Story of BCCI, the World's Most Corrupt Financial Empire* (Boston: Houghton, Mifflin, 1992); and Jonathon Beaty and S. C. Gwynne, *The Outlaw Bank: A Wild Ride into the Secret Heart of BCCI* (New York: Random House, 1993). Also relevant is the much less traumatizing approach taken to deal with the savings and loan scandal of the 1980s in the United States. See Kathleen Day, *S & L Hell: The People and the Politics Behind the $1 Trillion Savings and Loan Scandal* (New York: Norton, 1993).

31. For a critique of Libya policy by a non-Muslim see Fan Yew Teng, *The Continuing Terrorism Against Libya* (Kuala Lumpur, Malaysia: Egret Publications, 1993).

32. See Fuller and Lesser, *A Sense of Siege*, 49–50.

33. This gambling metaphor is borrowed from Mary Catherine Bateson's illuminating study of bias against and demoralization of women. See Bateson, *Composing a Life* (New York: Atlantic Monthly Press, 1989), 205.

34. For the complexity of this latter extension of Westphalian thinking see James Crawford, ed., *The Rights of Peoples* (Oxford, England: Clarendon Press, 1988);

William Felice, *Taking Human Suffering Seriously: The Importance of Collective Human Rights* (Albany, N.Y.: State University of New York Press, 1996).

35. A recent discussion of these conceptual issues in relation to the alleged erosion of sovereignty, with particular reference to intervention under the auspices of the international community, is to be found in Lyons and Mastanduno, eds., *Beyond Westphalia?*

36. For important extensions of the scope and orientation of human rights see Abdullahi Ahmed An-Na'im, ed., *Human Rights in Cross-Cultural Perspectives: A Quest for Consensus* (Philadelphia, Penn.: University of Pennsylvania Press, 1992), esp. chapter by An-Na'im, 19–43; Smitu Kothari and Harsh Sethi, eds., *Rethinking Human Rights: Challenges for Theory and Action* (New York: Horizons, 1989); Myres S. McDougal, Harold D. Lasswell, and Lung-chu Chen, *Human Rights and World Public Order* (New Haven, Conn.: Yale University Press, 1980); also Felice, *Taking Human Suffering Seriously*.

CHAPTER 9

1. Robert Jay Lifton, "Introduction" to Zlatko Dizdarevic, *Sarajevo: A War Journal* (New York: International Publisher, 1993), xv–xxvi, at xix.

2. Compare Helen Fein, ed., "The Prevention of Genocide: Rwanda and Yugoslavia Reconsidered," a working paper of the Institute for the Study of Genocide, 1994.

3. Lifton, "Introduction," xxvi.

4. The NATO campaign in 1999 relating to Kosovo raised many of the Bosnian issues in what appears to be a reversed geopolitical context. Instead of seeking an avoidance of engagement, there are grounds for believing that NATO, or at least several of its leading member governments, welcomed the opportunity for a military showdown. See Eric Rouleau, "Lessons of War: French Diplomacy Adrift in Kosovo," *Le Monde Diplomatique*, Dec. 1999. See also Henry Kissinger, "Our Nearsighted World Vision," Jan. 10, 2000, A19 and Noam Chomsky, *The New Military Humanism: Lessons from Kosovo* (Monroe, Maine: Common Courage Press, 1999).

5. See Richard Falk, Gabriel Kolko, and Robert Jay Lifton, eds., *Crimes of War* (New York: Random House, 1971); see also *In the Name of America* (New York: Clergy and Laymen Concerned About Vietnam, 1968) and James William Gibson, *The Perfect War* (Boston: Atlantic Monthly Press, 1986).

6. Of these shallow measures, lifting the arms embargo is the most likely to have reshaped the conflict. It would appear that the imposition of the arms embargo without an accompanying substantial UN/Europe commitment to protect Bosnia against Serb aggression was an instance of what might be described as "perverse" intervention (that is, it was helpful to the side responsible for producing the humanitarian crisis). Under this circumstance, lifting the embargo would at least have returned the situation to a more balanced situation of the sort that existed when the conflict originated. Again, assessment is problematic, since the probable effects of lifting the embargo, supposedly imposed to contain the magnitude and scope of conflict, were controverted and uncertain throughout.

7. For an impressive account of the conflict in Bosnia that stresses the causal con-

tributions of a shifting geopolitical scene brought about by the end of the cold war, see Susan L. Woodward, *Balkan Tragedy: Chaos and Dissolution After the Cold War* (Washington, D.C.: Brookings Institution, 1995). Woodward's conclusion that Western intervention in its shallow form aggravated, rather than moderated, behavior of the adversaries confirms the weakness of shallow intervention as a tool of an antigenocide diplomacy. See also Jasminka Udovicki and James Ridgeway, eds., *Yugoslavia's Ethnic Nightmare* (Chicago: Lawrence Hill, 1995).

8. European affinities were divided among the parties based on ethnic, religious, and historical considerations; support for the Bosnian Muslim leadership was never easy for Europe to swallow, given the tensions between Islam and the West, which remained an influential subtext throughout.

9. David Rieff, *Slaughterhouse* (New York: Simon & Schuster, 1995), 12–13.

10. Compare Saul Mendlovitz and John Fousek, "The Prevention and Punishment of the Crime of Genocide," in Charles B. Strozier and Michael Flynn, eds., *Genocide, War, and Human Survival* (Lanham, Md.: Rowman and Littlefield Publishers, Inc., 1996), 137–51, Mendlovitz's and Fousek's argument proceeds from the other orientation, namely, that of morally conditioned political advocacy.

11. For an explication of cosmopolitan democracy see Daniele Archibugi and David Held, eds., *Cosmopolitan Democracy: An Agenda for a New World Order* (Cambridge, England: Polity, 1995).

12. These considerations are intelligently discussed in Woodward, *Balkan Tragedy*, 322–23; for the wider rationale see Theodor Meron, "The Case for War Crimes Trials in Yugoslavia," *Foreign Affairs* 72 (1993): 122–35.

CHAPTER 10

1. Ken Booth, "Human Wrongs and International Relations," *International Affairs* 71(1995): 103–26.

2. See Booth, "Human Wrongs and International Relations," 103–26, esp. 118–19, for an enumeration of exceptions to his generalization, that is, a listing of authors who do provide normative assessments of international relations. See also Roy Preiswerk, "Could We Study International Relations as if People Mattered?" in Richard Falk, Samuel S. Kim, and Saul H. Mendlovitz, eds., *Toward a Just World Order* (Boulder, Colo.: Westview, 1982), 175–97; and Robert C. Johansen, *The National Interest and the Human Interest* (Princeton, N.J.: Princeton University Press, 1980).

3. Kissinger misleadingly conflates the triumph of Wilsonian rhetoric, relied upon by American political leaders to validate globalist projections of U.S. power, with the actuating grounds of policy and the contours of behavior, which conform closely to the dictates of realist geopolitics. For Kissinger's argument see Henry Kissinger, *Diplomacy* (New York: Simon and Schuster, 1994), esp. 804–35.

4. For example, see George F. Kennan, *American Diplomacy 1900–1950* (Chicago: University of Chicago Press, 1951); Hans J. Morgenthau, *Politics Among Nations: The Struggle for Power and Peace*, ed. Kenneth Thompson, 6th ed. (New York: Knopf, 1985).

5. For a clear delineation of the rationale for this conceptual framework in the

setting of the cold war see John Lewis Gaddis, *Strategies of Containment: A Critical Appraisal of Postwar National Security Policy* (Oxford, England: Oxford University Press, 1982). For a range of views that include realist adaptations to a post–cold war global setting see Sean M. Lynn-Jones and Steven E. Miller, eds., *The Cold War and After: Prospects for Peace* (Cambridge, Mass.: MIT Press, 1993).

6. The Gaddis article, "The Long Peace: Elements of Stability in the Postwar International System," was published as the lead piece in the influential anthology of Lynn-Jones and Miller (note 5) at 1–45.

7. In addition to the Lynn-Jones and Miller anthology, see Charles W. Kegley, Jr., ed., *The Long Postwar Peace: Contending Explanations and Projections* (New York: Harper Collins, 1991); for an entirely different interpretation see Samir Amin, *Re-Reading the Postwar Period: An Intellectual Itinerary* (New York: Monthly Review, 1994).

8. For a major study of warfare in this century that is admirably sensitive to overall human and societal consequences see Gabriel Kolko, *Century of War: Politics Conflict, and Society Since 1914* (New York: The New Press, 1994).

9. Ibid., 123.

10. For a generally well-intentioned, but rather confusing, advocacy of "global governance," see Report of the Commission on Global Governance, *Our Global Neighbourhood* (Oxford, England: Oxford University Press, 1995), esp. 1–7; for a more suggestive approach to governance see Johan Galtung, *There Are Alternatives! Four Roads to Peace and Security* (Nottingham, England: Spokesman, 1984); for earlier perspectives and proposals see Richard Falk, *A Study of Future Worlds* (New York: Free Press, 1975).

11. I think one of the strengths of Hedley Bull's work is to call sensitive attention to this unexplored normative potential. See Hedley Bull, *The Anarchical Society* (New York: Columbia University Press, 1977).

12. Of course, these world religions often operated on the basis of their own exclusivist ideas, but at least their worldview provided, and continues to provide, inspiration for inclusive perspectives. Consider, for example, the following rhetorical question put by Joe Nangle in "A Community of Nations?" *Sojourners* (October 1996): 42: "For people of faith living in the United States, and dedicated to building up of human communities at every level, the question becomes: Are we citizens merely of this country, or do we strive to exercise our citizenship in the entire human family?" For a range of views, in an American context, on the orientation of persons toward political responsibility, see Martha C. Nussbaum et al., *For Love of Country: Debating the Limits of Patriotism* (Boston: Beacon, 1996); some of the same issues are explored in a European context in Bart von Steenbergen, ed., *The Condition of Citizenship* (London: Sage, 1994).

13. This line of argument follows closely the arguments of Immanuel Wallerstein in *After Liberalism* (New York: New Press, 1995); see also John Gerard Ruggie, "At Home Abroad, Abroad at Home: International Liberalization and Domestic Stability in the New World Economy," *Millennium* 24 (1995): 507–26.

14. For a major effort at such a reconceptualization see David Held, *Democracy and the Global Order: From the Modern State to Cosmopolitan Governance* (Cambridge,

England: Polity, 1995), esp. 219–86; see also Martha C. Nussbaum, "Patriotism and Cosmopolitanism," in Nussbaum et al., *For Love of Country*, 3–17.

15. See I. William Zartman, ed., *Collapsed States: The Disintegration and Restoration of Legitimate Authority* (Boulder, Colo.: Lynne Rienner, 1995); and Robert H. Jackson, *Quasi-states: Sovereignty, International Relations and the Third World* (Cambridge, England: Cambridge University Press, 1990).

16. For one important exploration see Robert Jay Lifton and Eric Markusen, *The Genocidal Mentality* (New York: Basic Books, 1988).

17. For a persuasive assertion that the genocide in Rwanda was facilitated by the disruption of precolonial ethnic patterns of accommodation during the period of Belgian and French rule, see Mahmood Mamdani, "From Conquest to Consent as the Basis of State Formation: Reflections After a Visit to Rwanda," unpublished paper (1996), esp. 6–17.

18. See foundational international law text, *Convention on the Prevention and Punishment of the Crime of Genocide* (1951), esp. Articles IV–IX, in *Human Rights: A Compilation of International Instruments* (New York: United Nations, 1988), 143–47.

19. For expressive confirmation of this assessment see David Rieff, *Slaughterhouse: Bosnia and the Failure of the West* (New York: Simon and Schuster, 1995).

20. See Mamdani, "From Conquest to Consent"; see also Philip Gourevitch, "Neighborhood Bully: How Genocide Revived President Mobutu," *The New Yorker*, September 9, 1996, 52–57.

21. See Paul Lewis, "How UN Keeps Pace, With Fewer Troops to Keep the Peace," *New York Times*, May 4, 1997, 12.

22. For discussion of this complexity see Richard Falk, "Human Rights, Humanitarian Assistance, and the Sovereignty of States," in Kevin M. Cahill, ed., *A Framework for Survival* (New York: Basic Books, 1993), 27–40.

23. Such mobilizations of an exile community can be normatively oppressive, as in the case of anti-Castro exiles in the United States.

24. For a careful proposal along these lines see Saul Mendlovitz and John Fousek, "The Prevention and Punishment of the Crime of Genocide," in Charles B. Strozier and Michael Flynn, eds., *Genocide, War, and Human Survival* (Lanham, Md.: Rowman & Littlefield, 1996), 137–51.

25. Support for such an institutional innovation is contained in *Our Global Neighbourhood* (note 9) at 323–25.

26. See Mark Dery, *Escape Velocity: Cyberculture at the End of the Century* (London: Hodder and Stoughton, 1996), esp. 1–18, 227–319; Alvin Toffler, *The Third Wave* (New York: William Morrow, 1980); also John Heilemann, "The Making of President 2000," *WIRED* 3 (December 1995): 152–55, 218–30; and Immanuel Wallerstein, *After Liberalism* (New York: New Press, 1995), esp. 1–7, 126–61.

27. See the discussion of species-self in Lifton's *The Protean Self* (New York: Basic Books, 1993).

28. See Richard Falk, *On Humane Governance: Towards a New Global Politics* (Cambridge, England: Polity, 1995), and UNICEF Yearbooks.

29. Why military expenditures, as a public good, remain an exception for powerful countries has to do with the greater willingness of elites to protect inequity than to correct it, and with the social learning that supposedly validates a mil-

itarist foreign policy as the only true foundation of security in international society, especially given the predominantly nonterritorial character of the most dynamic modes of wealth-production.

30. Wallerstein, in *After Liberalism* (New York: The New Press, 1995), argues persuasively that social democracy and welfare ideas were primarily adopted as ways to contain the demands of the industrial workforce, but with the dilution of these demands, a less fiscally burdensome approach can be adopted.

31. For analysis along these lines, see Richard Falk, "The Making of Global Citizenship," in Jeremy Brecher, John Brown Childs, and Jill Cutler, eds., *Global Visions: Beyond the New World Order* (Boston: South End Press, 1993), 39–50; and Richard Falk, *On Humane Governance.*

32. This point is most comprehensively argued in David Held, *Democracy and the Global Order.*

CHAPTER 12

1. Richard H. Minear, in his important book on the Tokyo war crimes trials criticizes such a punishment because it rested on charges of "negative culpability," that is, failure to act rather than acting illegally, and also because there was no evidence introduced by the prosecution to demonstrate that General Matsui had either knowledge of the atrocities or the capacity to prevent them. Richard H. Minear, *Victors' Justice: The Tokyo War Crimes Tribunal* (Princeton, N.J.: Princeton University Press, 1971), 69–72. See also B. V. A. Röling and Antonio Cassese, *The Tokyo Trial and Beyond* (Cambridge, England: Polity, 1993).

2. As quoted in Paul Abrahams, "Japan's Wartime Ghosts," *Financial Times*, 28/29 November 1998, 7.

3. For text see Radhabinod Pal, "Dissenting Judgment" (partial text) in Leon Friedman, ed., *The Law of War: A Documentary History*, 2 vols. (New York: Random House, 1972), 1159–83; also see Minear, *Victors' Justice*, 213–14, where he notes that the forty-two volumes of the Nuremberg proceedings are available as an official U.S. government series but that the Tokyo proceedings, most of which are not even published, can be obtained only with difficulty, and then, in microfilm form.

4. This failure is one of the themes of Iris Chang's book. Iris Chang, *The Rape of Nanking: The Forgotten Holocaust of World War II* (New York: Basic Books, 1997).

5. For interpretations of this backlash see Edward T. Linenthal and Tom Engelhardt, eds., *History Wars: The Enola Gay and Other Battles for the American Past* (New York: Metropolitan Books, 1996); also, Robert Jay Lifton and Greg Mitchell, *Hiroshima in America: Fifty Years of Denial* (New York: Putnam, 1995).

6. In international law this practice is discussed under the somewhat misleading and self-serving doctrinal headings of "diplomatic protection" and "state responsibility."

7. Hedley Bull, *The Anarchical Society: A Study of Order in World Politics* (New York: Columbia University Press, 1977).

8. In World War I the United States reluctantly abandoned isolationism to turn the tide of war in favor of the liberal democracies. Despite the efforts of Woodrow Wilson to construct a new architecture of global security, the United States refused to take part, resuming its diplomacy of noninvolvement with

European conflicts. Even the rise of Hitler and Germany's expansionism did not rouse the United States to respond, and this despite the efforts of its popular leader, Franklin Delano Roosevelt, to nudge the country ever closer to participation. Isolationist sentiments remained predominant until America was attacked. It is also correct to note that isolationism was driven as much by self-interest as it was by a pacifist ethos. The elements of this self-interest included fiscal desires to keep military expenditures and human casualties as low as possible. Another aspect of the American orientation related to the conviction of many early leaders that military establishments and constitutional democracy did not mix. There was strong support, only narrowly circumvented, for including in the Constitution a total prohibition on "standing armies," that is, on a peacetime military.

9. For an important reappraisal of reformist initiatives in this period, see Cecelia Lynch, *Beyond Appeasement: Interpreting Interwar Peace Movements in World Politics* (Ithaca, N.Y.: Cornell University Press, 1999).

10. See, for example, E. B. Weiss, *In Fairness to Future Generations: International Law, Common Patrimony, and Intergenerational Equity* (Dobbs Ferry, N.Y.: Transnational Publishers, 1989).

11. Among these were the 1992 Rio Conference on Environment and Development (the so-called "earth summit"), the 1993 Vienna Conference on Human Rights and Development, the 1994 Cairo Conference on Population and Development, the 1995 Beijing Conference on Women and Development, and the 1995 Copenhagen Social Summit.

12. See chapter 2.

13. Booth, "Human Wrongs and International Relations," *International Relations* 71 (1995), 103–26.

14. The scale and character of the Rwandan genocide is graphically depicted in Philip Gourevitch, *We Wish to Inform You That Tomorrow We Will Be Killed with Our Families—Stories from Rwanda* (New York: Farrar, Straus and Giroux, 1998).

15. See Steven Erlanger, "Bosnian Serb General Is Arrested By Allied Force in Genocide Case," *New York Times*, December 3, 1998; for a broad account of background and approach see Roger S. Clark and Madeline Sann, eds., *The Prosecution of International Crimes* (New Brunswick, N.J.: Transaction Publishers, 1996).

16. For an overall evaluation of the Pinochet detention in relation to wider issues of justice as an element of world order see chapter 1.

17. See Abraham H. Foxman, "The Dangers of Holocaust Restitution," *Wall Street Journal*, December 4, 1998, A18; Foxman: "There is no place for ambulance chasers in this sacred undertaking."

18. A wonderfully realized expression of this spirit is found in the introductory essay by Carolyn Forché to her anthology of poetry collected under the title *Against Forgetting: Twentieth-Century Poetry of Witness* (New York: W. W. Norton, 1993), 27–47.

19. Ibid., 46.

20. For interpretation see Richard Falk, "Reflections on the War," *The Nation*, June 28, 1999, 11–15.

CHAPTER 13

1. For influential formulations of the case for an expanded notion of security, see Jessica Tuchman Matthews, "Redefining Security," *Foreign Affairs* 68, no. 2 (1989): 162–77; and Richard Ullman, "Redefining Security," *International Security* 8, no. 1 (1983): 129–53. For a well-reasoned rejection of arguments for an expanded conception of security, see Daniel Duedney, "The Case Against Linking Environmental Degradation and National Security," *Millennium* 19, no. 3 (1990): 461–76.

2. There are other concerns: To what extent does the UN Charter prohibition on the use of force presuppose that the collective enforcement provisions of Chapter VII have been implemented? How then, should the prohibition be adapted to the reality of nonimplementation?

3. This failure to promote enforcement ignored the Security Council responsibility as set forth in Article 94 of the UN Charter.

4. See Thomas M. Franck, *Judging the World Court* (New York: Priority Press, 1986), 35–76.

5. Thucydides, *History of the Peloponnesian War* (London: Penguin, 1956), 400–408; of many examples, see the use of the Melian Dialogue by Michael Walzer, *Just and Unjust Wars: A Moral Argument with Historical Illustrations* (New York: Basic Books, 1992); and Stanley Hoffman, in *Duties Beyond Borders: On the Limits and Possibilities of Ethical International Politics* (Syracuse, N.Y.: Syracuse University Press, 1981).

6. For classic critiques along these lines, see E. H. Carr, *The Twenty Years' Crisis, 1919–1939: An Introduction to the Study of International Relations*, 2nd ed. (New York: Harper and Row, 1946); George F. Kennan, *American Diplomacy 1900–1950* (Chicago: University of Chicago Press, 1951).

7. A distinction adapted from the very important work of the Finnish jurist Martti Koskenniemi, *From Apology to Utopia: The Structure of International Legal Argument* (Helsinki: Lakimiesliiton Kustannus, 1989); see also Freidrich Kratochwil, "Sovereignty as Dominium: Is there a Right of Humanitarian Intervention?" in Gene M. Lyons and Michael Mastanduno, eds., *Beyond Westphalia? State Sovereignty and International Intervention* (Baltimore, Md.: Johns Hopkins University Press, 1995).

8. But for the sort of Type II realist or geopolitical morality articulated by Hedley Bull as a matter of systemic moderation, such a narrowing would be appropriate given the character of international society; see discussion of Bull's approach in the second section of this chapter.

9. Actually, the emergent policy was in many respects an unsatisfactory compromise, amounting to a "geopolitics of gesture" that made superficial concessions to the Type III moral claims through such steps as sanctions on the former Yugoslavia, an arms embargo, and the establishment of a war crimes tribunal in The Hague; but for Type II reasons it withheld peacekeeping efforts needed to protect the victims of war crimes and ethnic cleansing and to protect the integrity of the Bosnian state.

10. Gabriel Kolko, *Century of War: Politics, Conflicts and Society Since 1914* (New York: The New Press, 1994).

11. For an important discussion of these concerns, see Timothy Dunne and Nicholas J. Wheeler, "Hedley Bull and the Idea of a Universal Moral Com-

munity: Fictional, Primordial or Imagined?" in B. A. Robertson, ed., *The Structure of International Society* (London: Pinter, 1996).

12. Semantics are confusing, as "morality" is used as counterrealism and geopolitics, ignoring the realist position on morality, which is to condition the relevance of values upon the character of the societal matrix, the sort of moral approach worked out so effectively by Hedley Bull in *The Anarchical Society* (New York: Columbia University Press, 1977).

13. Kolko, *Century of War*, at 139–79.

14. See Myres S. McDougal and Harold D. Lasswell, "The Identification and Appraisal of Diverse Systems of Public Order," in McDougal et al., *Studies in World Public Order* (New Haven, Conn.: Yale University Press, 1960).

15. Compare E. P. Thompson, "Notes on Exterminism, the Last Stage of Civilisation," *New Left Review* 121 (May-June 1980): 3–31; Jonathan Schell, *The Fate of the Earth* (New York: Knopf, 1982); Robert Jay Lifton and Richard Falk, *Indefensible Weapons: The Political and Psychological Case Against Nuclearism*, rev. 2nd ed. (New York: Basic Books, 1992).

16. For one of several far more coherent challenges, see Grenville Clark and Louis B. Sohn, *World Peace Through World Law*, 3rd rev. ed. (Cambridge, Mass.: Harvard University Press, 1966); by shifting war-making capabilities to the reformed UN it remains doubtful that such a system could on its own satisfy requirements for a Type III morality as specified in the next section.

17. Carr, *The Twenty Years' Crisis*, 168.

18. "Desire to cure the sickness of the body politic has given its impulse and purpose to political science." (Carr, *The Twenty Years' Crisis*, 3.)

19. Kant, as world order thinker, rather than a philosopher of ethics, is also best understood as a Type II or even Type III moralist.

20. Hedley Bull, "The Grotian Conception of International Society," in Herbert Butterfield and Martin Wight, eds., *Diplomatic Investigations: Essays in the Theory of International Politics* (Cambridge, Mass.: Harvard University Press, 1966), at 51–73; and Hedley Bull, *The Anarchical Society*. See also Martin Wight, "Western Values in International Relations," in Butterfield and Wight, *Diplomatic Investigations*, 89–131.

21. See Dunne and Wheeler, "Hedley Bull"; Richard Falk, *Explorations at the Edge of Time: The Prospects for World Order* (Philadelphia, Penn.: Temple University Press, 1992).

22. John J. Mearsheimer, "Back to the Future: Instability in Europe After the Cold War," in Michael E. Brown, Sean M. Lynn-Jones, and Steven E. Miller, eds., *The Perils of Anarchy: Contemporary Realism and International Security* (Cambridge, Mass.: MIT Press, 1993), 78–129, at 105–8.

23. Again see Mearsheimer, "The False Promise of International Institutions," 332–76.

24. A prominent recent example is the report of the Commission on Global Governance, *Our Global Neighborhood* (New York: Oxford University Press, 1995); for a critique along these lines see Richard Falk, "Liberalism at the Global Level: The Last of the Independent Commissions?" *Millennium* 24, no. 3 (1995): 563–76.

25. Part of the explanation can be found in Ethan B. Kapstein, "Is Realism Dead?

The Domestic Sources of International Politics," *International Organization* 49, no. 4 (1995): 751–74.

26. See Bruce Russett, *Grasping the Democratic Peace: Principles for a Post–Cold War World* (Princeton, N.J.: Princeton University Press, 1993); Michael Doyle, "Kant, Liberal Legacies, and Foreign Affairs," Parts I and II, *Philosophy and Public Affairs* 12, nos. 3 and 4: 205–35; 323–53; for a critique see John Mearsheimer, "The False Promise of International Institutions," at 121–24; Christopher Layne, "Kant or Cant: The Myth of Democratic Peace," *International Security* 19, no. 2 (1994): 5–49.

27. See, especially, David Held, *Democracy and the Global Order: From the Modern State to Cosmopolitan Governance* (Cambridge, England: Polity, 1995).

28. This position is well articulated in Hugh Gusterson, "Exploding Anthropology's Canon in the World of the Bomb: Ethnographic Writing on Militarism," *Journal of Contemporary Ethnography* 22, no. 1 (1993): 58–79.

29. That is, nonviolence is but one of several Type III possibilities.

30. Robert W. Cox, "Social Forces, States and World Orders: Beyond International Relations Theory," in Robert O. Keohane, ed., *Neorealism and its Critics* (New York: Columbia University Press, 1986), 204–54, at 237.

31. Ibid., at 238.

32. Robert W. Cox, "Future World Order and the UN System," paper presented at the Conference on the UN and Japan in the Age of Globalization, Yokohama, Japan, 30 Nov.–3 Dec. 1994; for a more general discussion along these lines see Richard Falk, *On Humane Governance: Toward a New Global Politics* (Cambridge, England: Polity, 1995).

Index